Patrick Vieira is a formidable powerhouse of a player whose ball-winning and passing skills helped drive the Arsenal team for nearly a decade. He played only two league games for AC Milan before joining Arsenal in 1996. He helped the Gunners to the 1997–98 League and FA Cup Double and again to the double in 2001–02. He was named as the new captain for Arsenal for the 2002–03 season following Tony Adams's retirement from the game, and guided them to the Premiership title in 2003–04 without losing a single league game. In addition, Patrick Vieira is a vital part of the French national side, a World Cup and European Nations champion. He has been capped by France over eighty times, achieving international recognition at the club more often than any other player in Arsenal's history. In July 2005, he moved to Juventus in Turin for a transfer fee of nearly £14 million.

VIEIRA

MY AUTOBIOGRAPHY

Patrick Vieira

with Debbie Beckerman

An Orion paperback

First published in Great Britain in 2005
by Orion
This paperback edition publishing in 2006
by Orion Books Ltd,
Orion House, 5 Upper St Martin's Lane,
London WC2H 9EA

Revised edition

1 3 5 7 9 10 8 6 4 2

A CIP catalogue record for this book
is available from the British Library.

ISBN-13 978-0-7528-7781-5
ISBN-10 0-7528-7781-X

Typeset by Deltatype Ltd, Birkenhead, Merseyside

Printed and bound at Mackays of Chatham plc,
Chatham, Kent

The Orion Publishing Group's policy is to use papers that
are natural, renewable and recyclable products and made
from wood grown in sustainable forests. The logging
and manufacturing processes are expected to conform to
the environmental regulations of the country of origin.

www.orionbooks.co.uk

To my mother Rose, brother Nicko and Mario for all we have been through together. Our unity is our strength.

To my wonderful wife Cheryl, for her support over the last eight years during good and bad times, and for much happiness in the future with her daughter, Cheries.

CONTENTS

ACKNOWLEDGEMENTS

To Jacques Autef from Dreux, Phillipe Leroux from Tours, Guy Lacombe and Richard Bettoni from Cannes, and, of course, Arsène Wenger from Arsenal, for all they have taught me and helped me to achieve.

Thanks to all my teammates, past and present, for helping me achieve goals, for great memories and hopefully many good times in the future.

To my grandparents, all my uncles and aunts and all my cousins for their love and support.

Jamie Jarvis for all his hard work, support and friendship.

Jonathan Sieff and all the staff at Global Brands.

Jonathan Harris at Luxton Harris.

Alan Samson, Lucinda McNeile and Emma Noble at Orion.

Patrick Vieira

My thanks to the following people:

Alan Samson for his invaluable help throughout.

Keith 'Stevie G' Jones for his essential advice and unwavering support.

Junior Gunners Nicholas and Natasha for being so understanding.

David Luxton and Jonathan Harris for being so nice to me!

Debbie Beckerman

LIST OF ILLUSTRATIONS

Where I am Now ... and Other Thoughts

Last night was the start of the new Italian football season. We beat Fiorentina 3–2 away and Zlatan Ibrahimović scored the winning goal. Business as usual, people might think. Except that, over the summer, both of us swapped the black and white stripes of Juventus for the black and blue ones of Inter Milan. And the way that happened was anything but business as usual.

Nothing could have prepared me when I arrived at Juventus in July 2005, full of excitement at what lay ahead, for the ups and downs of the year that was to follow. I don't think many players have gone through what I did, both at club and international level, in the space of just twelve months. At times, I have had to face brutal truths and harsh defeats, whilst at others I have experienced sheer elation and indescribable pride. It has been a crazy year for me, but one which I would not have changed for the world. Well, except maybe just one game...

My season with Juventus started well. On a personal level, I re-learned the Italian I had last used a decade earlier, and settled in to my new life in Turin with my wife Cheryl and her daughter Cheries. Professionally, I managed to adapt to the Italian game, ten years after I had last played in Serie A. In Italy, teams generally play a more defensive style of football, with a lot of passes building up into an attack. This is quite different from the typical English style which – with the exception of Arsenal – tends to make more use of width and crosses. Despite this, I did not change my own physical way of playing because that is what defines me as a player. In any case, I have always played like that and would be incapable of changing even if I had to.

I fitted in well to the squad, which was quite small, with only 17 or 18 players, and could not have asked for a better start to my career as a *bianconero*. We stormed ahead in the title race and I felt that on the whole my level of play was good and I was contributing positively to the results. Although we had a difficult patch mid-season, and had to fight to stay ahead, we always believed in ourselves and believed we would win the coveted league title, the *Scudetto*. As far as I was concerned, La Juve was where I belonged and, barring injury, that was where I would be for the next five years.

We did, however, have one big footballing setback in our season and that came at the end of March when we travelled to Highbury for the first leg of our Champions League quarter-final against my former club. There is no doubt that, for me, that game came too soon after leaving Arsenal and, to be honest, I would have preferred to play any other side rather than the Gunners that evening. You don't spend nine fantastic years at a club, guided by a unique manager whom you have incredible respect for, surrounded by great players, many of whom became close, personal friends, only to return there without a care in the world. No, this was a difficult game for me, make no mistake. I knew it was coming up, of course, and I was determined to prepare myself psychologically, and to try to eradicate all my emotions from the evening. But I'm only human, and, it turns out, so is Arsène Wenger, because I read afterwards that he, too, thought it was not great that I was playing against his team so soon after leaving and that it would be a tough match for them as well.

One of the reasons it was tough for me to return to Highbury just six months after leaving was that, at the end of the previous season, I had not been planning to go. Then, suddenly, certain things happened and, very quickly, by mid-July, I was transferred to Juventus. I did not know at the time that my last kick for Arsenal would be the FA Cup Final in Cardiff, where I had scored the winning goal in the penalty shoot-out that had clinched us the Cup. I had never had the opportunity to say my goodbyes to the fans in the way that Dennis Bergkamp was able to, for example, and I was sad about that. So I knew that by returning for the game in March, it would mean the fans and I would get to salute each other one last time, even though it was hardly the ideal occasion, given how important the game was.

As the day approached, I tried to focus solely on the game itself. I told myself that it was a game like any other, that I had experienced other tricky situations in the past and overcome them, so this was no different. I spoke to Thierry Henry and Robert Pires beforehand and we knew the game would be especially tricky for all three of us, but we all felt we were professional enough not to let it get to us. The strangeness of the situation began to hit me, though, when I was on the coach on the way to the stadium. I spoke to Titi on my mobile and it just seemed really bizarre for me to be saying to him 'Hi, I'm arriving in a few minutes, see you in there'! When we got to Highbury, I saw all these people I had worked with for nine years, people who had been a huge part of my existence for almost all my adult life, and I found myself embracing them, even though they were now the opposition. Then I headed not for the home dressing room, as I had done for so long, but for the visitors' one, and it took great determination on my part not to let my emotions overwhelm me.

This was just the beginning, though. I still had to play a football match and help my team win. That was what we had come here for, not to pay a nostalgic visit to my former club. When we ran out on to the pitch, I did not know what to expect from the fans and how I would react, and that made me a bit nervous. I started to warm up and out of the corner of my eye I could see my former team-mates warming up in the way that I had done for nine years. I knew exactly what they would be doing: I could have gone through their routine with my eyes closed. I tried to ignore it and get on with my own warm-up, but what I couldn't ignore was the noise of the fans applauding, cheering and chanting my song all around Highbury. The words were still the same, the singing as loud as ever. There was no way I could drown that out. It was as if I had never left and I felt torn in half: on the one hand, it was fantastic to hear these incredible fans – and I acknowledged them and thanked them from the bottom of my heart – on the other it was really difficult to stay concentrated and emotionally detached. All I could do was keep looking down, try not to make eye contact with the supporters and avoid seeing how pleased they were to see me.

The game itself went badly for us. Arsenal played really well and Fabregas and Henry scored two great goals. I picked up a yellow card after a tackle in which adrenalin and nerves probably played their part, and which prevented me from playing the return leg the following week. This was frustrating for me, as I wanted to play to try and help us overcome our 2–0 deficit. To round off a bad evening, we lost Camoranesi and Zebina to second bookings late in the game. By the time the final whistle came, my return to Highbury had taken a nightmare turn, and it was with mixed emotions that I headed back to Turin the following day.

Arsenal, of course, went through to the Champions League Final, and many people thought I might find this a tough situation to accept.

After all, I had had hopes of achieving success in that competition with Juventus, whereas Arsenal had never gone as far as I had wanted in all my years with the club. The truth is that, yes, I wanted Juventus to win our quarter-final and go through to the final. But I felt all along that if it was not to be for my new club, then I would rather it was my old club that qualified than any other. I am too old and experienced to be jealous of their success and the fact is, they are one of the clubs that have progressed the most in terms of results, preparation, coaching, and improvements in infrastructure. Everything about Arsenal has improved – they have become a highly professional club, one of the big players in Europe, and much of that is down to the vision and determination of one man, Arsène Wenger. He is the one who made it possible for all that to happen, and he deserved to win that trophy. I watched the final on television and I know how hard he has worked towards trying to achieve his goal and how much it would have meant to Arsène to win. So I was disappointed for his sake that Arsenal did not beat Barcelona at the Stade de France. And they came so close!

Although our exit from the Champions League was our biggest footballing setback that season, another, much larger one occurred soon after that was to have the sort of consequences for the lives of everyone at Juventus that few could have predicted. In early May, just when we needed one more point to be crowned league champions, the Italian media broke the news that some of the biggest clubs in the country were embroiled in a huge corruption and match-fixing investigation and that officials at Juventus were at the heart of the allegations. Luciano Moggi, our general manager, was particularly implicated in the scandal, as he was accused of influencing the choice of referees for certain key fixtures and therefore of affecting the results of the games.

Along with my team-mates, I immediately realised that, if these allegations were true, this was very serious indeed; moreover, if the proposed sanctions against the club were carried out, there was no way I wanted to be starting the following season as a *bianconero*. I was really shocked by the news, as were all the players. I had a good relationship with Moggi, as well as with Antonio Giraudo, our managing director; Juventus was a club with a great, family-type atmosphere, where everyone got on well and trusted each other. Amongst the squad, we discussed the situation at length over the next few weeks. If one of us read something in the paper, or heard about some new development, he would share the information with his team-mates. As far as we were concerned, we had been playing our hearts out, putting every effort into getting the best results. What sickened us most was that we felt we deserved the league title, the *Scudetto*. We had battled hard over the winter months to keep hold of our lead, we had ended the season at the top of the table and we had won it fairly and rightfully. Then, suddenly, at the eleventh hour, it was going to be taken away from us.

As things stood it looked as if everything I had worked for over the previous nine months was going to be wasted. Suddenly, I was plunged into total uncertainty, my future was unclear and the World Cup Finals were looming large. I had thought I would be able to prepare for them serenely, comfortable in the knowledge that my move to Juventus had reaped rewards. Now, none of that was the case and I felt cheated in so many ways.

It quickly became clear that, if the Italian FA confirmed its suspicions – and, given the telephone conversations involving Moggi that the whole of Italy was now listening to on all radio and TV stations, the evidence looked damning – Juventus would be relegated to Serie B and given a huge points penalty, preventing any hopes of immediate promotion after one year. The verdict was due the week after the World Cup final. It was at that point that I spoke to my business manager and told him I had to move: it was out of the question for me to play in Serie B, so I needed to find another club. Preferably fast.

It was against this unsettled background that David Trézéguet, Lilian Thuram and I travelled to Germany to begin France's World Cup campaign. Many of our Juventus team-mates from other nations were in a similar situation. I spent the entire time on the one hand trying to concentrate on the games we had to play and, on the other, trying to work out and organise my future professional career. That was tough, definitely, and not what I had hoped for, because as it was, the France team had enough pressure going into the tournament without some of its squad anxiously waiting for calls from agents and clubs during the build-up to crucial games.

France were in Group G, along with Switzerland, South Korea and Togo, and although many people, including journalists, were saying that we would qualify fairly easily for the knockout stages of the tournament, we all knew that, firstly, there is no such thing as an easy group when you get to the World Cup and, secondly, we had to take all three teams seriously. Switzerland were a good side, with some great talent, South Korea had had a really good World Cup last time round and could not be dismissed lightly, and Togo were an unkown quantity. Like all African nations, they were capable of surprise results and a large part of the team were based in France and were familiar with our way of playing.

Our first match, against Switzerland, was a 0–0 draw during which we played nervously. We could feel the tension, we couldn't seem to get into our stride and it showed in the result. The same thing happened in the next game against South Korea. Thierry Henry gave us the lead after nine minutes – our first World Cup goal since 1998 – but even that was not enough to free us up. We knew that a one-goal lead was too slender to be able to relax and, sure enough, in the 81st minute, the Koreans equalised in one of their rare bursts of attacking play. To make matters worse, Zizou picked up a yellow card in the final minutes that means he was suspended from the next, all-important game.

By the time the third and final group match came round, against Togo, all the French press were criticising us and, in particular, our coach, Raymond Domenech, who had been under enormous pressure during the long build-up to the tournament and during the round-robin matches. There were all sorts of rumours flying around about alleged arguments and rifts between individual players, and between the players and the coach. The media said that certain factions of players did not agree with the manager's tactics or with his team selection. All I can say is that the media have to fill their pages – and I understand that – but they made mountains out of molehills on a daily basis. The squad and the coaching staff came to Germany determined to work together, and to make an effort to all get on. And that's exactly what happened: the players, the coach, everyone made an effort, differences were set aside when it mattered, and we talked things through whenever there were any problems. The journalists never actually saw any of that or knew exactly what went on inside our camp. We had no contact with the media, other than during official press conferences; nor did we read what the papers said about us. We spoke to our family and closest friends on our mobiles but otherwise we were quite cut off from the outside world, which was good because it allowed us to bond as a group, and to gain confidence in ourselves as a team without having to read the opinions of all the doubters and critics.

We had to win against Togo by two clear goals in order to go through to the next stage of the tournament, but even this assumed that South Korea did not beat Switzerland. With Zizou suspended, I stood in as captain for the game, which happened to fall on the day of my 30th birthday. I still felt we needed to free ourselves up and play as I knew we were capable of playing, but I also knew that the main thing was to qualify, not whether we played beautiful football.

The first half was tense and ended 0–0. We had several opportunities and were even denied a goal when David Trézéguet was judged to be offside. It turned out to be a very questionable decision and one that could have cost us dear. In the end, our efforts finally paid off and, in the 55th minute, Franck Ribéry suddenly burst through down the left into the penalty area and passed the ball to where I was in the middle of the box. I turned in an instant and sent the ball flying into the far corner of the net. It all happened very quickly and it gave me such satisfaction: I was having a good game, I was the captain, plus it was my 30th birthday. So the goal was very much the icing on the cake. Not that I had any time to savour the moment, as we still had to score at least once more. My goal finally seemed to energise us and, five minutes later, I set up Thierry for him to score and stretch our lead to 2–0. It was enough. When the whistle blew half an hour later, we were through.

We knew we could play a lot better than we had in those three group matches. We had the players, we knew what we were capable of, we had worked hard to become a team, so the fact that we were now into the knockout stages of the tournament gave us a real boost. Somehow, that liberated us, gave us confidence, and took a lot of pressure off us, because the press had been doubting that we would even make it this far.

Our next opponents were Spain, who had been playing well throughout their group matches, had scored a lot of goals and finally seemed to be fulfilling expectations. They had always been one of the underachievers of the World Cup but now the media were saying that maybe, with no clear favourites this time round, they could go far. We went into that game as the underdogs, the ones who many people thought would lose. We were expected to be on the next flight home. What happened instead was that our pride was stung by all the criticisms, and we showed that we wanted to prove everyone wrong. Everything came together for us in that game and it became one of the best matches of the tournament. Beforehand, Raymond Domenech had stuck his neck out and talked about us going all the way to the final, and most people thought he was deluded, off his head. But he had the guts to stick to his guns, to believe in us, when all around us did not. He showed enormous strength of character and, for that alone, deserves great credit.

The fact was that his hard work, his organisation of the team and of the way we trained, his faith in us, all these elements finally paid off in that match, which was a difficult one, not least because of the racist comments that the Spain manager had once expressed concerning Titi. We ignored all that during the game, and although we went 1–0 down after a dubious penalty awarded to Spain, we now believed in ourselves, and kept going forward. Finally, just before half time, I fed a ball through to Franck Ribéry, who raced through, danced round the keeper and slid the ball into the back of the net.

In the second half, both teams came close to scoring but in the 83rd minute, as extra time was fast approaching, Zizou lobbed a free kick into the box, and although Xabi Alonso reached the ball first he only managed to head it on to where I was standing, unmarked at the far post, ready to nod it in. Two goals in two matches for me, and this one the probable match-winner – simply the best feeling in the world! But we weren't finished and, in the 92nd minute, Zizou ran down the left, cut inside, shimmied past Carlos Puyol and slammed the ball in just before the final whistle went. We ended on a high, full of renewed confidence and self-belief, and a real sense that we were working together as a team, not just a collection of players. Now we couldn't wait to meet our next opponents, the World Cup holders Brazil, for a rematch of the 1998 final.

The quality of football didn't match the previous game but the all-important goal for us came in the 57th minute when a Zidane free kick delivered from way out on the left found Thierry unmarked by the far post. He volleyed it home to give us the winner and our ticket into the semi-finals. Who cares if it wasn't our greatest match? What counts is the result and it's always immensely satisfying to beat Brazil, and to beat the holders, in a World Cup.

How quickly things can change, though, and how quickly people do a U-turn in their opinions. Suddenly, the press were speaking of us as the possible winners of the whole tournament, not as the unhappy, ageing losers we were supposed to have been at the start of it. It's because of situations like this that I have long since learnt never to attach much importance to what people say about me, because I know everything can change in an instant.

When it came to the semi-final against Portugal, we knew that it wasn't the best team who would win, it was the one who played the most effective football. Portugal are a difficult side to play, because they play a similar game to us. Other people thought we already had our ticket through to the final, but Portugal were actually the best team we played against. I know that will surprise many English fans, and, sure, they don't play like the Spanish or the Brazilians. But they were a powerful team, they worked hard on the pitch, they had players who could turn a match, and they were a very organised side that resembled ours in many ways. And their manager, Luiz Felipe Scolari, had a track record that spoke for itself. That's why the match was our toughest of the entire tournament. Added to which it was a World Cup semi-final, perhaps the hardest game to play psychologically, because the stakes are so high. Nobody wants to lose, but especially not in the semi-finals. It's worse than losing in the finals.

I know England couldn't believe that they lost against Portugal, and on penalties as well. I followed England's progress during the tournament and watched all their matches because I had friends playing in the team and, having played for so long in England, I was naturally interested in their progress. I find it strange that, despite having some fantastic players (Ashley Cole, my ex-team-mate, being one of them, but Steven Gerrard, Wayne Rooney, John Terry, and Frank Lampard are amongst some of the others), they couldn't deliver when it came to the matches. They just don't seem to work together as a team, they haven't figured out what to do. I hope that will change under their new manager, Steve McLaren, but it seems such a waste that all these good players were unable to function as a group. I know the England media reacted to the loss by saying that Portugal like to dive and to wind players up, but we had no intention of their supposed reputation getting to us. As far as we were concerned, Portugal simply fought hard – in the right sense – and we had to make sure we fought back.

The match was certainly a battle, and in the 33rd minute Thierry was tripped in the penalty area by Ricardo Carvalho. Zizou stepped up for the penalty and fired it low into the left-hand corner, just past the keeper, Ricardo, who had dived the right way but was not able to save the ball. From then on, it was a tense night. The Portuguese kept attacking, but we had more opportunities to score. However, we were also strong in defence and that allowed us to keep our lead. It wasn't the most elegant, inspired display by either team, but we showed great determination and at the end of it we were through to another World Cup final. For those of us who had already lived through it once, eight years before, this was huge. For those who had yet to experience it for the first time, it was simply out of this world. And for Zizou, it was to be his last ever game of football.

The key thing now was not to get carried away with ourselves or with our thoughts. On big occasions, it's crucial not to start playing the match in your head in advance of the day itself. Otherwise, when you get there you are mentally and physically drained. Raymond Domenech understood this completely and he made sure we did not change in any way the routine that had got us through to this stage. So we prepared for the final in exactly the same way as we had prepared for all the other games. Nothing was different. The only thing that had changed was that we'd had to move the day before the final from our headquarters in Western Germany to Berlin in the East where the final was taking place. Otherwise, we did the same training, and the same warm-up and warm-down exercises the day before the game, and on the day itself, we went for a stroll in the morning, as usual, then had lunch and had a siesta in the afternoon, also as usual. We did no more and no less than we normally did. Similarly, the coach did not say anything different. We watched videos of the Italians and analysed their game in as much detail as we had for our very first game against the Swiss. Nor was there any need for the coach to come up with big motivational speeches or deep insights into the importance and historic nature of the game we were about to play. What would be the point? Firstly, it would make us more nervous, and secondly, if you can't get motivated and energised by a World Cup Final, then you are in the wrong business.

Psychologically and physically, therefore, we were prepared and in good shape by the time we walked out on to the Olympic Stadium pitch that evening, in front of 70,000 people. I had a completely different feeling for this final from the one I had had in 1998 at the Stade de France. This time round, I felt much more involved, more implicated in what had gone before and what was about to happen. In 1998, I had hardly played in the lead-up to the final, and had only gone on as substitute towards the end of the game. This time round, I had played in all the matches and was very much a pillar of the team, part of the 'old guard'. Hearing the national anthems, seeing and hearing the fans packed into the stadium full of flags and banners from both countries, I couldn't help but be moved by the experience. It was a beautiful, fantastic moment that I told myself at the time I had to treasure for ever.

Once the game got underway, I banished all emotion and put all my effort into concentrating on the task ahead. In the first minute of play, Titi's head collided heavily with Fabio Cannavaro's shoulder and he looked down and out, which was a worrying start, as it would have been a huge psychological blow to have lost him so early. Eventually he got up and, just six minutes later, we were awarded a penalty when Marco Materazzi – the man whose name was to feature in several key incidents that evening – brought down Florent Malouda. Zizou stepped up to the spot, took his usual very short run-up and delivered the sort of cheeky chip down the middle that only he would have had the guts to attempt in a match of this importance, where you rarely get many opportunities to score. Never, ever, would I or my team-mates have thought that he would try such a trick shot. We almost had to laugh, particularly as the ball bounced not that far inside the goal line. It just went to show how confident Zidane was and what sort of mental strength he must have. In some ways, that penalty was typical Zizou.

We were 1–0 up but little more than ten minutes later Marco Materazzi headed in an Andrea Pirlo corner to equalise for Italy. That goal is particularly painful for me as I was supposed to be marking Marco. At the time, I didn't have the chance to torture myself about it, because everything happened so fast and there was no time to reflect, but it is something that I played back in my head and blamed myself for in the immediate aftermath of defeat.

At the start of the second half, all seemed to be going our way. We were outplaying the Italians when suddenly, about ten minutes in, I felt a sharp muscle spasm in both hamstrings. I had just dribbled the ball and passed it when the pain shot through me and forced me to pull up immediately. I couldn't walk, let alone run, and although I tried to run it off, I quickly knew that I would have to come off. I was bitterly disappointed to be substituted, as I felt I was letting the team down, and I still had a lot to contribute. But I had no choice. You can't play in a match of that importance if you are not 100 per cent, so I had to sit out the rest of the match from the dugout with an ice pack on one leg. And watching is far, far harder to do than playing.

By the time extra time came round, it was clear that the opposition were playing for penalties. They defended very well, even when they got really tired, and I think they just decided that they weren't going to score, that the only way they were going to win was to defend like crazy, and to pin all their hopes on the penalty shoot-out. We, on the other hand, kept trying to press forward. David Trézéguet had come on during extra time for Franck Ribéry who had run himself into exhaustion, and Sylvain Wiltord had come on a few minutes later for the injured Thierry Henry. We hoped that some fresh pairs of legs might just win it for us in the dying minutes.

Then, with ten minutes of extra time remaining, just when everyone's nerves were getting frayed, and energy levels were almost spent, something happened that no one will ever forget. Zizou's loss of control when he headbutted Marco Materazzi in the chest was not seen by the vast majority of fans and players. It wasn't seen by me on the bench. It wasn't even seen by the referee. But some members of the Italy team went crazy and alerted the referee to what had happened, and the fact was that Materazzi was lying on the ground, seemingly in pain. For a split second, Zizou started reaching for his captain's armband, as if to take it off. Then he stopped. But deep down, he knew it was only a matter of time, because once the man in black became aware of the situation, Zizou would not be staying on the pitch for a second longer. Sure enough, with television cameras relaying the incident, which they had not initially picked up either, around the world, the full scale of what had happened began to emerge. We on the bench were all numb with disbelief. We simply could not understand. It was so out of character that it was impossible to explain. In my mind, it still is. I have been asked so many times about it, and all I can say is that nobody really knows what went on in Zizou's head, what the lead-up to the incident was and what precisely was said by Materazzi. I can only explain it by taking into account the weight of the occasion, the pressure, the strain, the fatigue, the things that may have been said during the previous 110 minutes, plus the fact that this was his last ever game; all these factors must have contributed to his moment of madness.

It was all over very quickly. Zizou walked straight off the pitch and into the changing room without saying a word to anyone, whereas we barely had time to take on board the magnitude of the sending-off before we were into the penalty shoot-out. Time flies by, you almost enter another dimension whilst the list of penalty-takers is drawn up. With Henry, Ribéry, myself and Zizou now absent from the potential takers, it fell to five brave men to step up to the spot. The final was going to be decided by a form of Russian roulette. It's never great for these huge games to be decided in this way, but you just have to accept it.

At 1–1 on penalties, it once again fell to Marco Materazzi to see if he could help keep his country in the final. He duly converted his penalty with confidence. Next up for us was David Trézéguet, who is a regular goal-scorer and penalty-taker at Juventus. In addition, he had a fresh pair of legs, which is important in these situations. Nothing led me to think he could not equalise. But fate, luck, call it what you will, deserted him on this occasion. Whereas Zizou's early penalty had hit the underside of the crossbar and bounced the right side of the line, David's also hit the crossbar but agonisingly bounced just the wrong side. At that moment, the blood runs cold, you're not sure you can believe your eyes, even on the television replays. But unfortunately, just ten centimetres was all that separated us from victory. On such fine lines are battles won and lost. And it still hurts to think about it.

All the other penalties, both the French and the Italian, were successfully converted, so when Fabio Grosso's went in, giving our opponents an unbeatable 5–3 lead, it was all over. David was devastated, as were several other members of the team who were in tears. I tried to console him, because the fact was, he had had the courage to step up to the plate, which took guts, and anyway, we all know that penalty shoot-outs could just as well be decided by a roll of the dice.

The medal ceremony afterwards was especially tough, because Zizou was missing. Everything felt very hollow and all we wanted was to get back to the dressing room. Zizou had gone by the time we got there, whisked off, presumably back to his hotel room. The atmosphere was one of total dejection and disappointment. There was nothing much to say. We didn't talk about Zizou's red card, because that was pointless, and what hurt more was the fact that we had lost, not that we had lost him in the way we did: we felt we had played well, much of the time better than the Italians, but in the end, luck had not been on our side. End of story. We met up with our wives and girlfriends back at the hotel and that helped, but I found it incredibly difficult to get any sleep that night. I kept replaying the whole match in my head, telling myself that I could have done this better, or that better. It's a horrible, frustrating feeling.

The following day, we all flew back to Paris where we were expected at the Elysée Palace for a reception with French President, Jacques Chirac. I have to say that the welcome we received from thousands of people when we touched down on French soil really warmed our hearts and helped to heal our pain a little bit. The fans were fantastic, telling us we'd played brilliantly, we had done our country proud and that they would continue to support us no matter what. That was great to hear, and although it was an emotional homecoming, I felt better hearing all this.

What was difficult, though, was going our separate ways afterwards. We had been together every single day since 21st May – almost eight weeks – and we had lived through some incredible experiences. What was more, the team spirit had been really good, we were pleased to come down to breakfast every morning and to see everyone, we enjoyed eating together, working together. We had had some unforgettable times, so to leave each other was very sad.

For me, I left the rest of the squad with my future still in the balance. Throughout the whole World Cup, I had awaited the verdict of the Italian FA's investigation into the allegations of corruption, although I assumed, along with my other Juve team-mates, that the club would find itself relegated. By the time the verdict was announced, coincidentally, on the 14th July, the first anniversary of my signing for Juventus, I was not surprised to hear confirmation of the relegation, along with a 30-point deduction. In addition, we were stripped of our title, although as far as I am concerned, this makes no difference: in my mind, we were still the 2005/2006 league champions. Nonetheless, the challenge now was to find a club where I would be happy. I knew I would find a club somewhere, but you never know in football what might happen, there are no guarantees for a player, so the worry was trying to find a club that had the sort of aspirations Juventus, and previously Arsenal, had had and where I would feel content for the next few years of my career.

I was fortunate because I soon had some interesting offers from various clubs. But the club that immediately emerged as the front-runner was Inter Milan. There was talk in the media about me going to Real Madrid, Barcelona and even Manchester United, but I can say that all that was pure speculation because none of those clubs even contacted me. On the other hand, Inter showed at once that they wanted to sign me, their coach really wanted me and the terms were very good. There was no bullshit from them, none of this 'one day they want you, the next day they don't' that can so often go on in transfer negotiations. They had ambitions as a club, they had everything I was looking for as a player, so the contract was signed a mere ten days after the inquiry's verdict.

Thierry Henry was asked soon after how he would have felt if I had returned to Arsenal − an unlikely prospect, I know − and he had replied that he would have loved me to return to Highbury. Or rather the Emirates! He would happily have handed me back the captain's armband. But that since I was now going to Inter, he joked that perhaps I could give Marco Materazzi a bit of a punch on his behalf! And beware if the Gunners ever played us in the Champions League. Actually, I'm really happy for Titi that he chose to stay at Arsenal. I believe that he belongs there, and for him I know it was the right decision.

Several of us left Juventus: Zlatan Ibrahimović signed for Inter as well, whilst my good friend Lilian Thuram went to Barcelona. Several others, however, such as David Trézéguet and Gianluigi Buffon, the best keeper in the world, and a World Cup winner, stayed. To say that it's a waste of their talent for these players to be in Serie B for at least a couple of seasons is a total understatement. But for whatever reason, that is where they are, and I hope the situation is not too frustrating for them.

Similarly, in England, the Ashley Cole transfer saga had repercussions that spread far and wide. I have heard what he said and what William Gallas, my France team-mate, said, and although I obviously don't really know what went on behind the scenes, my main reaction is that it's a real shame that Ashley went. Ashley, even more than Thierry, belongs at Arsenal. It's the club he grew up in, he came up through the ranks, from when he was a boy through to being a professional. As I said when I wrote the rest of this book last year, he should have been their next iconic captain, in the way that Tony Adams, who is forever associated with the Gunners, was. I cannot understand why Arsenal did not fight tooth and nail to keep Ashley, because, as I know, when they really want to they make sure they keep a player. They should have made every possible effort. Instead, they allowed him to get away. As for William, who spent five years at Chelsea and who put in a lot of hard work and dedication, I find it incredibly disappointing that a great club like Chelsea should sink to making allegations about William's commitment and about what he may or may not have said. There was absolutely no need to do what they did, it belittles them and I think less of them as a result.

I am now settled in Milan. I was obviously teased quite a lot when I got there by the other Italian players, but I get on well with everyone. And no, I have no issues with Marco Materazzi, who is actually a very likeable, respectful guy, not the racist yob the media depicted him to be after the 'incident'. In fact, it saddens him as much as it does Zizou that the whole matter took on absurd proportions and that people talk about that moment more than the fact that Italy won the World Cup and that he scored their one and only goal.

France is now involved in trying to qualify for Euro 2008 and we have a tough group, with Italy, the Ukraine and Scotland, who are playing good football. I am now captain once again, which is a great honour. We had a difficult game to play in early September because we had a rematch against Italy, at the Stade de France. There was so much to play for: not only maximum points, which would leave us in a good place in the table, but there was also a lot of pride at stake and our defeat to avenge. We badly wanted to show that we were better than them, even if that would never change the result and bring us the World Cup trophy.

Our 3–1 victory was therefore very satisfying, although José Mourinho again soured things by saying that the continuing use of Claude Makelele and Lilian Thuram, (who had changed their minds about retiring from international football after the World Cup) was akin to them being slaves to their country. I like to think that the Chelsea manager did not realise how inflammatory the word 'slave' can be when talking about two coloured players, and that he spoke off the top of his head. I hope so, because the word has heavy connotations, and is a harsh and ugly word when used to describe those two great players who have so loyally served both their clubs and their country. As for me, I shall continue to do the same for as long as both club and country want me, and as long as I still derive pleasure from the game. I hope that will be for many years to come.

1

Juve: A Black and White Move

I'm sure it's hard to believe but I was one of the last people to discover that Juventus wanted to sign me. Cheryl and I had decided to get married at the end of May and we tied the knot in Vence, a beautiful medieval village in the hills above Nice on the French Riviera. The English football season had well and truly ended and I was looking forward to a month-long honeymoon. The first half was spent in the Bahamas, whilst for the second we went off to Miami. One of the best aspects of the two weeks spent in the Bahamas was that my mobile phone wouldn't work there, so I was left in complete peace by everyone back home! That was a rare luxury. However, by the time we got to Miami, I had hundreds of messages on my phone from friends saying things like 'Huh, didn't realise you were leaving Arsenal' or 'So, why Juve?' What on earth were they talking about? So when I returned their calls I just told them I didn't know where they had got all that stuff from but I could assure them it was all rubbish.

I returned to London in early July and began a week of work with my own physical trainer in advance of Arsenal's pre-season training. I have often done this – when I have not been injured, that is – because it shakes off the cobwebs that accumulate after a few weeks off. It also shakes off a few pounds I might have gained and gets me in reasonable shape before I start serious training.

One evening, I called Arsène. We had a long conversation. I asked him about what our objectives were for the coming season, how he saw us as a team, what his plans for us were. In short, we had a long discussion about the future for Arsenal. He didn't say anything about Juventus and I didn't ask. I simply assumed that all those phone messages and rumours were just red herrings.

God knows, in the past, I had had enough regular approaches or alleged approaches from clubs and the media had always reported them, whether they were true or false. So I wasn't going to get too excited by this latest lot, particularly after the previous summer when I had so nearly gone to Real.

Within twenty-four hours, however, David Dein was on the phone to me.

'What do you want to do, Patrick? Juventus want you,' he told me.

I was staggered.

'What do you mean? I don't understand. I have heard the rumours, obviously, but you're saying they have been speaking to you?' I replied.

David told me that, yes, Juventus' director general, Luciano Moggi, had already been over to London to discuss a possible move.

'They are offering a good contract,' he went on. 'And we're obligated to let you know about any approaches that are made to the club.'

I wasn't too pleased by what I was hearing. Things had obviously been going on behind my back. Also, in the past, the club certainly had not felt duty-bound to inform me every time a club approached them, which was just as well, given the dozens of times that had happened. It would have left me with little time to think about anything if, every time a club had been in touch with Arsenal, I had been summoned to consider the approach. But this time, apparently, was different.

Then David told me that, as far as this particular offer was concerned, 'We are neutral. We are giving you the choice of deciding what you want to do.'

That was the moment when I got cross and from then on, let's just say I struggled to keep the tone of the conversation relaxed. 'What do you mean, you're neutral and you're giving me the choice?' I asked David. He repeated what he had said and that the offer was a generous one. It would be up to me if I chose to leave Arsenal or not. Whilst he was talking, I was thinking to myself, 'Hang on, I've spent nine years at this club. If a club really wants to keep a player, it fights tooth and nail to do so. It doesn't "leave it up to" that player to decide.' That, for me, was the issue. It wasn't that the proposed contract was good or bad. The issue was that the club was neutral, that it was leaving it up to me to decide. Those were the words that swung it for me. 'If that's how it is,' I quickly concluded, 'whatever happens now, I'm off. And I'm off to the club of my own choosing. Because I believe I will be able to choose.' So I informed David of my decision.

Sure enough, Juventus and I quickly reached an agreement on the terms of the contract and a deal was struck in no time at all. On 14 July, a day symbolic for me as that is the day that all Frenchmen celebrate the Revolution, a revolution took place in my career: I signed for Juventus and immediately left Arsenal, the club that had been my wonderful home for nine glorious years. That said, I believe everyone was happy in the end. Arsenal were, because they got a good sum of money, Juventus were because they got the player they wanted, and I was because I would be furthering my career at one of the greatest football clubs in Europe.

Once I had had time to think about the way in which things had been done, I realised that it was just a typical football transfer. The fact is, when you are a young player, just starting out, yet to reach your potential, a club will hold on to you if it can, and will prevent you going off elsewhere if it can at all help it. Once you are older and more mature, further along your career path, clubs aren't always very transparent about what goes on behind the scenes. They are happy to blame a player when he decides to move, but they don't always come clean about their own dealings. In the end, I realised that what had happened was just normal: that's business and, in particular, that's football. It all boils down to the fact that clubs have to look after number 1, i.e. themselves, in just the same way that we, the players, have to as well. And if a club wants to get rid of you, for whatever reason, then you have to understand where it is coming from. Young players don't necessarily realise that that's how it works, but when you have reached my age, you do. The problem is that, all too often, it's the supporters who are caught in the middle, in a cloud of misunderstanding made all the more impenetrable by the inevitable rumours and press inaccuracies that fly around at the time. And I feel for the fans, because they don't understand what has happened, and feel let down by all sides. In my case, though, the bottom line was that Arsenal had done little to persuade me to stay.

In the end, I didn't blame David Dein or Arsène Wenger. I still have the immense respect for them that I always had and we parted on good terms, although my last meeting with the boss was obviously not easy, as we had been through so much together. We had arrived at virtually the same time, I was his first signing, and I was now his captain. I went to see him in his office on the morning of my departure from the club. We had a really nice talk about the last few years, about how he had viewed me over that time, how he had seen me progress, not just as a player but also as a person, and how he thought I could still improve. He said some really kind things which I shall always treasure. From my side, I know I shall miss him, and I owe him so much I will never be able to thank him enough for all he has done for me.

When the time came to say goodbye to my team-mates and all the Arsenal back-room staff, it was even harder. I had to go to the training ground to clear out my belongings from my locker, so I picked the moment before the squad all went off to train to do it. It was tough saying goodbye, firstly to the physical trainers, the physios, in fact all the technical staff with whom I had worked for so long, and who had made sure I was always in the best possible shape to play. We had gone through so much together, so many difficult times when I had been injured and they had helped me back to fitness. I had also shared so many wonderful moments with them, often away from the cameras at the training ground when I would come in early to have breakfast with them and catch up on things. Then, of course, there were the players. Ashley, Sol, Dennis, Robert – guys that I wouldn't be seeing again for some time. Thierry I would probably see more often playing for the French national team, but Robert is not currently being selected, so he was amongst those I would not be seeing for the foreseeable future. Those goodbyes were emotional. I was setting off into the unknown, leaving behind everything and everyone I had loved for nearly ten years – for almost all of my adult life, in fact. And it had all happened so quickly. There had been no time to come to terms with it, no chance to reflect on the departure calmly. No wonder I found it hard to speak when it came to closing the door.

Before long, though, I had left Arsenal and London and been whisked off to Juventus and Turin. Just twenty-four hours later, in the club's trophy room, I was being presented to a huge gathering of foreign and Italian media as the new '*bianconero*' (as they nickname the Juve players). It so happened that I was to have the number 4 shirt, just as I had done at Arsenal, but in all other respects, things were clearly very different. I was certainly pleased to be coming back to Italy. 'I am coming back to win,' I told the assembled group. 'That's why I have come to Juventus. I have already won many trophies with Arsenal and I am here to continue along that road.' Given that this is the club that has won the Italian league title, the *scudetto*, the greatest number of times (twenty-six in total) I felt I was giving myself a good chance of doing just that.

Inevitably, I was asked about a statement I had made a few years previously about not playing in a country where racism from the stands is seen and heard on a regular basis, as it also is in Spain. 'I may have said that, but it's a minority of people who do it and that shouldn't prevent me coming to Italy to play. If I am to be a victim of it, so much the worse, but I'll be ready for it,' I replied.

Basically, I felt I had picked the right club to take me to the next stage of my career. Yes, I had signed a five-year contract guaranteeing my wages at a fixed level, but what I really liked was the fact that this was a club with a huge tradition and a strong work ethic, which I shared. In addition, I already knew several of the players well (notably my French team-mates David Trézéguet, Lilian Thuram and Jonathan Zebina), not to mention their head coach Fabio Capello, who had done so much to encourage me at AC Milan at a time when things had been far from easy. The prospect of playing for Fabio at this stage in my career had been incredibly tempting. Finally, I knew that I would find a group of people who would feel like a family, very much like I had found at Arsenal and that, too, was vital in order for me to feel happy. Those were the main reasons why I had chosen Juventus over other clubs that might have been interested.

The next day, 16 July, just two crazy, whirlwind days after leaving London, I was already training with my new team-mates at their training camp $1\frac{1}{2}$ hours from Turin, at Salice Terme. I was staggered to find a crowd of around three thousand people at the ground, waiting with excitement to see me put through my paces. I hadn't expected there to be so many, but I had forgotten how public football can be in Italy.

At the same time as experiencing my first training session, I was also trying to remember all the Italian I had learned ten years before at Milan and, at first, I found it almost impossible to come out with anything that made sense. Fairly soon, though, words began to come back to me. Luckily, Italian is so close to French that, if in doubt, I would just make it up, sticking an 'o' or an 'a' on the end of a French word. Surprising how often that worked!

At Salice Terme, I shared a room with Lilian, which was great because we have always got on so well. After that first training session, I got changed, went down to have dinner, returned upstairs, went to sleep and woke up the next morning completely confused. There was Lilian next to me, sleeping away, when surely it should have been Thierry, the guy I usually room-shared with? Where was he? 'Oh, OK,' I told myself, 'I'm with Lilian because we are about to play an international' (that's who I shared with when the France team got together). It took me quite a while to work out where I was, and why it was that Lilian was in the room with me. Not only that, but for the next couple of days, whenever I saw him in the room, I had this instinctive feeling that we were about to play for France, not for Juventus. I just couldn't get my head round the fact that I was no longer with Arsenal! That was a really bizarre experience.

The irony was that over the years, whenever I'd see Lilian, we always used to say that it was about time he came to play in England. The plan had always been for him to join me, not necessarily at Arsenal, but at least in England. But things had turned out completely the opposite and it was I who had come to Italy to join him! We had a good laugh about that.

When it came to the actual training, it was similar to what we did at Arsenal where we had twice-daily sessions. In the morning, we would work on the physical side of things – fitness, endurance, flexibility – go for runs, do stretching exercises. In the afternoon, we would concentrate on ball skills, set pieces and tactics. The main difference in the morning sessions was that, whereas with the Gunners everyone did the stretches on their own, stretching out whatever part of the body needed it the most, at Juventus we all stretched together as a group, using the same parts of the body! There was no question of individual choice in the matter. That seems to be very much the Italian approach. Similarly, I rediscovered the tradition, also in place at AC Milan, that when eating together, we all had to wait for the captain to have finished before we could get down from the table. In Italy, teams operate very much as a group. Maybe that helps them to cope when the pressure starts to mount. Because without doubt, in Italy you feel the pressure to perform on a daily basis. The pressure to win every time is stoked by the media, and in the end, the only thing that counts is getting a result time and time again. In England, whatever people might think, the fans are much more cool about winning and losing, as are the papers. Incredible, but true, believe me!

I found a fantastic group of players at Juventus. Some were legends already, both in Italy and in their home country, but all made me feel welcome. On the pitch I played in tandem with Emerson, the former Brazil captain. He is a magnificent, combative player and we formed a really powerful partnership. Defender Fabio Cannavaro, the Italian team captain, is someone who I instantly struck up a good rapport with, not least because he is one of Lilian Thuram's great friends. So I got to spend time off the pitch with Fabio and I can say that he likes to have fun and have a laugh. As a player, he is one of the game's survivors, and, although only 1m 76cms (5' 9"), he has shown that he is one of the country's most effective centre backs. Club captain, striker Alessandro del Piero, had been at Juventus for twelve years and was incredibly warm and open to me from the start. He's a very easy-going, simple guy who is not interested in playing the fame game. Coincidentally, we had bumped into each other in Miami when I was on honeymoon but little did we know then that fate would bring us together again so quickly and in such a way.

As for my two compatriots in the team, David Trézéguet and Lilian Thuram, I was so lucky to have them. David, who I call Trézégoal because of the number of goals he scores, is the most skilful player in front of goal that I have ever seen. He is both discreet and effective on the pitch: you might not notice him for fifteen minutes, but suddenly he will come up with a pass or a goal that turns the game. He is also discreet off the pitch and as a result is someone that I enjoy going out to dinner with because I know he's not courting publicity. Finally, to Lilian, my great friend. We have been international team-mates for years and know each other incredibly well. I can talk to Lilian about anything and everything. Born in Guadeloupe, he is interested in the world around him, and as a result is interesting in his own right. He gets involved with good causes, and fights for what he believes in. Above all, the two of us seem to share a very similar vision of life, so we are on the same wavelength for everything. He also happens to be a fantastic defender, one of the pillars of the French team (he came out of international retirement to represent France once again) and, with Fabio Cannavaro, I believe they formed the best defence in Europe.

Over the years, France has had quite a lot of players who have sported the famous black and white shirt from Turin. Michel Platini and Didier Deschamps both had success at Juventus in the past. I was hoping to carry on that tradition but, sadly, events prevented me from doing so for longer than one season. My future now lies in a blue and black shirt.

2

Diambars and my Senegal

Diambars means 'warrior', 'champion' and 'winner' in Wolof, the most commonly spoken dialect in Senegal. The idea for the Diambars Academy came from Jimmy Adjovi Boco and Bernard Lama, the former French international goalkeeper. Jimmy is from Benin and Bernard is Guyanese but met at Lens football club where they became great friends. Bernard subsequently moved on to various other clubs, including Paris St Germain and even West Ham, where in the end he stayed for just one season in 1997 but he and Jimmy kept in touch because they both had a long-standing idea of one day giving something back to the sport that had given them so much, which is how they came up with the idea for Diambars. Bernard and Jimmy talked to me about this project about two or three years ago. It was something that they were intent on doing and they wanted to set it up in Africa. They had chosen Senegal even before speaking to me about it because it was the most politically stable country in that continent.

Having made their decision, they asked me if I was interested in joining forces with them. For me, it was a fantastic idea, the ideal project. The initial concept – which has remained unchanged since – was to create not only a football academy but also a place of education. Life in Senegal is a bit better than it was but there are still areas where it is very tough. All three of us felt that it was really important to put the emphasis on education. There are other football academies in Africa but on the whole they are just interested in turning out young footballers who then get bought by foreign clubs. If those youngsters do not then make the grade as professional footballers, either because of injury or because they are not quite good enough, they often have nothing to fall back on when their clubs discard them. They are good for nothing because they have barely had any proper education. We wanted to make sure that Diambars would not be like that but would help these kids in every way possible to stand on their own two feet when grown up and to follow whichever path they wanted to choose, the sporting or the non-sporting one. Only then can they help themselves and, as a result, help Africa. In order to do that, though, we have to make them understand that they can only succeed in life by working hard. At first, there were kids at the institute who could not read or write. Now they all read books, write stories – and then they play football. We emphasise to them that it is very difficult to become a professional footballer and that only a few of them will succeed. They have to understand how important their education is because it is something they will always have, whatever the outcome of their sporting career. We pay for boys to come to university in Europe so that they can return to Senegal one day. In that way, they can give themselves a better future and help their country. That is why I passionately believe in what we are doing with Diambars.

It took me a long time, though, to go back to Senegal. Almost twenty years, in fact. I'm not too sure why I took such a long time to do it. For over five years, I was constantly delaying this homecoming. At the last moment, I would decide to go off somewhere else, friends would invite me to somewhere fantastic for a holiday, or there would be a major tournament such as the World Cup to play in. It was as if, subconsciously, I was slightly afraid of facing up to reality, so I would convince myself that there was always a good reason why I could not go that particular year. Above all, I dreaded the thought that I might disappoint those people who had waited all this time for me. Perhaps I was not yet ready to dive back into the past. By 2001, though, I had reached an age where I had a lot of questions that needed answering. In the end, I understood what was going on and admitted to myself that I was missing something. Before then, I had probably been too young to have understood this. When I was growing up in France, I had never wondered about my roots and about the first years of my life. Maybe because I didn't want to know about them. Later on, I didn't ask myself any questions because I was living in a sort of football bubble. But all this began to change in 2001, during the Confederations Cup, when I spent an evening with various other French players, all of whom had unusual backgrounds. I was with Robert Pires, whose roots are in Portugal, Marcel Desailly, Laurent Robert, Nicolas Anelka and Sylvain Wiltord, who originates from the West Indies. It made me realise that, although I was French, I also had a part of me that still felt a very strong attachment to Senegal, my country of origin. From that moment on, I began to want to go back there but felt I needed something positive to offer, which is why Diambars, for me, was extraordinary. It was the perfect opportunity.

From the moment I arrived back in Senegal, what hit me was the sheer number of children begging in the streets of Dakar. I hadn't realised there were so many in Dakar itself. It really shocked me to see these children, who had barely any shoes or clothes.

Today, we're still trying to raise about £800,000. In total, the academy costs between £1.5 and £2 million. Over half of this has been financed by sponsorship, private donations and business. When I spoke to Adidas about Diambars, I was under contract to them. They are going to supply the kit for the centre and, on top of that, they will help us financially. Adidas France and Adidas UK have been incredibly supportive.

I badly wanted to go back to Senegal. The memories I had of the place were getting dimmer and dimmer and it was really important for me to go back. I was asking myself lots of questions about my true roots and wondered what the place I grew up in was really like. I had some idea but it was all too vague, so I wanted to see for myself – except I didn't know when to go back. Every year, I would tell myself, 'Right, this is the year I'm going.' And every time, I would postpone the trip. It was almost as if I needed something to take me there, to push me to go. Diambars turned out to be the catalyst that made me go back.

I did not have to choose French nationality, contrary to what I have sometimes heard said. My grandfather fought for the French army, so I am Franco-Senegalese by birth. That is why I have never had a problem over my nationality, nor any choice to make. I went to Senegal in July 2003, a year after the World Cup. With the Diambars project in my pocket and in my heart, I told myself that this was the dream opportunity to go back. I was not going empty-handed to Senegal. It was important for me to go to my country of birth with something to offer.

Before the trip, the closer it got to leaving, the more I became full of doubts. I worried about how things would go, whether people were going to welcome me. In the end, however, everything went unbelievably well.

My mother could not accompany me, so she let me go on my own. I was tense during the journey. My hands had started to sweat. I didn't know what to expect; I was anxious as well as emotional. I was not worried about being disappointed. Rather, I was worried because I didn't know how things would go and how I would cope with moments of intense emotion. Because going back to the country of one's childhood is not an easy thing to do.

When I landed at the airport, it was as if the President of the Republic had arrived. There were so many people! It was awesome. There were at least 500 people waiting for me. The kids from my school in Dakar were there, cheering away. The tom-toms were playing, the atmosphere was electric. It was an amazingly powerful moment. I didn't get tearful because I managed to control myself but the emotion was very much there, inside me. I don't know if the crowd noticed but, the truth was, I was deeply, deeply moved.

My godmother was there to greet me and various uncles as well. I hadn't seen my godmother in a long time. She had come to visit us once in France but it must have been at least ten years since I had last seen her. I went to the hotel to get changed, then we all went out for dinner.

I stayed for a week. During that time, I think I must have met every single person in the country! The President of the

Republic, Abdoulaye Wade, as well as his Prime Minister, the Minister for Sports and the President of the Football Federation. I met all the leaders of Senegal! When my parents discovered that I had met the President of the Republic, they were both proud and happy. That's the great thing about football. Without it, I would never have been able to meet all those people. Yet I found it all a bit too much. I was never alone for a moment.

I went to the neighbourhood where I grew up. I was with my aunts, my neighbours, people who had carried me on their shoulders when I was little. Everyone was outside their homes, it was like a giant street party. I instantly recognised the street itself, Dara Street, which means 'zero' in Wolof. Yes, I know, I come from zero street! It's a small, well-kept street, though, with only about thirty houses and not far from the suburb of Grand Dakar.

At one stage, I was standing outside the little house where I had lived when something happened that hit me like a hammer blow. I turned and suddenly recognised the garage door opposite my house which we used as a goal when we played football. It still had a number seven painted on it, just like it did all those years ago, and seeing that sent me spinning back in time. It was a really powerful moment for me. This was where it had all started, my love of the game, my obsession with it. It was there, in front of this garage door with its number seven. And here were all these people from my childhood talking to me and telling me all sorts of things.

It felt, though, as if I no longer had any memory. I was in Senegal surrounded by people who I had grown up with; they knew who I was but, as far as I was concerned, they were adults that I did not know. Physically, they had changed, just as I had as well. We had gone our separate ways when we had been seven or eight years old. Twenty years on, we were no longer the same people yet they were telling me about all the places we used to hide in when we had done naughty things. The problem was, I had no memory of any of this at all. In the evening, when I went back to my hotel room, I would ask myself, 'How could you have forgotten all this?' It bothered me a bit. When the people I had grown up with told me about these moments from our childhood, I could see the emotion on their faces, even though I couldn't really remember what they were talking about. One man presented me with a traditional shirt and some photographs of the two of us together when we were boys. There was a little group of women who teased me that I used to terrorise them when I was little. I was so surprised because I had no memory of them. Also, I did not want them to think 'He's changed, he doesn't remember us, or his country, or his street.' I was embarrassed, ill at ease. I thought about that a lot. I wondered how it was possible for memories, especially childhood memories, to disappear like this from one's mind. I know I left Senegal when I was very young but I don't think it was the fact that I left when I did that was the cause of it. I think it's more that I had lived through a lot for someone who was still only 28. I think football has made me fast-forward through a lot of life at a young age. Football has given me so much, and in return I have given it my all, I have dedicated myself to it every single day. I am not offering excuses, simply reasons.

My greatest moment of joy was the day I went to a school and was welcomed by the children who had put together a show and a mini-football tournament. The girls sang, then the boys played football. It was wonderful. That was the most moving part of my trip to Senegal. To see so much joy in the eyes of those kids was easily enough to make me incredibly happy. They enabled me to understand that I was one of them, not just an outsider who was paying them a visit. I obviously recognised a part of myself in all those kids. Just like them, I knew how to be content with the basics: eating and playing football. It was a pleasure to see them because they were totally unaffected and exuded expressions of sheer happiness. In Africa, people know how to be content with what they have. I have been raised with that attitude and I have never let myself stray from it.

Laying the foundation stone for Diambars was a moment of great pride for me because the project was, and continues to be, a tough undertaking. But we were quickly encouraged by the fact that Senegal really helped us. They gave us the land within a few months of our project becoming official; in total, there will be four football pitches. The opening is set for the start of 2006. The foundation stone was laid in Saly, 45 minutes by road from Dakar. There were a lot of people there, who kept thanking us for what we were doing for Senegal, because people are genuinely touched by this sort of act.

On the whole, Africans are a bit disappointed that there are not more footballers who help their country. They would like more of them to follow the example of George Weah who is from Liberia, or the Ghanaian Abedi Pele, both of whom are now fantastic ambassadors for their sport and for their continent. Both these players had a lot of success in Europe but nowadays devote themselves fully to life and to football in their country. These are the sorts of comments that people made to me.

It was a wrench when the time came to leave Senegal. The week had flown by too quickly. I had the impression that I had seen nothing and visited nowhere. It was too early to be leaving. I felt terrible and already I want to go back. The good thing is that, thanks to Diambars, I know that I will.

For the time being, given all the games and all the travelling, it's a bit difficult but I would like to be more committed to the Diambars project. But, if it works well in Senegal, the long-term aim is to have a Diambars project in each African country.

Since I was a child, I have never asked myself questions about my colour. It has never been an issue for me to be black and to be the captain of the France football team. I am not the first and I'm sure I won't be the last either. I was already the captain of the under-21s. It's not something that shocks me or that makes me reflect upon the situation. As far as I am concerned, I have never suffered as a result of the colour of my skin.

I never had any problems with racism in my childhood, nor have I had as a player. Well, only the usual one-off incidents such as the one with Mihaljovic during an Arsenal game against Lazio, or in Spain against Valencia and Vigo. But otherwise, in France, I've never had any problems. I know very well racism exists, I'm not that naïve. It exists everywhere. But in my own career and in what I do every day, I have never come across it either in France or in England. And from my point of view, I never differentiate and get on equally well with white people and black people. Diambars is not a project to combat anything in particular. It's a positive project, something that was created to advance things, not to prove anything specific.

As is so often the case in this world, the works have been a bit delayed and I need to go back to Senegal for the inauguration. On 3 February 2005, at the Landmark Hotel in London, we organised a fund-raising evening. It was a fantastic night. Lots of players turned out for us. My team-mates were there: Sol Campbell, Ashley Cole, Robert Pires and Thierry Henry. But other friends were also there: Mickaël Silvestre, William Gallas, Salif Diao, Andy Cole, Brad Friedel. There was a superb dinner and an auction where we sold off club shirts from all over Europe, as well as objects, holidays, and even Charlene Spiteri's guitar which Titi managed to buy. There was Maldini's shirt which brought about heated bidding between Sol and Ashley. Ronaldinho's shoes were also sold. In addition, we have created a Diambars shirt, a 1,000 limited-edition one that costs from £1,000 to £10,000, depending on the number. I was really proud of the fact that Senegal's President Abdoulaye Wade bought the number 1 shirt. Maybe President Chirac of France and Tony Blair could buy numbers 2 and 3. That would be really fantastic! The first Diambars dinner was a fabulous and very successful evening. I got the feeling that a lot of players supported our project but not just because they were my friends. They could tell that we want to do something new and different, something that will make a real difference and I was very touched by their support. That evening we raised a total of £200,000.

With Bernard and Jimmy, everything runs very smoothly. Jimmy, who travels between Senegal, France and England, is really the one who looks after everything. He's the co-ordinator. Bernard is the President of Diambars France, and I am the Diambars UK President. In other words, Bernard is my counterpart in France. He goes out looking for sponsors and partnerships, for brands that believe in us and our academy. But

Bernard is also much more than that. When I started off playing for France, he was the one who made me realise lots of things. He used to say to me regularly, 'He who doesn't know where he comes from finds it hard to know where he is going.' He opened up my eyes, and he did the same for Lilian Thuram. He made me understand how important my roots were and especially how significant it was for me to go back to the land of my birth. In the end, I could no longer make do just with photos and my mother's anecdotes.

I love the slogans that accompany our project – 'creating champions for football and for life', 'reading the game and books' and 'enabling the water-carrier to carry through his dreams'. They symbolise everything we believe in. Football is neither a pretext nor an end in itself. It is the key to the foundations of what we are building. Diambars is something that is very important in my life and has become a part of me. It symbolises my everlasting ties with Senegal.

3

My Childhood

I don't have many memories of Sicap, the neighbourhood in Dakar where I grew up. I left Senegal when I was seven. When I went back there in 2003, it really jogged my memory. My mother and stepfather sometimes talk about what I was like when I was young. Apparently, I was a 'naughty little boy'. We were lucky compared to others in the neighbourhood because we had a TV. Not many of us did. Each time my brother Nicko – who is a year older than me – invited any of his friends back to watch TV, I refused to let them in. I would throw stones at them so that they would go home! My parents and my grandparents tell me that I was a real hard case. The street where we lived was not very big and there were some small covered play areas where we used to go and play football. A couple of minutes away from our house was a sand-covered area where I would meet up with my friends and we would organise some matches. I used to play in my little plastic shoes. We would muck around. We were five, six, seven years old, so just played for the sheer fun of it, because from as young as I can remember, I have always loved to kick a football around.

I never knew my father who apparently was a student from the Gabon. My parents divorced when I was very young and in fact my name, Vieira, is my mother Emilienne's surname. I am told my father once came to see me in Dakar when I was little and that I wanted to go off with him! That's what my mother told me. But I have never seen him since. If I was asked today what he looked like, I couldn't say. If ten people lined up next to each other and I was asked to identify which one was my father, I would be incapable of recognising him. I have no idea what he looks like. My mother – who is known to many people as Mama

Rose – comes originally from the Cape Verde islands which are about three hundred miles off the coast of Senegal. She remarried in 2004 but has been with my stepfather for over fifteen years. She met him in France and he is the one I think of as my dad. He was very good to me and my brother.

My natural father has a twin brother and one day, he came to see me. He said that my father would like to make contact with me and to meet me. This was after an international game. On a different occasion, another uncle gave me a letter from my father saying that he wanted to meet up with me. He was writing to me because he felt the need to see me again. But I didn't follow it up. I have never particularly felt a need to know him. I grew up in a house with four uncles and a grandfather, so I have always had male role models and have never felt I lacked anything in that part of my life. My mother has four brothers and three sisters. I grew up in an atmosphere of harmony, with a real family. My mother was very strong during the hard times that we lived through. She was both the mother and the father figure.

We left for France to have a better life. It was hard in Senegal and life was difficult. Because Senegal was a former French colony, going to France was an opportunity to escape from hardship and poverty. When we first arrived – my brother and I, our mother and a few uncles – we went to live in a flat on the outskirts of Paris with another of my uncles, my mother's older brother, who had been the first to settle in France. I didn't experience a shock. The dominant feeling was more one of excitement at boarding a plane and travelling far away.

My mother's older brother had already been in France for a while and he had found this flat in Trappes, in the western suburbs of Paris. When we got there, we went straight to stay with him. There were five or six of us there. At first it was difficult, although at least the language was the same. But everything else was so different. We had left behind everything we were familiar with – all our friends, our family, our African culture and our way of life. Only later on do you settle in, find your bearings, develop your little habits. And you learn to become strong, which is a good lesson to learn in life. But being uprooted and having to fight to establish ourselves in our new country is probably one reason why our family is so close, so bonded together.

We all came to France. The first ones to arrive found work. My mother initially got a job as a cleaning lady but she also went to secretarial college. She's now forty-seven. When she got her diploma, she changed jobs.

I don't remember having any particular problems when I first arrived. I have to say that we had settled in a neighbourhood full of immigrants, in particular from Africa. Although life was not easy for people, it was generally a safe neighbourhood at the time. I did not experience any racism, we were never on the receiving end of insults. We used to get in to fights, like all kids do, but there were never any major problems. I joined the local football club in Trappes; I must have been about eight or nine years old. But it was just to get a game, nothing more. I have always liked football, and was always drawn to the sport. It was a group activity and this allowed me to make friends quickly. I played in Trappes for a couple of years before leaving for Dreux, a satellite town about 100kms north-west of Paris. We moved there when my mother found a more secure job, and we settled in quickly. We lived with my grandparents. My brother was with me. The two of us used to kick a ball around but my brother never took football seriously. For him, his mates were all-important. Even though he had more talent than I did, the fact was, he couldn't care less about football. He preferred hanging around with his mates and chatting up the girls.

As for me, I didn't take football seriously either for a long time. I immediately loved the game but it was a source of pleasure, that was all. In Dreux we started off playing in a covered play area and the guy who supervised us also ran the local club. He asked me to go and play for them. I wasn't against the idea but I said that if I went, then my mates also had to come with me because I wanted to carry on playing with them. So it was in Dreux that I really started to play properly, that I started to take football a bit more seriously.

Throughout my childhood, I was always a lot taller than kids of my age. That's why I used to have problems whenever we played against other teams or took part in tournaments. There has always been a problem with inaccurate dates of birth, with what is referred to by officials as 'the presumed date of birth'. That was tough, despite the fact that it is quite clear what day I was actually born on. There is no controversy over that, even though I admit that the same cannot always be said for some of the other players from Africa. It's funny because that remains my worst memory of that whole time – people wanting to check my passport because I was taller than the other kids. I was always allowed to play, it never stopped me from taking part in any tournament, but even so, the suspicion was always there and I found that tough to live with. I had the impression that other people thought I was a cheat. And I have never cheated when it comes to football.

Like a lot of talented youngsters, I played in a more attacking position at the time. I was the playmaker. But I was also a team player. Even when I was little, I used to get hold of the ball, dribble it up towards the goal then pass it so that another team member scored the goal. I have always had that attitude. I get as much pleasure from seeing another player score as I get from scoring myself. I played for the under-15s at Dreux, then the under-18s. I left the club the same year as we were promoted to the under-18s national league, known in French as the *cadets nationaux*. I had the choice whether to do another year with them or go to Tours. There was also Châteauroux and a number of other clubs in the region that had contacted me but the one I was most interested in was F.C. Tours which had, at the time, an excellent reputation.

My years with Dreux were an extraordinary time for me. We used to set off in our minibus, having prepared our little Catalan-style sandwiches in advance. We would play in the afternoon. The journey there would be quite long, so we had to have our sandwiches ready to eat either before or after the games! Tuna sandwiches with tomato ... Sitting in our 15- or 20-seater minibus, we would eat those sandwiches with crisps, tell each other stupid stories, slap each other as a joke. The atmosphere was great! The good times that I spent with my mates going to and from football matches are what really made me love the game.

When I look back at the fantastic results we have had with the French team, I am convinced that the atmosphere within the squad was a key factor in our success. When there's a good atmosphere amongst team members, when they like being together, then that creates a real sense of solidarity between them. You actually want to go tearing into another defensive position simply to help a mate out that you love. With the Blues, the personal journey we embarked on proved to be as wonderful as the sporting one. But going back to F.C. Tours: it was my first professional club, they were in the second division at the time. Philippe Leroux was an important person in my life during that period. He was their coach at the time and was instrumental in helping me to settle in, in enabling me to progress in football, and he was the one who made me move back into a defensive midfield position.

Tours was an enormous change for me because I suddenly found myself boarding at the coaching academy. I had left my parents and was all alone. That was really hard because, although I was a gangly 6' 3" tall, I was still barely sixteen years old. At home, my mother looked after us all so well and she cooked all these delicious African dishes for me. I knew that I was going to miss all that! I still felt very African at the time. And I have never lost that culture, even today. It's deep-rooted and still very much there at home. Whenever we have big family meals, that's the atmosphere I love going back to. Our traditional dish is the *tié bou dienne*, rice and fish. It's fantastic. Just talking about it makes my mouth water. When I'm home with the whole family, we eat it from a huge bowl, seven or eight of us. The men all eat from one dish, each with his own small spoon, and the women are next to us, eating from theirs. That, too, is typically Senegalese. And that sort of tradition will always be important for me, wherever I am, whatever I do.

At Tours, I was all alone. I shared a room with Armand Rimbaud who was the goalkeeper. We soon got on really well.

But Tours was not a coaching centre like the others. There were only eight of us who boarded; the other players lived in the area, so they got to go home in the evening. The eight of us who stayed behind became really close. There was Armand, Vincent, Stéphane ... We had a very close bond. I never saw nor felt any difference in where they came from. The main thing was to have a lot of fun. Beyond that, in terms of football, it was fabulous! It was when I was at Tours that I met the Cameroonian José Touré who had been going through some difficult times in his life. Tours had given him the opportunity to sort himself out.

Obviously, sometimes, we would do a bunk. We were about an hour's walk away from the town centre, but being four mates who got on really well, we wanted to go clubbing, meet girls. So we jumped over the wall several times. To make it worse, there was an Alsatian dog, or something similar, that guarded the centre. So we would wait until he was at the other end of the grounds before we made a run for it. It would be very late by our standards, 11 pm, or even midnight. The lights would be out and everyone asleep. We would leap over the wall at the back and start to walk. We would walk for a whole hour just to go clubbing. We would always get in because, in the end, they got to know us! The first time I did this, I thought I was going to die; I didn't think I would ever reach the nightclub! We would leave at about four or five in the morning. Then we had another hour's walk ahead of us! But those are some of my happiest memories. We never got caught. That's how good we were! But when I think that I would walk for one hour just to go to a nightclub – that's completely crazy, nuts. Still, we had so much fun.

I have always been shy with girls! I grew a bit more confident after I became more successful in life and in football, but at first, before I went over to speak to a girl, she had to be a 'dead cert'. I have always been someone who is quite reserved, not the sort to chat up the birds. But once I'm on the pitch, that's completely different: I know why I'm there, I know what I want. I'm determined and I am not afraid to say what I think.

I was seventeen when I left for Cannes. Tours had just been

declared bankrupt because they had had some big financial problems and it was the Mediterranean club that came after me. I had had offers from Cannes, Auxerre (in Burgundy) and Nantes (in Brittany). I chose Cannes for two reasons. Firstly because Richard Bettoni, their scout at the time, had been the first to go and see my parents. And secondly because Cannes was in the south; there was the sun, the sea. I am still very attached to that town. But at first it was tough for me to decide to go there because it was so far away. Tours was just two hours from Paris by TGV train, three hours from my parents. Being at Cannes would mean that I could no longer go home to see them very often. But I was won over by what Richard Bettoni said, as were my parents. He told them that I was not just being offered a normal contract but that he would look after me as if I were his son. He would oversee my education. And that last point was very important for my mother.

With Tours, when the best of the Centre region went to play in a tournament, I was always picked. It was the same thing when I was picked for the Eure et Loire region's team. I was carving out my little path, but always in the same way ... nonchalantly!

When I got to Cannes, Bettoni and Guy Lacombe, who was the youth coach at the time, got all the youngsters together and made two teams, one for the third division and one for the fourth. It had all been decided on the basis of some physical tests. And mine had been disastrous! All this was completely new to me. I am not someone who likes to run. He had obviously watched me doing some of these exercises and told himself, 'That one, he can go straight in with the reserves.' I let them make their choice. They made their two groups. I went into division four. As far as I was concerned, that was how it was and I didn't even ask myself whether it was fair or not.

I didn't stay long in the fourth division. A couple of weeks, that's all! I was better than that. It wasn't as if I had something to prove, I was just playing how I normally did. The training sessions were run by Guy Lacombe and Richard Bettoni. But Richard Bettoni looked after the discipline side of things in particular. The training ground was at Cannes La Boca. I shared a room with Frédéric Malayeude who was the spitting image of Richard Gere.

When I first got to Cannes, I would go for a swim in the sea every evening. It was fantastic to have the sea there. But then the novelty passed! At first, it was brilliant, but after three weeks, I had got used to it. Cannes, for me, represents comradeship. I had my two best friends there, Jimmy Capoue and Bernard Lambourde, the Guadeloupe-born defender who subsequently played for Chelsea. They used to come and get me in the evening and I would do a bunk. They had a flat and a car, so they would come and get me and take me clubbing. Afterwards, I would go back to bed. And again, I never got caught! Nobody thought I might be up to that sort of thing, but that's because I hid my cards well. Whether I was in Dreux, Tours, or on the Croisette in Cannes!

At first, the games were tough. They were a clear notch above the level I had been used to. But I was a very quick learner. I quickly learned to raise my game, both in terms of my positional play and my one-on-one match-ups. My physical strength improved as well. Guy Lacombe was an outstanding coach. There was not a single training session where we were bored. (Well, maybe Tuesdays. Because on Tuesdays, we would go running in the woods or round the golf course.) Guy Lacombe is one of the best coaches I have ever come across. Football was his life. We would finish our training sessions and go home, but he was always there. He would arrive at eight o'clock in the morning and leave at eight o'clock at night. He was always in his office watching tapes of games. There was an extraordinary generation of players who came from Cannes and it was in large part down to him that many of them went on to have successful careers after learning their trade at the club.

It took me a year to break into the first team which by then had just been promoted to the first division. When I started to play in it, Luis Fernandez was the coach. A former defensive midfielder, he had been capped 60 times for France and won the European Championships with them in 1984 when Platini had been in the team. At club level, he had played for Paris St

Germain before finishing his career at Cannes. In fact, he had been one of the players that I most admired when I was growing up. Luis was incredible as a coach. He had come to watch a reserve team game and that day, I had been rubbish. Even so, when I emerged from the changing room, he was waiting for me and told me, 'Monday, you're training with the first team.' So I trained with them all that week and on the Saturday, I played my first A-team game.

For a youngster to be with the players that were in that team – it couldn't get much better than that! There was their key striker, Franck Priou, Mickael Madar, who later spent a season at Everton and was known, amongst other names, as Mad Mike and Ma-Darlin (I'm not sure why but maybe because he had long, black hair), the goalkeeper François Lemasson, my mates Lambourde and Capoue, and the team captain Franck Durix. They were all real characters. We had such a laugh! When you are young and starting out in that sort of atmosphere, it's fantastic. They adopted me straight away. But they also put me under a lot of pressure, every one of them. They all wanted the ball. When I had the ball and I passed it to Madar, I would get bollocked by Priou. And when I gave it to Priou, I'd get the same earful from Madar. They were all crazy and it was brilliant!

At the training ground, we would get changed in the changing room but to get to the ground itself, we had to take our cars. We would get to the ground and wait for Luis who was always the last to arrive. We would bring the balls and the guys would start shooting at goal. One day, Luis was calling out to everyone but nobody was listening to him. He got annoyed so he shouted 'We're leaving.' We had only been there for five minutes. Back in the changing room, I saw him at the back of the room playing cards with some of the guys as if nothing had happened. We had a little pit and an artificial grass pitch where we had some incredible four-a-side games. The quality of players there was really high.

Nantes–Cannes: 1–1. I remember the game and the score very well, even though my memory is not really my strong point, because it was my first game in Division One for Cannes. I remember that towards the end of the ninety minutes, Georges Eo, Nantes' joint-coach, had verbally laid into the referee. This had happened near to where I was standing and I had been really shocked. The ref had not given a penalty at the end. I didn't know you could talk to match officials in that way.

The game was fantastic. The fans at Nantes, the game, everything that day was extraordinary and it had gone really well for me. I was very pleased. My mother was so proud. She wasn't there on the day but I know she was very happy for me.

I knew this was only the beginning. I realised that I had a golden opportunity, now that I was at the coaching academy of AS Cannes. I had told myself when I got there that my stay might enable me to make a career out of the game, to be a professional footballer. Beforehand, it had been more a question of spending time having fun with my mates, and of doing a bit of sport.

When I got to Cannes, I was still studying. I was doing an accountancy diploma, which I got. It was really just to say I had done it because what I really wanted was to be a professional footballer. After my first game, I never once played for the reserves again.

I am proud of myself when I sit here and think about Senegal, Cannes and everything else. I have managed to progress and I am proud of that. Nothing has ever been handed to me on a plate. I was lucky enough to meet some good people. There has always been somebody to guide me in all my clubs, from Dreux and Tours through to Cannes. And there has always been somebody to whom I have become attached. At Dreux, it was Jacques Autef. He would come and collect me at home, take me to training, then bring me back afterwards. Sometimes, I would spend the weekend with him and his son Tony. He would give me little gifts and would look after me as if I was his son.

At Tours, that special person was Philippe Leroux. He was responsible for the coaching centre. He would give me advice and try to make me understand that I had what it took to succeed and that I had the opportunity to do so. He would talk to me about my game but also about everyday life. There was a real closeness between us.

At Cannes, I had Richard Bettoni. Then Guy Lacombe. Guy is someone who has passion. Luis, on the other hand, is a nutter. What I loved about him is that I never felt under pressure. He introduced me gently into the job. He was such a fun and crazy guy that all I could think about was having a laugh. Whatever advice he gave, he would give it whilst we were playing. He was always playing with us. In fact, in order to win, you had to be in his team. You could never win against him! Because then, he would stop laughing.

I scored my first goal, a header, at Strasbourg. I have so many wonderful memories of my time with Cannes that it makes me feel ill to see the state that the club is now in, languishing in the lower divisions of the French league.

My grandfather and my mother have kept all the newspaper cuttings about me, right from the start of my career. They have all these scrapbooks in which they stick everything that they have cut out. Even my little cousins do it.

I don't remember what the very first article about me said. I am not someone who keeps all his mementos, his first shirt or whatever. I tell myself that it's done now, it's in the past, I have to move on to the next thing. Anyway, I have all these people around me who do the gathering of memories for me. I love the game for what it is. I don't keep a thing. I should do, because they represent wonderful memories, but I just don't. I don't even watch my own games.

What I love is the game itself. I don't think I could play for a club where there was not a good atmosphere. It would be too difficult for me to play for a team where everyone was in it for himself.

At Milan, it was tough because that's exactly what it was like, everyone was in it for himself. And that's really not my mentality. Arsenal, though, was a family club. Players spent time together – going out to eat, socialising. I prefer that sort of set up. I need all of that to succeed, to feel relaxed, to be pleased to go to training every day.

At Cannes, I won the Coupe Gambardella, played in the Paris suburb of Issy-les-Moulineaux. It's the French junior championships, and it was my first cup. I was already regularly playing with the pros but this final meant a lot to me. It was a game for my generation of players, for my mates and my coaching centre. For all of us, this game represented the culmination of all our hard work and of the training methods of the club. To add to the excitement, we even paraded the trophy at the Parc des Princes. Obviously, I have held aloft a few trophies in my time but this one had a particular meaning for me. It just goes to show that we don't necessarily have a logical hierarchy of victories in our minds. If that were the case, the Coupe Gambardella would have disappeared long ago from my memory. But you never forget that first cup, that first big emotion. Never.

4

It Was Like Being Kidnapped

While I was still at Cannes, I was selected for France's under-21 squad that, under former French international Jean-François Jodar, was preparing for the European under-21 championships. Jodar, who now manages the UAE team, had a clear idea of who he wanted in his final line-up, so although I was the only one in the squad playing in the first division, and, at eighteen years old, the youngest captain in top-level football in France, I never seemed to be part of his plans. I was playing with Mickaël Madar, Franck Priou, Frank Durix and I had Luis Fernandez as a coach. They were all crazy guys! But to be honest, it was ideal for a young player to kick off his career surrounded by characters like that. It was like living in a dream, because we had a great team and we were always laughing.

Jodar was forced to pick me because I was in Division One but I felt that he didn't really want to. I could feel that he was under pressure to do so, although I don't know from where or who that pressure came, but I could sense that he picked me against his wishes. I felt it because I could see how he was with me. For two or three years beforehand, he had been getting his squad ready for the European Championships and now here was this player that he had never called up, who played at the top level, and had come out of nowhere. It was as if someone had said to him 'You have to take Vieira.' He wouldn't talk to me and it was obviously a complete pain in the arse for him to have me around.

The under-21 team played at Cannes against Italy. We drew 0–0 and it went well for me. So he brought me into the squad for the European Championships. Just before the very first game, something really crazy happened: my boot fell apart. I only had the one pair, and on top of everything, they had moulded studs, so it's true I wasn't making it any easier for myself. Also, I take a shoe size 44, which is a $9\frac{1}{2}$. I didn't have too many options so was forced to play with bandages wrapped around my boot. We had gone round the shops to find another pair but we hadn't been able to find one, so I played that first match and after that was on the bench and hardly played again.

I remember that time because even though I was very young and didn't say anything, I didn't think the coach's attitude was very good. None of that affected my self-confidence, though. Things were starting to go well for me at AS Cannes in that autumn of 1995 and I was regularly playing first-division football. And that's when I went off to Milan. It was a lightning quick departure that took place in the most extraordinary way.

Not many people know what really happened. One day, I turned up for training at Cannes, only to be told, 'You're not training today, you're off to Milan, you're going to sign for AC Milan.' I said, 'What? Who am I signing for?' I didn't even have time to work out what was happening, or let the news sink in. Before I had had even the slightest chance to think about the situation, a car whisked me away to the airport where a private jet was waiting to fly me to Milan. It was almost like being kidnapped.

I therefore found myself at AC Milan's headquarters. There were photographs of the players everywhere, as well as a lot of silverware on show. We sat down in the office of Ariedo Braida, AC's manager at the time. In the plane, I had been accompanied by various people, including Alain Miglascio, an agent, Francis Borelli, AS Cannes' President, and even the then mayor of the city of Cannes, Michel Mouillot, which was certainly unusual. The situation was far from clear and it was obvious that something important was going on. I was only nineteen years old. When I boarded the plane, I had told myself, 'That's pretty cool, signing for AC Milan.' Obviously I was pleased because even just the name of this illustrious club was enough to make the kid that I was dream.

But once I was in Ariedo Braida's office, I asked Miglascio, who was in there with me, if I could call my parents. 'I need to get hold of my mother to tell her that I'm in Milan and about to sign for AC,' I said. I thought I was asking for something simple and totally legitimate. I thought I should at least speak to my parents to let them know what was going on before I made such a big career-changing move. I wasn't being difficult and I wasn't asking for a big favour but he replied 'No, go on, sign. This is AC Milan, you won't get another opportunity as good as this.' They left me alone in the office for five minutes. I was sitting there all on my own. Thinking. Quickly.

AC Milan had Paolo Maldini, Franco Baresi, George Weah and Marcel Desailly. So I signed. It was a four- or five-year contract, I can't remember which. As for my salary, I didn't understand a thing about it. It was all in Italian lire and I had absolutely no idea how much we were talking about. But I still put my signature at the foot of the document.

I was pleased to have signed for AC Milan because at the time, to be part of such a high-level club at nineteen years of age was really not something that happened very often. But deep down, my conscience was not clear. Something was bothering me, something was not right. I wondered whether it was the fact that I had done it without having talked it over with my mother beforehand, because I used to talk to her about everything, about all the approaches that I used to get. I remember my frame of mind very clearly. I felt a mixture of joy and real pride but at the same time a feeling of having done something bad. I was overcome by a definite sense of unease.

I returned to Cannes to get my things ready. My agent at the time was a guy called Marc Roger. He had been completely pushed to one side, and I had not had time to talk to him about the whole business. I had turned up for training one day, then off I'd gone in that private plane bound for Milan. I had not suspected a thing either. I had told Braida and Miglascio that I worked with Marc but they had replied that they would sort it out with him. All this bothered me enormously, so when I got back to Cannes, I called him. 'Listen, Marc,' I said, 'I think I've just fucked up big time. I was in Milan and I've just signed for AC. I don't really understand what happened. Do you think you could have a look at the contract?' Marc was really unhappy with what I told him. I sent him over the document I had just signed, he took one look at it and said that he would take care of it at once.

I flew to Paris and went to see him at his office. The papers were already saying things about it and *l'Equipe* even had the headline, 'Where has Vieira gone?' I had signed for the following season and had to finish the season with Cannes. Everyone was looking for me but I was already with Marc. He then went to see the people from Cannes and Milan and he told them that this was no way to conduct business, that they should never have taken me off to Milan just like that to sign a contract, given that I was a client of his. He told them, 'Either we start again from scratch if you really want him, or we sue you.' In the end, when we looked at the contract in detail, it became clear that it didn't correspond at all to what I had been told. And because everything had been worded in Italian lire, I hadn't known what all those unfeasibly long numbers had meant and that in fact they didn't amount to very much.

In the end, we drew up another four-year contract. And this time, I knew what my salary would be! At Cannes, I had an apprentice's type of contract, but because I had started to play with the professionals, Borelli had altered certain elements. I earned about 60,000 French francs per month, gross, which amounted to around £75,000 per year. By going to Milan, I would be multiplying my salary four-fold. I had a good relationship with Borelli who treated me like a son. That was also the case with many players; in fact, he had a fantastic relationship with everybody. When it came to football, his relationship with the game was one of total passion and love. He remains, though, one of the most superstitious men I have ever come across.

Borelli, the Cannes President, had understood that it was in my interest to move to Milan. My mother, on the other hand, couldn't quite get her head round the fact that I had signed without being conscious of what I was doing. She had trouble understanding, which is completely normal, the sheer pressure that a youngster can experience when he is surrounded by so many great names. Also, she had difficulty appreciating that for a very shy youngster, it was unsettling to find myself whisked off in a private jet with a load of people that I didn't really know. I hadn't initially seen the downside of the whole business, even though in the end, I realised and came to my senses quite quickly.

It was only a few years later, when I went back to Cannes and was able to talk about it once more to people, that I finally realised what had actually gone on. It seems that not a lot of my £2m transfer fee had actually found its way into the club coffers. If I take into account what the agents, and people here and there took as well, and when I see the state that AS Cannes is now in, I'm absolutely livid.

When you look at all the players that learned their trade at the club, including Zinedine Zidane, Johan Micoud, Sébastien Frei, David Jemmali or our own Gaël Clichy, and when you see the club languishing in the 'National', the equivalent of England's Second Division, I tell myself that it's a complete scandal, that it can't be true. That's why I am part of a foundation that tries to help this special club which has in turn helped mould so many players.

At the time, I was heavily criticised, along the lines of 'the youngster who is off to AC Milan', but people did not know me. I had not played much in Division One in France and I was taking a big risk by leaving for this renowned European club. Also the whole thing happened before the Bosman law which, amongst other things, allowed EU players who were out of contract to transfer freely within clubs in Europe. But that was not the case for me when I arrived at AC Milan where I was the sixth foreigner under contract. Already there were Paulo Futre, the Portuguese international whose career was ultimately cut short by long-standing knee problems, Dejan Savicevic, who came from Montenegro, Zvonimir Boban, the poetry-writing Croatian midfielder, George Weah from Liberia, and the future France captain Marcel Desailly. In other words, the squad already contained some very big foreign names. And only three out of the six of us could be on any one team sheet. Three players were almost automatic selections: Desailly, Weah and Savicevic. When one of them got injured, it was often Boban who played. He was the captain of his national side and went on to lead them to third place at the 1998 World Cup, so he was no mean player. Paulo Futre, who later on had a spell at West Ham, was also frequently injured, so that left me maybe three or four matches per season that I would play in. It was a strange situation.

I left Cannes with a heavy heart. Cannes was a small family club and the people there were fantastic. Now is the right time for me to pay tribute to a player with whom I started out: Frank Durix. I have never seen a player as tough as him. I have played against or with some of the biggest names in football today but Frank gave me some unforgettable memories. Come rain or snow, a dry or a waterlogged pitch, he was always there wearing his moulded studs. Durix was a real magician.

When I arrived at Milan, I discovered other magicians, starting with none other than the coach, Fabio Capello. He was amazing. He knew full well that I was not yet ready. But he was constantly saying 'Keep working! Keep working, it always pays off.' He never sidelined me, he always made sure that I was involved in the group. Saturday mornings, for example, he worked on tactics. He would take the eleven he had picked for the next day's game and practise positional play. The others in the squad would then do some drills. A favourite one was where a group of players passed the ball to each other and one or two others would try to intercept it.

Capello would always tell me to get behind the midfielder Albertini or Desailly who was a central defender, and copy their every move. I followed them around like their shadow and, by doing exactly the same as them, I learned about defensive tactics. I was the only player allowed to do this and I was really pleased. I was young and Capello knew I needed to learn. And as a result, I was happy because I felt involved. At the end of training, he would often tell me to go and do more work, or some physical training with the fitness coach. So that's what I would do.

Some days, he would tell me to stay with the other players to work on something specific, so I would stay. I had the impression that he was always very considerate towards me and because of his attitude, which I consider to be that of a true professional, I never felt ignored and never got discouraged. Naturally, there were some tough times as well because I was dying to play, to run around, to let off steam. And after training, when I went back to my apartment, I would feel very alone. Although my mother would come every now and again, that feeling of solitude never really left me. I lived next to the San Siro stadium which is fifteen minutes away from the city centre – in an apartment block owned by Berlusconi. I don't know about other clubs but when it comes to organisation, AC Milan is right up there with the best. When I arrived, Ariedo Braida took me round all the offices and introduced me to everyone. After training, he showed me my room at the Milanello training headquarters which are about fifty kilometres from the centre of Milan. It's a fantastic place and every player has his own room there. He gave me my keys, the room even had a little TV in it – in fact, it had everything!

I stayed in a hotel for only a couple of weeks which is extremely rare for a professional footballer just arrived in a new town, especially when he has moved to another country. The club wanted me to live in the Berlusconi residence because I was still young. There were quite a few other players living there as well, such as Roberto Baggio and Marcel Desailly. I visited a few apartments, lavish places with four or five bedrooms, and I could pick whichever one I wanted. So I picked one. Two or three days later, I was taken shopping to select video equipment, a TV – everything I needed in fact. Within a week, the whole flat was completely kitted out. Cutlery, TV, beds, sheets, a cleaning lady booked in. Everything was sorted. Two or three days after that, a car was in the garage. It was an Opel – the English players got a Vauxhall – because they were the official sponsors.

If I had the slightest problem, I had a phone number I could dial to call someone 24/7. When my parents came over, there was a car to meet them at the airport. In terms of being looked after, it doesn't get any better than that. I haven't yet met a single player who thinks that his club is as well organised as AC

Milan. It's an unbelievable club when it comes to that. Ariedo Braida believed that if the club focused totally on our needs, we could be 100 per cent focused on the pitch. I met Silvio Berlusconi twice but, being nineteen years old, I didn't really take on board everything he stood for. I have fantastic memories of how well I was looked after throughout my whole time at AC Milan, even though I have more bitter-sweet memories of the season I spent there. I played two games having been on the bench to start with, and I think I played one game for the full ninety minutes. In total, I must have played half a dozen games, plus the two European Cup games we played against Bordeaux.

Those two Bordeaux games are painful to remember. We had won the home leg at San Siro 2–0 and we had told ourselves that the hardest bit was over. In addition, that had been one of my first games and I had been playing against Zizou. I was marking him a bit because we more or less covered the same area of the pitch. We had calmly won and I was so happy! For the return leg, I played right midfield. We took a bath. In fact, things went so quickly, it was incredible. And we lost 3–0. For the French, it was one of the greatest European games ever. That was the evening when Zidane's aura took on an extra dimension. It was also the evening when Christophe Dugarry scored the two goals that got him signed ... to AC Milan the following season!

I lived in the same apartment block as Roberto Baggio. When I arrived, he immediately invited me over for dinner. His wife was there, as well as his kids. He couldn't care less that his name was Baggio. I had just arrived and I was only nineteen, so when I got back to my place, I called my mates to show off. 'Guess what, I've just been for dinner at Roberto Baggio's!' I was so proud. He was the one who had invited me because he knew that I was all alone. He was always asking me to go for a coffee or to come over for dinner. He had real class and he wasn't the only one to be like that.

With George Weah, though, it was something else. I was his protégé. My room at Milanello was next to his. He was the one who taught me how to knot a tie, a very important skill to have when you play in the Italian league. George was always behind me, and whenever I needed anything, he was always there for me. It's no surprise to me that he is now standing for the Presidency of his country, Liberia. There is something about him that says 'born leader' and, since retiring from football, he has done a lot to help his war-torn country. Even the legendary Pelé named him recently as one of the top 125 greatest living footballers.

Another who helped me a lot when I first arrived was Paolo Maldini, the great left back who has only ever played for AC Milan. He has been at the top level of football for twenty years and has won almost everything there is to win in the game, yet he was so friendly to me when I first arrived as a complete nobody and I will never forget that. He was fantastic and it's for that reason that he is one of the players I admire most in football. It's not enough for a player just to be a great footballer on the pitch; for me to admire him, he has to be great off it as well.

One of the players who I felt was not particularly helpful when I joined was Marcel Desailly. At the time, Marcel was already a French footballing icon. He had won the Champions League with Olympique de Marseille. I was slightly in awe of him and I was hoping he would help me a bit, give advice and support but his attitude, at least at the beginning, somewhat surprised me. As far as he was concerned, if I was at AC, it meant that I was good enough to be part of the squad, so I just had to get on with things. The fact that I was there meant I had what it took, and the rest I had to learn on my own. It's not that he couldn't care less, it was just his way of being. I love Marcel, now, he makes me laugh. I love going for dinner with him because I know I'm going to have a lot of fun. He's a great guy and has a way of seeing things that only he can understand. At Milan, though, when I was young, I was all alone and though we spoke the same language and had sort of similar roots – we were born abroad but had grown up in France – we weren't that close. I must have gone to his place once or twice because he'd invited me, but that was all. I did not have the same relationship with Marcel as I had with George. I expected more from Marcel because he seemed the perfect example for me to follow. We had the common bond of an African heritage and that should have united us. So I was a bit disappointed and I held it against him to a certain extent. But over time I matured and began to get to know him. I realised that he did not ignore me – it was just the way that he was and how he lived his life. And nowadays he probably does not regret the fact that he didn't help me!

Franco Baresi was also quite distant. He didn't talk much. In fact, he was probably the one who spoke the least. When he did say something, though, everybody listened because he was a leader and everyone respected him. By the time I arrived at the club, his playing career was almost over. He had been the outstanding central defender of the Italian national team from 1982, when they had won the World Cup, right through to the final they lost on penalties in 1994 (he missed one of the penalties). He could read the game so well and knew how to control the pace of play. Like Maldini, he too had spent his entire career at AC Milan and by the time he retired in 1996, had played an incredible 444 games for them. In fact, he was so idolised by the fans that his number 6 shirt was retired by the club, something which hardly ever happens in Italian football.

The player who amazed me the most, though, was Dejan Savisevic, nicknamed 'il Genio' by AC Milan fans. He was the one with the most talent but actually he trained very rarely. For a Sunday game, he would only really show up from the Friday onwards. I never saw him do a full week's training and sometimes fans accused him of lethargic performances. Usually, though, come Sunday, he was the one who would win a game by making that decisive pass or scoring a goal. His dribbling and his creativity set him apart from everyone although he had a problem accepting authority and hated being on the bench or being substituted. Because he was amazingly talented, though, Capello was intelligent enough to let him do his own thing.

Capello is a great coach. It's not very original to say this because everyone knows it. A former Italian international himself, he is currently the Juventus head coach, so I'm really looking forward to working with him again. He led both AC Milan and, later, Real Madrid, to European Cup victories and he has also won national championship titles with four major clubs in four different cities, Milan, Rome, Madrid and Turin, which is an unbelievable achievement. What surprised me most about him was the way in which he handed out forfeits to anyone who stepped out of line, regardless of who they were. He would argue with Maldini or Panucci during training, for example, because he's got a really strong character. Christian Panucci, I think, considered him to be a bit like a mentor, though, because he subsequently followed Capello to Real and then to AS Roma. At the table, when we ate together, even if you had finished, you had to have the captain's OK to be allowed to get down from it, so there was a definite sense of discipline at AC Milan.

By the early summer of 1996, I knew that Milan wanted me to leave. In fact, they wanted to sell one of their foreign players. And amongst all the foreigners, I was the one who had played the least and who was the least known. On the other hand, Braida, who had bought me from Cannes, really wanted me to stay. But one foreigner had to go and it turned out to be me.

At the time, I had several offers. I could have gone to Ajax or returned to France and to Bordeaux where Roland Courbis was the coach. When I was at Milan, I had regularly come across Arsène Wenger because I often sat in the stands at San Siro. We had talked on several occasions. He had told me that he was taking over at Arsenal and would I be interested? Of course I would be, I used to reply. It was 1996 and two years later, the World Cup was taking place in France. I was desperate to play and I knew I had a good chance of making the squad but I needed to be playing football week in, week out. That was not going to happen if I stayed where I was. Arsène already knew my game well because he had been the boss at Monaco and that was another big reason why I followed him. I could sense that there was a good rapport between us. Before that, though, I had almost signed for Ajax. I had spent three days there in Amsterdam and had met all the directors of the club. I had talked things over with them but in the end, we had not been able to agree on financial terms because the deal they were offering me was a lot worse than what I already had at Milan. It was still the period when Louis van Gaal was there but the best players were beginning to leave. In fact, Seedorf, Davids and Reiziger were to join Milan when I left for Arsenal, where a wonderful adventure awaited me ...

5

First Few Steps with Arsenal

Until I went to Milan, I had never met Arsène Wenger. That was incredible given that I had been at Cannes when he had been the coach at Monaco. There were barely forty miles between us, yet we hadn't yet come across one another. At Milan, we were always chatting. I would talk about my situation, about football, about anything and everything. Then one day he asked me if I'd be interested in going to England because he was leaving to manage Arsenal. At the time, I was already thinking about such a move because I had talked with Raymond Domenech who in those days was the under-21s France coach. He had told me that I had an opportunity to make the France squad for the 1998 World Cup but, in order to do so, I had to be playing on a regular basis, which was absolutely not the case at AC Milan. Ever since Domenech told me that, it was clear in my mind that I had to find myself a regular first-team place at a club. I wanted to impose myself and earn my place in the national squad for that forthcoming World Cup which we were hosting.

Arsenal, however, were not the only club I was looking at. I had already spent three days with Ajax. I was tempted by the Amsterdam club because of its great facilities and its style of football. It was an attractive proposition for me. We talked a lot but we couldn't reach an agreement on my salary. In addition, Roland Courbis, the Bordeaux coach, had been in touch. He wanted to get me back playing in the French championship as soon as possible.

The reason Arsenal won the day over these other two clubs was of course Arsène Wenger. I was convinced by what he told me, because he had first been interested in me as a person before he had thought of getting in touch with me the player. In the end, it all happened without fuss. Arsène really wanted me to join and he did everything he could for the negotiations to be finalised as quickly as possible, which is what happened.

I actually arrived at the club before Arsène did because he hadn't yet completed his contract in Japan. I arrived in London at the same time as Rémi Garde, another French international midfielder, who was on a free transfer from Strasbourg and who ended up staying three years before heading back to France. I was lucky he was with me because those first few weeks were tough.

During the negotiations over the contract, because Arsène wasn't yet at Highbury, I was dealing with David Dein and it was with him that I signed my first four-year contract with the Gunners. I will always remember a particular incident that had a great effect on me and which, many years later, seems to me to be highly symbolic. After signing and initialling the contract, we talked about which number shirt I should wear. It might seem unimportant but that was the moment when I realised how much the club believed in me. When I arrived, there were only a few numbers free, including the number 14 and 18 shirts. Out of numbers 1 to 11, only the number 4 was still free. As it happened, I wasn't too keen on that number, though today I can't for the life of me remember why. I therefore had a preference for the number 14 or something similar. But David Dein said to me, 'You're going to be an automatic first-team choice at Arsenal, so take the number 4 since you will be in the starting line-up.' I accepted, and throughout my years at the club, I owned that number, and I loved it.

At the time, there were no other Frenchmen at the club. Writing that sentence today is really strange when I look at what happened in the nine years that followed. I arrived, therefore, with Rémi Garde, and I remember how difficult those first few weeks were. I didn't speak the language and, in England, more than anywhere, that's a handicap that you have to get over very quickly. The English think that not speaking their language shows a lack of respect and, in the end, they are quite right. However, Rémi could get by a bit and he would translate for me.

We arrived at a strange time for the club because they had just sacked their previous manager, Bruce Rioch, and Stewart Houston and Pat Rice were temporarily in charge of the first team. Yet they would leave us completely alone in our corner. We would train with the reserves, and we would play with the reserves. Occasionally, we were allowed to train with the first team, but at other times not. We were constantly yo-yoing between the two, included one moment and out in the cold the next, and it was really unpleasant. I was getting frustrated, because I didn't want a repeat of what had happened in Milan. So I spoke on the phone to Arsène – who was still in Japan – and he told me not to worry, to keep fighting. 'It won't be a problem. Just be strong and hang on,' he said.

Arsène arrived a few weeks later. His first game in charge was a UEFA Cup match against Borussia Mönchengladbach who had the temperamental German international midfielder Steffen Effenberg amongst their ranks. For us, the atmosphere seemed really strange. It was very British. The team consisted only of English and Irish players and had a reputation of playing very defensive football. It was in an odd phase.

The first big thing that happened as soon as I arrived – before Arsène had, in fact – was that Tony Adams announced he was an alcoholic. I remember, one day after training, he gathered us all together because he wanted to speak to us. He stood there in the middle of the dressing room and began to talk about his problems with the bottle. He spoke totally naturally and openly and at the end of his speech, everyone began to applaud him. Meanwhile, I hadn't understood a single word of what he had just said, so I had no idea why they were clapping! I felt as if I had landed on Mars. So I asked Rémi if he had understood but, even with the little English he spoke, he too had missed the important word 'alcoholic', so was as much in the dark as me. Eventually, we asked around and the other players explained. I then understood what a major thing Adams had just announced. I also thought he must be a very strong man to stand in front of everyone and admit this thing to them. But instead of wondering what on earth I was doing here, I realised that I must have come to the right club if a man – the captain – could stand up in front of his friends and team-mates and tell them about something like this and, moreover, if these people could then help him through his problems. For me, Arsenal *was* Tony Adams. He symbolised everything about the Gunners, in terms of his career, his aura, his permanent will to win, in fact in terms of everything he stood for. To see him open up in that way about such a difficult, personal subject, really surprised me but also deeply impressed me.

The team at the time was made up of the back four – Nigel Winterburn on the left, Lee Dixon on the right, central defenders Steve Bould or Martin Keown, and Tony Adams. They were the key back four. In goal was David Seaman. They played a typical English game, hard and powerful, a real warrior's game. It wasn't based on technique or on an attacking strategy. They won by closing down the opposition and by playing the long-ball game. When we did our first Double, in 1998, the quality came from individual players such as Dennis Bergkamp and sometimes Marc Overmars; otherwise, the rest of it was down to mental strength and organisation. We played a whole series of games that we won 1–0. In 1998, our strength lay in the fact that we didn't concede many goals.

At the time, we used to train at a ground in Barnet, near their Underhill stadium. Coming as I did from Milan, where everything was unbelievably well organised and easy, where we all had our own room at the Milanello training ground, where the pitches were fantastic, I got a bit of a shock when I came to Arsenal. We got changed, five or six of us together, in little prefab huts. In winter, it was freezing cold. Later on, the huts caught fire, so we would get changed at the Sopwell House Hotel, near St Albans. This is a fantastic country club and spa hotel in a Georgian manor house, set in enormous grounds. We would take a minibus to the training ground ... and the same thing for the way back. We would eat at the hotel. Actually, we still do that, as it is convenient. Nowadays, though, we train at

London Colney, a ground that is also near St Albans, where the facilities are very different from the ones at Barnet. Over the years, things have changed beyond recognition at Arsenal. But at the time, the club was still in transition. If you compare what the club was like the year I arrived to the way it was when I left, it's like comparing night and day. It has changed beyond recognition.

In any event, when I arrived, I was barely twenty and I must say that the first few months were really hard, even though things sorted themselves out after Arsène arrived. Maybe people assumed that it was easy settling in off the pitch because things went well on it, but it took me a while to acclimatise, to get used to things, and I suffered a lot. For a start, I lived in a hotel room for the first four months. I know that for 'normal' working people, the idea of living in a hotel room for so long probably seems incredible. But it actually happens quite a lot to footballers. Not every club owns property and apartment blocks in the way that Silvio Berlusconi does in Milan and it is often quite difficult to find a place to live in a city you don't know, especially if you are a foreigner. In Milan, also, I always had someone I could turn to when I first arrived if I needed help with anything. That wasn't the case in London, where I was left alone to do what I wanted and to get by as I could. That meant, though, that I had a lot of freedom to come and go as I pleased, so I enjoyed being a tourist at first, visiting the capital which is always so busy and lively and which I immediately thought was fantastic.

I waited until I'd got to know London and its surroundings a bit better before deciding where to live. Although in the end, finding living accommodation was not the hardest part of what I had to adapt to. What was harder was the way of life in general. The pace of life in London is completely different from that of France or Italy. I couldn't speak English at all when I first arrived. The mentality, the culture, everything is different and, unless you speak the language, it's difficult to understand how people live and hard to integrate. Here in England, people happily go and have a beer at two o'clock in the afternoon. That is not exactly what happens in France! So initially, it was everyday life that I found hardest to adjust to. Having said that, I soon got to love the mix of so many different people. When I first arrived, I was impressed when watching TV that there were people of all colours and races on it – black people, Asian people, reading the news, presenting popular programmes. That doesn't happen in France or Italy. There is a special tolerance in Britain and certainly in London. I think that will always be the case, despite what happened in the capital in the summer of 2005.

On the pitch, however, I have the sort of attitude that allows me to adapt quickly wherever I am, so everything went very well. And the guys in the team were great. Martin Keown, David Seaman, Ian Wright, Dennis Bergkamp – who had arrived the year before me – all helped me to settle in really easily at Highbury. There were two players who I never saw lose their temper – David Seaman and Ray Parlour. They would turn up every morning with a smile on their faces, and it was the same when they left. With guys like that around, I had no trouble settling in. And we often used to have a good laugh during training. So with them, everything was so easy!

I must also talk about the particular characteristics of English football. I'm not talking about the matches, which anyone can see are different from any other league in the world. The commitment, the all-round game, the will to win, everyone knows about that. No, what I am talking about is the way in which players train in England. For example, the fact that teams have a rest day right in the middle of the week; that they don't regularly go away to a hotel the night before a game. Obviously, I liked that a lot and, having spoken to many foreign players, especially to French ones when they first arrived in the Premiership, I can report that they were all very pleased and surprised by these new habits. In the French league, following a Saturday game, you would have a Sunday session to wind down, a rest day on the Monday, and a night away in a hotel the day before the next match.

In England, when the game started at 3 pm, we would meet at 10 am at the hotel, all have a light meal together at 11, then go straight to the ground. Personally, that sort of rhythm suited me well. But when you are sometimes used to going, as is the case in Italy, two whole days without training just before a game, it felt strange. That said, I adjusted very quickly!

If I had to give an award to the guy who made me laugh the most in the dressing room, it would have to go to Ian Wright, without a doubt. He and Martin Keown were known as a right pair! Having a guy like Ian Wright in a group of people makes for an incredible atmosphere. But it was more than just an atmosphere; it was pure happiness that flooded the dressing room. I wasn't playing for Arsène's first game against Borussia Mönchengladbach. I was sitting in the stands. We had lost the home leg 3–2. We also lost the return leg by the same score. Even so, after the game there had been music in the dressing room. That was new for me, too. Ian Wright was dancing away to Michael Jackson! Arsène was looking at Ian strutting his stuff and, because I had joined before him, he turned to me and asked if Wright was like that after every game. I replied that, yes, since I had been at Arsenal, I could confirm that the atmosphere was indeed like that after every game, whether we had won or lost.

Knowing Arsène like I do now, I can imagine how surprised he must have been and what must have been going through his head when he saw this. But it wasn't something anyone could change. I think Ian Wright would always have behaved like that, whether he had just played in a World Cup final or a friendly game. Arsène, to his great credit, understood that he should not try to revolutionise things. He understood that there would have been no point in arriving and trying to impose more 'continental' ways of doing things straight away. He brought rigour in bit by bit. He also adapted to British football as well. And we know how successful he has been.

One story always comes to mind when I think of Ian Wright. It was 1998 and we had just completed the Double. For the final game of the season, the roads around Highbury were teeming with people. At the time, if you opened the windows in the dressing room, you could look out over the crowds. On that occasion, after the game, with all our fans celebrating out in the road and looking up at our dressing room, Ian Wright opened the window. Everyone saw him do it and started to chant his name out loud. That's when he literally started flying. He took our shirts, our clothes and began to throw them all out of the window towards the fans! There was a complete riot. The police even had to come and ask us to stop! What happened after that? Well, they blocked up the windows so that you couldn't open them any more. All that because of Ian and his complete craziness. He's really extraordinary, in the literal sense of the word. He never did anything ordinary because that was boring for him. On the pitch, he was capable of exploding with anger at any moment. If he didn't receive the ball quickly enough, he would turn round and insult the culprit. Then, at the final whistle, he'd come over and embrace him. It was done with and everything was fine again.

Tony Adams was an altogether different character. He was, and still is, Mister Arsenal. When I arrived, Tony very quickly came up to welcome me and make me feel at home. During the following seasons, I noticed that he did the same with all the newcomers. He would welcome them to the club as if it was a tradition. I have a lot of respect for him. He has had some serious problems in life and to come back and have a whole new career like he has, creates respect.

There are some things, though, that I don't like about Tony. I think that, once he left the club, he felt we would struggle without him. After all our successes there may be a hint of jealousy from Tony. I am disappointed that a great Arsenal icon cannot just be proud to be a former teammate. He is a legend and should be content with that. Arsenal will always be Arsenal, whatever happens, because it is bigger than its players. But Tony was an incredible competitor and I think he found it really difficult to stop playing, achieving and especially winning. I think he really missed all that. He found it difficult to give way to others and sometimes, in some interviews he gave, he reveals himself to be a bit too critical for my taste and so I don't always agree with what he says in them. For example, he feels that, because of my playing style, I am going to find it tough to compete at the top level in to my thirties. But I disagree with him: I have an understanding of the game and a technical ability, as well as a determination to stay at the top, that I firmly believe will allow me to do so. I know it's not going to be easy, and in modern football it's going to be more and more difficult for a midfielder like myself to still be at the top of the game in his mid-thirties, like Roy Keane is. That said, I look after myself well and my desire to play top-class football drives me on. Deep down, though, I don't begrudge him his views because personally I learned a lot when I was with him. He had such charisma. Yes, I was surprised by his problems with alcoholism and even more so by the fact that he made them so public. I wasn't used to that. That is something that doesn't happen in France. At the time, I was stunned, and a little ill-at-ease. But as the years went by, I realised that there were quite a few players who were in a similar situation in the English league. There had already been Paul Merson and his drug addiction. Then I discovered that there were other Arsenal players who also had alcohol problems, although from their performances on the pitch, you would never have known about it. These guys would run around as normal. I couldn't understand how they could be mentally prepared on the pitch, how they could have worked so hard beforehand. But they had this desire to play at all cost, whatever knocks they had taken, whatever problems they had, and that's what English football is all about. That's what I learned during my nine years there.

I am also like those players in the sense that I have always wanted to play, and win the mental battle, even when I was injured. I love being on the pitch. The older I get, the more experienced I become, the more I realise that it's rare to play a game and be a hundred per cent fit. The more your career progresses, the more you realise that your body always hurts somewhere or other. You might have a slight niggle with your heel, a small problem with your knee. You are never really fully fit. You have to learn to live with it, to train and to win with it. And it's perhaps even more satisfying when you do.

I remember my first game with the Arsenal reserves, although

I don't remember who our opponents were. It was at Highbury. We had earned ourselves a free kick about 20 yards out, slightly to the left of goal. So I said to Rémi, 'Let me have a go.' I shot and sent the ball right up into the stands, on the right. After that brilliant attempt, I looked at Rémi and we fell about laughing. The guys must have wondered where I'd come from!

My official Arsenal first-team debut came one Monday evening against Sheffield Wednesday, on 16 September 1996, to be precise. Sheffield were one of the best teams in the Premiership that year and needed a win to return to the top of the table. I was on the bench that evening but the match got underway half an hour late because there had been a power cut and the electronic turnstiles hadn't been able to let people in. Eventually, the game kicked off. Before long, we were 1–0 down. After fifteen minutes, things were not looking good and Stewart Houston told me to warm up. Ray Parlour had to come off injured. This was my chance. I was about to make my Arsenal first-team debut. As I came on to the pitch to play alongside David Platt, I'm sure most of the fans took one look at me and thought, 'Patrick who? Who is this tall, gangly French guy who we've never heard of? Let's see what he can do.' I had not had a chance to prove what I could do at AC Milan so, as far as they were concerned, I was a completely unknown quantity. They were understandably wary of this lanky, skinny guy. Plus, I was only twenty, so maybe I wouldn't be able to handle the situation. I guess they just thought they would wait and see before judging me. As it was, I played a really good game that night, passing and moving around with confidence. It wasn't the easiest situation to come into but I was ready for it. It's what I had wanted for so long. The training sessions were as competitive as the games, so I was able to get into my stride at once. Anyway, this was my style of play. I loved the commitment, having to fight to win the ball, having to make that crucial tackle. We won the game 4–1 and by the time the final whistle blew, the crowd knew my name. They soon invented a new chant: V-I-E-I-R-A, Wo-oh-oh-oh, V-I-E-I-R-A, Wo-oh-oh-oh, He comes from Senegal, He plays for Arsenal. I don't know if Arsène had anything to do with it, whether he called Stewart before or after the game but in any case, after that night, I was never out of the first team.

A lot of people have asked me if I ever had doubts at the beginning about my choice of club. But I never wondered how things were going to go on the pitch. I never sat there in my hotel room wondering 'What the hell am I doing here?' I knew that my time would come. And I am very adaptable. For example, within a couple of months of making my debut, there were two matches where I had to play out of position. The first was against Wimbledon at Plough Lane where both Steve Bould and Tony Adams had gone off injured. The second was at Newcastle where Tony Adams got sent off after bringing down Alan Shearer in the penalty box. Despite being down to ten men for three-quarters of the game, we managed to win 2–1, Ian Wright scoring the winner in the second half. In both those games, I was switched to centre back. I don't really like playing there because you don't see enough of the ball but I still quite enjoyed those matches. Wimbledon were playing the long-ball game and I really had to fight to win the ball. I think they were quite surprised by what they saw of me. As for the Newcastle game, we played with typical Arsenal grit, to the extent that Arsène Wenger, who had only recently taken charge, said afterwards, 'I thought we would lose when Tony was sent off, but there is something special about this team. They have a good team spirit because they have been playing together for a long time.'

Arsène understood how well the team worked together. When he changed it, he did so slowly but surely. When he first took over, there were several players over the age of 30, such as Nigel Winterburn (whose testimonial season it was), Lee Dixon, Tony Adams and Paul Merson, who it seemed had been there for ever. Ian Wright himself was already 33. But Arsène didn't tamper with the squad, as some managers do the minute they arrive at a club. Instead, he nurtured a group of players who were capable of blending themselves into a team but who could also live with the atmosphere of a big stadium.

David Platt was the first person with whom I shared a room.

Except that he never slept! He's a real businessman. He was always on his laptop conducting business. I would try to get some sleep, but all I could hear was the sound of him tapping away on the keyboard. He never had a siesta. Eventually, I had to have my own room because, in the afternoons, I like to sleep!

I started to tell myself that this was the club for me in the summer of '97, at the end of my first season. We had finished third in the Premiership which was good, considering how unsettled things had been managerially for a while, and things had gone really well for me. Above all, I was happy because I was playing! The atmosphere in the team was great. We all had a good laugh, I felt really at ease, relaxed, part of things. On the pitch, things were also going well. This was a club with huge potential. It was ambitious. And I was as well.

Arsène's presence was obviously very important. There was something about him, a sort of total serenity. He's someone who likes to communicate and who is always measured in what he says. He has always possessed those qualities. He is really gifted when it comes to communicating. He can talk to Tony Adams about his alcohol problems and to me about my behavioural problems on the pitch. He always has an opinion on every subject, or a piece of advice to give.

On a personal level, I had really made my mark and began to achieve a certain recognition after that first season. I felt I had found a secure place within the structure of the team, able to pick up any pass from the defence and distribute the ball in virtually any direction. I was also getting to the stage, which was particularly satisfying for me, where I was able to find the freedom to move forward. What surprised me at first about Arsenal's game was the pace and the commitment. There was no down-time, it was 'everybody forward and let's try to win this game'. That attitude has never changed even though there are now a lot of foreign players in the Premiership. Fundamentally, that culture and mentality still exist and they are really important. In fact, they are epitomised in a certain way by Arsenal.

I have always loved physical commitment. Given my physique,

I know I can allow myself to say that. My physique is one of my strong points. And that's also why I loved the English league. Physically, I could really assert myself. On the pitch, I'm not afraid of physical confrontation, of sticking my foot in, and I'm not afraid of putting my head where another guy might put his boot. I think Sir Bobby Robson once said something to the effect that I was 'such a monster it's like tackling two blokes'. I was pleased to hear that!

I remember those first few difficult years and how things gradually improved. Game by game, I felt more and more at ease on the pitch and with the other players. The main reason I settled in, though, was because I played well from the start, because I proved I could do it, not because I was a nice guy! So I couldn't have wished for a better debut, when all was said and done. It was gentle enough to enable me to make a mark but tough enough to earn myself a place with the Gunners. I showed everyone that I had the same attitude as the others in the team. Because in the end, it's what you do on the pitch that determines whether others accept you or not. That's the bottom line and it helps form everyone's judgement.

My first goal for the club came in January 1997 against Everton. At half time the score was 0–0 and there was no indication of what would happen in the second half when, within two minutes of each other, Dennis and I both scored spectacular goals, mine a shot that I blasted in from 20 yards out – better than my attempt in the reserves – leaving Neville Southall, their goalkeeper, stranded. The final score was 3–1 and the papers were beginning to look at Arsenal in a different light for the first time since Arsène Wenger had taken over. We were casting off our defensive, 'boring Arsenal' tag and beginning to play a more flowing and passing game that all agreed was much more attractive. And I was loving every minute of it.

Generally speaking, the English are passionate about their football in a healthy manner. In Italy, it's different and more complicated. If you are doing well, you are the king of the castle, everyone welcomes you with open arms; if, however, you lose two or three games, people start to throw stones at you. In

England, when you win, you are also king of the castle; but when you lose, they say 'Better luck next time.' There's huge respect for players in England. All the foreign players who come over notice the difference. English supporters are not very aware of it because they don't travel abroad that much. When you play in England, you don't feel caged in, you can still have a life. You can meet a Tottenham or a Man U supporter and he might tell you that he supports another team but he won't insult you.

When it came to supporters, though, the first ones to really impress me were the Liverpool fans. When they sing 'You'll Never Walk Alone', it's unbelievable. The atmosphere in their stadium is magical: it's the ultimate football atmosphere. Even the visiting team can't help but be taken aback because it's an incredible experience. When the fans all put their arms up in the air and sing that song, it's fabulous. When I played at Anfield and heard them sing, it sent shivers down my spine. It's an unforgettable stadium because of its fantastic atmosphere and everything that Liverpool represents. Paradoxically, although playing at Anfield obviously gives the Reds an extra impetus, their opponents also benefit in the same way because they want to excel themselves, to be worthy of the place, of the ground on which they tread, of the history they are contributing to.

My first house was near Edgware, to the north of London. As time went on, I lived further and further away from the training ground and nearer and nearer to the centre of London. My first place was a pretty little house, ten minutes from the training ground. I always bought my houses, I never rented them. I was always told that in England you had to buy because you never lost money on them when you came to sell up, and that at worst you sold for the same price as you bought. I did well out of property. The house was quite secluded, almost in the country-side. It was surrounded by several other little houses, in that typically English fashion. The neighbours were all Arsenal supporters. It was quiet. I stayed 18 months. After that, I moved to Barnet. From there, it took me twenty minutes to get to the training ground. The house was a bit more isolated, being down a private road. After Barnet, I moved to Hampstead. There, I was fifteen minutes from the city centre and half an hour from the training ground. I lived there for two years and I loved every minute of it. I found a really fantastic house and I think I got a bit of a bargain. But at first, I have to admit that I was surprised by house prices in England. They're crazy, worse than in Paris or Milan, in fact worse than anywhere I have ever known. For the price of my house in London, I could buy a house in Paris with an indoor *and* outdoor pool!

As for the language side of things, I had English lessons for three or four months. After that, because only Rémi and I spoke French, I learned pretty quickly by speaking to my team-mates. Shortly after the end of my first season, however, three players were signed from abroad who were to begin changing Arsenal from primarily an English team to one comprised of players from all over the world.

The first to be signed was Luis Boa Morte, then a Portuguese under-21 forward with Sporting Lisbon. He was signed for £1.75m. At the same time, Arsène Wenger managed, after a mammoth transfer saga, to sign Marc Overmars for £7m from Ajax. The Dutch international winger signed a five-year contract and everyone hoped that, for that amount, he had fully recovered from the leg injury that he had struggled with all year. Finally, on 12 June, Arsène bought Emmanuel Petit from AS Monaco, the club he used to manage. He had been instrumental in developing Petit's career who, at 26, hadn't yet reached his peak, although he was already a regular fixture in the France team. The great thing about Emmanuel was that he could play at centre back, left back or left midfield, so he was able to slot into the team really easily.

I was excited by these three arrivals as, to me, it definitely showed that the manager had a long-term plan in mind. The team that had largely been put together by George Graham a few years back was in need of fresh blood and, as far as Arsène Wenger was concerned, he was going to look abroad for it. I had been the starting point of that search, things had gone well with me and now he wanted more where that came from. By the end of my first season at the club, I felt very confident not only about what I was capable of, but about the club's future as well. I couldn't wait for the new season to begin.

6

My First Steps in Blue

A few weeks after Euro '96 in England, I was supposed to go to Atlanta to take part in the Olympics. I had been preparing for the tournament for the last two years, when, bang! As soon as I arrived there, I got injured. I'd stretched some anterior cruciate ligaments which meant being out of action for three weeks. I would have preferred to have done my knee in at the start of the build-up for the Games because I would not have been so annoyed. Luckily, I have a lot of great memories of the start of those Olympic Games. We were staying in Auburn, a small town near by. The people there were nice, they were welcoming and they put themselves out for us. And on top of that, we got on well with the other sportsmen and women who were with us: the table-tennis players, the boxers and the gymnasts. We had a really good time with them. We talked about sport, pressure, training; plus we were living beyond the usual world of our own disciplines. So the Games remain a happy memory for me, despite the injury.

I played my first international for France against the Netherlands. I even exchanged shirts with Dennis Bergkamp, who was already one of my idols. In fact I had three at the time. Frank Rijkaard was the first. I liked him a lot as a player. He played in the same position as me, he had a not-dissimilar build, so I was very much inspired by him — by the simplicity of his game and by his calm strength. The great AC Milan team had three great Dutchmen — Marco van Basten, Ruud Gullit and Rijkaard — but people only ever talked about the first two because they were strikers and they scored goals. They never talked about Rijkaard, even though he was the most important one out of the three, the one who did the most work. In any case, in his five seasons there, he and his fellow countrymen won the European Cup twice and the Italian league twice as well.

After him, there was obviously Zidane. I have already talked about how and why I so admired him, both as a person and as a player. For me, Zizou is the guy who likes to make others shine. Dennis Bergkamp has that same quality. That's how I see those three players. They all have a unique ability to enable a team to play well and that is a trait which definitely comes with age and experience. But it's something that I always admired in them.

Dennis knows very well that he no longer has the legs to make all those constant sprints or to take the ball and dribble past three or four guys. Though still playing at the highest level, at his age he can no longer count on his physical qualities. He has to rely on his sense of the game and on his will to win – those are the things that now carry him through. There are other players that I admired from the past – like Luis Fernandez who, again, I have already talked about. But if I had to pick three international players from more recent years, they would be Rijkaard, Zidane and Bergkamp.

For my first international, I was proud to be able to swap shirts with Dennis. We were playing for the same club and, in any case, he was already amongst the best players in the world. When I discovered that I had been called up for the first time, I was surprised of course. I had never been so nervous, although in the end, it was all OK. This was the senior France team, not the under-21s. I was now with guys like Laurent Blanc; this was the big time, and I was rubbing shoulders with the big boys. I was of the same generation as Robert Pires. That game must have been Robert's second or third for France and he was practically the only guy there that I already knew. I don't remember who I shared a room with. I was a bit in awe of everything and everyone. I tiptoed around at the beginning. I didn't know anyone, I didn't know what you were supposed to do, how you were supposed to conduct yourself. I arrived looking like a rabbit caught in headlights, but I made sure I looked around me in order to learn.

During my debut call-up, the guy who most impressed me was

Lilian Thuram, even though, he too, was one of the young guys. Well, perhaps not the young guys but he certainly wasn't part of the old guard. We didn't know each other at the time. But Lilian always had the ability to reach out to people and to the new recruits in particular.

There wasn't anyone who frightened me or made me feel ill at ease. Nor was there anyone who was domineering or who used to show off. But there were some good-time guys, guys who liked to have fun. I was young, and I was able to stand back from all that. When I finished training, I was more likely to be found in my room than screaming and shouting in the corridors or in the TV room! When Laurent Blanc talked with Marcel Desailly or Didier Deschamps, I would stay out of it. I wasn't going to try to break into their conversation. I would take a step back and try to listen.

After Euro '96 in England, there were a certain number of players who were no longer playing international football for France. There was a new generation, to a certain extent: a new chapter in the story was about to begin. Cantona had stopped playing, Ginola was no longer there, Bernard Lama had been replaced by Fabien Barthez. When I was called up for that first game in 1997, I told myself that I now had a chance to make the squad for the World Cup Finals the following year. Raymond Domenich had already lodged that thought firmly in my head. The previous season at Arsenal had gone well. Obviously, I was ambitious but I didn't want to shout it from the rooftops. At first, I told myself that it was fine for me to be on the bench, given that Didier Deschamps was the first choice. I decided it was better for me to make the most of his presence because I wouldn't be able to find a better teacher than Dédé. And he was already a very good one. I remember there was a time when certain journalists were saying that Dédé should no longer be playing and that I should take his place, even though I didn't actually agree with them. Despite that, the atmosphere was always very good between us. I have a lot of respect for Dédé. I think he's great. I like the man a lot. Beyond that, some people rate the player, others don't. But that's another matter. Despite all the rumours to the contrary, his behaviour towards me never changed. I never got the feeling that he considered me to be a threat. Our relationship has always been the same, right from the start when he would talk to me quietly and calmly.

He's someone you can talk to easily. We would talk a lot about positioning, how to cover for each other on the pitch. I'm convinced that he likes that – exchanging ideas, talking tactics. That role suited him really well. I think he valued me as well because I was someone who knew my place. I never made any mileage out of the criticisms that journalists directed at him, I never tried to stab him in the back. I always showed a lot of respect for him, both on the pitch and through the pages of the newspapers. And I think he recognised that.

My main recollections from that first game were that we won and that I swapped shirts with Dennis. And I have kept that one! I have his shirt at home, along with Paolo Maldini's from France–Italy's World Cup quarter-final in 1998 and another of his from AC Milan. I also have Roberto Baggio's from that same France–Italy game. I have Salif Diao's Senegal shirt from the World Cup Finals of 2002. I'm not normally someone who collects these sorts of things but I like to swap shirts with guys I have played against or who I know well. I keep them in a bag so I know where they are. Those are the shirts that I will frame one day and put up on my wall. Also I have Thuram's shirt from Juve and Antoine Sibierski's from Manchester City because he's a good mate of mine and I love him dearly. Rijkaard's AC Milan or Holland shirt would be really nice to have, on the other hand. I'd take either one straight away! Aside from those, I've got a box-full of other shirts, but those will go to my brother.

A year before the World Cup, we played in a friendly international warm-up tournament in France in 1997, called the Tournoi de France. I didn't play the first game against Brazil. I played against England, however. Christian Karembeu was injured, so I was picked. That was a good memory for me. It was my first 'big tournament' with France. I loved the enthusiasm and energy surrounding the team, even though that was the period when people were attacking us. The newspapers used to really lay into Aimé Jacquet. The way in which the media treated him was incredible. For me, it was completely over the top.

I felt good in the squad. The more you are picked, the more you get to know people, and they get to know you, and the better you then feel. I often used to hang out with Thuram, Bernard Lama, Christian Karembeu and Robert Pires as well. Robert, he was the mate of us black guys!

At the time, no one could have predicted what would happen a year later. My debut at the Stade de France was strange. It was the inaugural game and we played against Spain. It was freezing cold, the ground was frozen as well. I was in the dressing room when Aimé came in and told me that I wasn't playing. 'Why aren't I playing?' I asked him. He answered, 'The ground is frozen, you're too tall, you're not sufficiently stable on it.' I was really shocked that he should tell me that, which is why I remember his words so well. So in the end, I didn't play for the entire match. I was on the bench, but I didn't get to go on at all. I didn't even get to warm up. I had a feeling of incomprehension because for me, there was no logic to the decision. It was an excuse, as far as I was concerned. I would have preferred it if he had said nothing at all to me. I didn't have any doubts when it came to the World Cup, but I did wonder why I didn't play that evening. I couldn't see what his logical reasoning had been when it came to that game. But I also knew that I wasn't the first choice for that position. There were one or two things that Aimé Jacquet told me like that which still make me react, even today.

7

Happiness is a Team Called France

The Tournoi de France hadn't gone that well. We had drawn against Brazil and Italy and lost against England. At the time, I was still young, so I was able to distance myself from all that. I didn't experience the pressure in the same way that the older guys did. I knew though that this was a crucial period leading up to the World Cup in France a year later. It was a difficult time for the France team because of their indifferent results and all the media attention. A lot of criticism was coming their way, both from journalists and supporters. Nobody thought for a moment that we were capable of winning the World Cup. The friendly games that took place between the Tournoi de France and the World Cup hadn't been great for us either. It's tough to play them, because there's nothing really at stake. Despite that, though, we remained pretty serene.

I had always hoped I would be in the squad. I was just starting out, there were a lot of other good players, so I just wanted to get my foot in the door, and to gradually work my way in to the team. But I always had my doubts. I never knew if I would find my place in the squad or if I was just passing through. So when I saw that I had made it on to the list of 28 players, I was happy. In fact, I was very satisfied. I still held back a bit, though, because I knew that, of the 28, six would be sent home from the training camp at Clairefontaine and would therefore not be part of the huge festival of football that would be the World Cup Finals. I was very pleased because I had played in the Tournoi de France and had been recalled after every subsequent game. On the other hand, in midfield, there were already other established players such as Manu Petit, Christian Karembeu, Dédé Deschamps and 'Bogo' Boghossian. There was also Sabri

Lamouchi who had a certain aura about him and who was often selected. Martin Djetou was also as hopeful as I was of being picked. So when I arrived at Clairefontaine, I wasn't as calm as I might have appeared to be.

We all had the same doubts in our minds. Well, maybe not all of us. It was more the younger generation of players, like myself, Thierry Henry, Nicolas Anelka, Robert Pires. Robert was perhaps a bit calmer than us, but we were all worried about being sent home. For example, there was a guy like Pierre Laigle who was an established player but was nonetheless one of the ones who was asked to leave. In addition, there were a lot of defensive midfielders. I really didn't know how it would all work out. There wasn't a strange atmosphere, though, and the relationships between the players remained good throughout. But we would nevertheless discuss this thing every evening. When we were on the pitch, or training, we didn't think about it too much. But at meal times, or watching TV or in the massage room, when we started to talk to others in little groups, then the subject would keep coming up. My little group was made up of Thierry, Robert, Martin (Djetou) and Nicolas. The youngsters, in other words! We all knew that some would stay and some would go and, inevitably, that created a certain tension between us.

I remember very well the evening when the six left. We had finished our evening meal and Henry Emile, the assistant coach and Aimé Jacquet's right-hand man, went to see various players to tell them that the boss wanted to see them in his room. He went to see first one, then another, then a third, a fourth. And as he didn't come to see me, I soon understood ... We were playing pool, or watching TV, I don't remember which. That was when I told myself, 'That's it, I'm in the final World Cup squad.' I was happy and proud. I called my family at once. My mum, my uncles, my aunts, my grandparents and Cheryl. Everyone, it turned out, had been as stressed out as I was!

I have to say that it was a really tough moment to live through. The guys who left had come to Clairefontaine with the same hopes and dreams. Some players didn't need to have any doubts because they were certain to stay, but there were others who were asked to leave who had also been sure they would be staying. Ibou Ba, I think, was one of those who was almost sure he would stay. Nicolas Anelka as well, because he was in one of his really good periods. I'm not too sure how I would have reacted not to have been selected at the last minute, after having completed the training camp. I don't know if it can wreck a career, but still, it's really tough to live through. No one can know for sure how it feels because those to whom it happens just say 'Those are the choices that have to be made, that's how it is, that's life.' But psychologically, for the rest of your career, it must be hard to bear.

I remember that Nicolas had gone off to pack at once and left immediately. I felt close to him, so it was difficult to find the right words to console him. It's hard to know what to say. You can't say that it's not important because it is. You can't say that you're sorry because you're the one who is staying. So I think that in these situations, it's best not to say anything. That's what I did, in any case.

I have always thought, and I still think so today, that it would have been better to have picked the final 22 from the start, because it's so tough to tell six guys that they are no longer part of the squad. On top of that, the World Cup was taking place in France, so we and all our families were hoping to experience it fully from the inside. If I had been the coach, I'm not sure I would have been prepared to do what he did. It must have been tough for Aimé Jacquet as well. But I reckon he must have had his reasons for doing what he did. Maybe he wasn't sure about some of the players and wanted to see them perform over a week, to see how they behaved on a daily basis within a group.

One of the main reasons we went on to win the World Cup was the atmosphere that existed within the squad as a whole. There was never the slightest tension between those who played and those who didn't and there was always a lot of mutual respect. Those of us who weren't picked much didn't feel out of the loop. And I think that, in order to create that sort of atmosphere, Aimé Jacquet had to pick a group of players who were capable of accepting that they weren't going to be playing.

The sort of guys who, even if they didn't play a single game during the entire tournament, would still be fully behind the team and would never mope around because they hadn't played. That's what Aimé Jacquet needed to check out. And once we won the World Cup, everyone agreed with what he had done.

I set out with the attitude that I was not first choice. I told myself 'I'm part of the France squad and I'll see what happens from there.' I reasoned with myself that if I played one game, that would be good, and if I went on during a game, that would be too. But it was a big mistake on my part to think like that. It showed a huge lack of personal ambition. I was satisfied just being in the France squad. I hadn't set myself a target of trying to play as often as possible, of earning myself a place in the team. I was sufficiently pleased just to be part of the squad. Once I became part of the 22 players, there was a period of training which changed things for me quite a lot. I remember that I wasn't as determined or ambitious as I should have been at the time. After a week or ten days, Aimé called each player into his room to talk about his preparation, his training, his behaviour. And he told me something that, without shocking me, still haunts me to this day and, I think, always will. He told me that he believed I had set out to play in the World Cup. When he looked at everything I had achieved up until then, he knew I could have become first choice, but he had been disappointed by my level of training, by my commitment during this period of preparation. Compared to a player like Emmanuel Petit who had involved himself completely in the training sessions and during all the friendly games, I had shown less commitment. Manu had earned his first-choice place during this period of preparation for the World Cup, whereas I had quite simply lost mine.

Even after the coach told me that, I never had the impression that I was too deferential towards my famous team-mates. The respect was always there. And I always had a lot of admiration for Didier Deschamps, as well as for the other players. On the pitch, I have always been determined, I have always had the same attitude. But I think that, when it came to that World Cup, I arrived on tiptoes and I lacked ambition. What Aimé Jacquet told me made me think, and with hindsight, I tell myself that he was right. In fact, I could have done a lot more.

In France, there weren't too many people who thought we were capable of winning the World Cup. The team had many critics. We obviously talked about that a lot amongst ourselves. We knew that our level of play was barely acceptable. Plus, the press never missed an opportunity to knock us after every game. The worry was there because there was huge pressure on us. We knew very well that, if we wanted to win the World Cup, we were going to have to play a lot better. Most of us had never experienced that level of pressure. This was the World Cup, in France, an event that we would only ever live through once in our careers and even in our lives, full stop.

Little by little, the pressure lifted. The first game against South Africa freed us up a lot because we won 3–0. I didn't take part at all. Nor in the second game, against Saudi Arabia, which we won 4–0. On the other hand, I played the whole of the game against Denmark. Then, in the last sixteen, against Paraguay (we won narrowly 1–0 after extra time), I didn't play, nor in the quarter-final against Italy which we won even more narrowly on penalties after the game had ended goalless after extra time. I didn't play in the semi-final against Croatia either and only went on for the last quarter of an hour in the final against Brazil.

Despite that, I didn't experience the World Cup Finals as if I was spectating. I honestly felt fully part of the group. Perhaps that was the problem – I felt too good, and I was satisfied with what I already had, even after Aimé Jacquet's words. Certainly, he had jolted me awake a bit, but by then it was too late. It took me a while to understand and by then the tournament was on the verge of starting. Then we won our first game, and the second, so it was difficult to change things. I admit, though, that what he said was to prove really helpful in the future. So even though I was mainly on the bench, the tournament went really well for me. There were some difficult matches, notably the first one which suddenly became easier for all of us once Christophe Dugarry's header gave us the lead. There was no doubt we had been tense. It was good that we played the Saudis because that allowed us to really get into the tournament, to gain in confidence and to play a more attacking game. After that, we beat Denmark 2–1. It was a good match. I was pleased with how I had played, I had felt good out there. Unbelievably, though, I ended up playing in the final itself and, for that, I have to say a big thank you to Marcel. Given that I had hardly played all tournament, I hadn't been expecting to go on. I was on the bench, quietly watching the game, enjoying it from the sidelines. Then, Titi went to warm up, David Trézéguet did the same, then Dugarry. They were mainly the guys who attacked, because things were looking good for us with our 2–0 lead. Then Marcel got sent off. During the tournament, Manu and Dédé had been the defensive midfield first choices. But I came on, without truly being aware of what was happening and of the importance of the situation. Marcel got red-carded, he came off, I came on, with the intention of not going further up than midfield. The aim was to defend, at whatever cost. I soon found my place on the pitch. I didn't have time to think about things too deeply. Everything happened too fast. That's why I got into the game really well. I didn't have time to think, to ask myself lots of questions. In the end, I even created the third goal for Manu after a counter-attack. For me, that move changed everything. In the final quarter of an hour we counter-attacked, I fed it to Manu and, with one touch, he scored.

I always felt involved during the World Cup. You had to be ready. Roger Lemerre, who at the time was the assistant trainer, would talk to us. We never felt side-lined, because he always followed what we were doing. We always had to prepare because you could never tell how things would pan out during a game, whether you might be needed after all. When it came to that final fifteen minutes, however, I felt like someone who had won the World Cup. That will go down in history. In ten years' time, when people talk about the France team who won the World Cup and when they show the three goals, they will see my deciding pass. That's a real source of pride for me.

After the final whistle, it was complete madness. But it went too fast. Much, much too fast. At the time, you know you have won the World Cup, that you have just achieved something extraordinary but you don't really take on board quite how significant that is. You are too close to it all. It's hard to tell yourself that this is the World Cup and that you have just beaten Brazil. It was the dream final. And we had beaten them 3–0. That was unbelievable. There was a party atmosphere on the pitch. The moment when I lifted the Cup was when I told myself, 'That really is the World Cup.' You take it in your hands, you look at it, you embrace it, you lift it up high. We have all watched so many players do just that on TV. I was completely engrossed in what I was doing. When I was a kid, I used to watch Pelé, Beckenbauer and the like lift the World Cup. When you watch the last few World Cups, you can see in the eyes of the players that it's a dream to win it. And when it's your turn to lift it, you tell yourself that you are truly living out a dream. You can now say to yourself, 'I too have lifted the World Cup.' And I can tell you, it's very heavy!

I remember certain images. David Trézéguet, at the end of the game. He gives the impression of being a bit of an unemotional guy, but there he really let it all out! But my most outstanding memory is of Youri Djorkaëff's joy. After the game, when we got back that evening to Clairefontaine, we had a party, and were celebrating. And Youri was like a kid, he was so happy. Djorkaëff is the guy who surprised me the most when it came to the emotion he showed afterwards, because of the contrast with his normal everyday behaviour. I never thought I would see him behave like that. He was jumping around, singing, dancing – like he was in heaven! There was a party organised for us afterwards but we decided to spend the evening all together at Clairefontaine, even though we had just spent six weeks there. That's why to have had such a good team spirit had been so important on a day-to-day level. Although Clairefontaine is a great place, and a magnificent training camp, after a couple of weeks you tell yourself 'That's enough!' What was extraordinary, though, was that during the whole of the World Cup there was never the slightest tension between anyone, no hassles, nothing in fact. The relationships that existed between us were magical. As was the fact that all the players created the 'Association France '98' afterwards which organised charity games. There is still the same respect between us, the same fantastic atmosphere.

Despite all that, I didn't miss Clairefontaine at all. Once we had left the training camp, the first thing that hit me was the atmosphere in the country as a whole. I had seen it on TV but I never expected people to go as crazy as they did about the France team. We had a parade up the Champs Elysées, and it was absolutely amazing. Two months before, we had done the Double at Highbury, and that was incredible enough as it was. But winning the World Cup, seeing the Champs Elysées like that, was pure magic. I wasn't frightened. I didn't think that all these people – and there must have been over a million of them – could have got trampled or suffocated to death. I was just soaking up the happiness. When we had been sequestered away at Clairefontaine, we couldn't get a sense of the enthusiasm there was for us. We were cut off, to a certain extent, from the outside world. We watched TV, and we could see the reaction of some of the people. On the way to the final, there had been all these people following the coach, as well as a helicopter that hovered over us. That too had been a crazy scene.

After all that, it was time for us to go our separate ways. There was a real sense of nostalgia because everything had gone so unbelievably well. We had lived through and achieved things that we would probably never do again. And we were probably not able to savour them long enough, to talk about them amongst ourselves, to tell each other what we had really felt. After the parade on the bus, everyone went on holiday separately. We didn't take the time to savour our happiness. Later on, though, we would call each other to talk about it after the event. That created a strong bond between us players. We had each lived through a real personal adventure.

From the moment we had set foot on the pitch, everyone had concentrated on the job in hand. What impressed me the most was the communal effort, rather than only one player in particular. If I had to pick out one player, it would be Marcel. He was incredible. But there were also Bixente Lizarazu, Lilian

Thuram, Laurent Blanc, as well as Fabien who was amazing too. Liza and Thuram are two hugely experienced players who have always worked unbelievably hard to stay at the top and there can't be many like them around. They are workers, grafters. You only have to see the way they warm up, the way they train during each training session, to know that. They are what I call real pros. I have so much respect for those two because of their attitude. Marcel is always ready to go for all his matches. When the coaches say 'you train just like you play', that sums Marcel up completely. When there is an important game, he's always there. The way he looks after himself, the way he knows himself so well, is unique. The self-confidence he has and which he exudes is fabulous. If there is one thing I most admire in Marcel, it's his self-awareness. Laurent Blanc, though, is the business, he personifies class. Everything is done with simplicity. There's never a misplaced word or gesture. It had been a real blow for us to have him sent off against Croatia, in the semi-final, because that meant he would be unable to play in the final. The Croatians had milked the incident for all it was worth. And although he can't deny what he did to the other guy, Bilic hammered it up disgracefully. That's what annoyed us the most.

Great players are extraordinarily tough mentally, irrespective of how strong they are technically. Mentally, we were a team that held firm throughout. We set out our objectives and in the end we achieved them because mentally we were so tough. Some players were incredibly important. Lizarazu, Lilian, Marcel, Dédé all played a dominant role. Not only on the pitch, but also in our everyday life and in training.

When it comes to Lilian Thuram, in my opinion, he still doesn't know how on earth he managed to score two goals against Croatia and, what's more, with his left foot! But it was just his day! When you compare that with what he had achieved up until then, both in his professional and in his private life, it was a well-deserved reward. He was destined to, I'm sure. We were also destined to qualify for the final by scoring those two goals. It was written in the stars. As for Zizou in the final – magic. He headed in two goals. That's the definition of a great player, playing a great game when he needs to. He was pivotal when it came to us winning the World Cup.

After the World Cup, we received the Légion d'Honneur, the highest honour a Frenchman can receive, from the Head of State. It was a source of great pride, of enormous satisfaction, given what it represented for me and my family. For my grandfather to be able to say that his grandson had received the Légion d'Honneur was fantastic. I think he was as proud of that as of me winning the World Cup. The Légion d'Honneur really symbol-ised something for him. I never wear the little red decoration on my lapel, it's at home in my safe. When I'm older, though, I'm sure I'll wear it . . . to go the stadium!

After our victory, we became unbelievably popular. We were like gods, almost. It wasn't just that we were popular as a team or as individuals; football in general soared in popularity. Us winning the World Cup in France raised the profile and the prestige of the game immensely.

Between the World Cup and Euro 2000, we changed coaches. Roger Lemerre took over from Aimé Jacquet. I started to be selected more and more, even though I still wasn't the automatic first choice. Before Euro 2000, I was already more confident than I had been before the World Cup. In some strange way, playing those final fifteen minutes of the World Cup Final had been a great confidence booster for me. This meant that I was calmer and consequently able to make more of a mark. Without being big-headed, I think I was making myself heard a bit more, and was less shy and retiring within the squad, although I was still very respectful towards Dédé and Marcel, as well as towards 'Bogo' Boghossian who was before me in the pecking order and was still being picked more often than I was.

I felt a certain pressure from the media who were pushing for me to be the automatic first choice rather than Didier. We both felt that pressure. I knew that the newspapers were angling for me to be in the starting line-up and that put me ill at ease. I didn't really know how to position myself relative to Dédé. I didn't want to do or say anything that might offend or upset him. He's someone I like enormously and I think Dédé felt that.

During that time, he came to see me and said 'Whatever the papers say or write must never come between us. Whatever happens, let's make sure of that.' He had expressed things perfectly and I admire him enormously for that. Given all the pressure he had on his shoulders, he could have come to see me to try to break me, or to scare me or shake me. Maybe he valued the fact that I had been discreet and had never said anything to the newspapers along the lines that I deserved to be picked or that I wanted to play. I always kept that distance between us and that respect for him.

Even so, deep down I believed that I deserved to play. But the team was winning, despite the fact that it had had trouble qualifying for the European Championships. And it's difficult to change a winning team. When Bogo was playing rather than me, I found it hard to understand. But I never said a thing. On the other hand, you need someone like Dédé on the pitch. Perhaps I could have brought more to the game than he did because I was better at going forward and had more attacking qualities than he did, but I didn't think I could contribute as much as Dédé when it came to his positional play and his ability to read the game.

During the World Cup, the French team had banked on the strength of its defence. At Euro 2000, it would rely on the strength of its attack. Obviously, it's the quality of the players that makes the difference. During the World Cup, we had had Guivarc'h and Dugarry up front. During the European Championships, they had been replaced by Thierry, Nicolas Anelka and David Trézéguet.

We didn't have a single easy game during Euro 2000, and we only won the key matches by slender margins. For me, though, that tournament remains an exceptional time, and gave me much more intense moments than the World Cup did – not in terms of the emotions that I went through but in more general terms. As far as I was concerned, the memories were much stronger, much more powerful. The way I prepared for it and the way in which I lived throughout the tournament was much more intense. I wasn't in the starting line-up for the first match against Denmark but I was for the second against the Czech Republic.

That was the start of a run of playing a few games in a row and I got the feeling that I was playing my way into being the automatic first choice.

Against the Netherlands, we were leading 2–1 in the second half. Edgar Davids had been one of the five or six best defensive midfielders in the world over the previous ten to fifteen years. I have always loved playing against players with personality. He's a real fighter, a winner. He hates to lose, he hates being pushed around. That was a fantastic match. Even though we lost, we came away with a feeling of having really enjoyed the game. Afterwards, we realised that in fact it suited us to have lost because we would be able to continue the competition in Belgium rather than have to go off to the Netherlands. That said, when we went on to the pitch, it was always to win.

I think that it was psychologically crucial for me to have played that last quarter of an hour against Brazil in the World Cup. After that, for Euro 2000, even though I wasn't in the starting line-up for the first game, I had nonetheless prepared myself differently, because I had remembered what Aimé had told me. In the lead-up to the tournament, I had wanted to show that I really wanted to play, that I was as ambitious as Manu Petit.

There was no difference for me between Aimé and Roger. It never matters to me who is coach. And in the France squad at the time, we had everything. We had quality; we had a unified, ambitious group of players. There was the same solidarity amongst us at the European Championships as there had been at the World Cup. There were no problems between us. In order to go all the way in those sorts of tough competitions, it's essential that all the players get on incredibly well together. There have always been different little groups. I'm not talking about cliques because those are unhealthy for the atmosphere. You can't help feeling closer to some players than to others, as you do to people in everyday life. We had our little group – Nicolas, Thierry, Robert – there were five or six of us in it. We have never laughed so much. We would listen to music in the evenings. In fact, we had a really nice time at Euro 2000.

Thierry gained a lot of confidence during the tournament. He attempted a lot of new things. When he plays for France, I can sense, because I know him so well, that he holds himself back just a little bit. With Arsenal, he's capable of taking the ball, beating two or three players, crossing it or scoring. For France, though, he doesn't feel free enough mentally to do that. But at Euro 2000 he was. For me, Thierry is part of that new generation of strikers who can do everything.

The quarter-final against Spain in Bruges was perhaps one of the best games I have ever played in. It had everything. Emotion, tension, goals, reversals of fortune. At the end of a match like that, you're physically and mentally completely exhausted. When you win games like that, all you want to do is play like that again. That day, I played with Dédé in midfield. Manu was ill with a virus and couldn't train at all for a while. Afterwards, against Portugal, all three of us played. That was a very complicated match. In the others, we had always scored first, but against Portugal in the semis, Nuno Gomes scored an incredible goal. We really had to pull ourselves together to get back into the game and equalise. That required mental strength above all else. But we showed we were equal to the task. In that game, we showed our determination. Fabien was fantastic throughout the tournament. I remember the expression on Portuguese defender Abel Xavier's face. There had been a corner or a free kick and I was supposed to be marking him. He headed it and Fabien saved it, I have no idea how. I must have taken four or five seconds to realise that Fabien had just saved my life. If Xavier had scored then, we would have been dead. It could have changed the course of my career. A penalty was given away by our opponents at the end of extra time. Everyone saw the handball except the referee who hadn't seen it from where he was standing. Luckily, the linesman had been vigilant. And Zizou struck the penalty as if it was a free kick. He curled it into the top right-hand corner. After that, he ran straight towards Dugarry on the bench. That was a good moment.

We were very wary about playing Italy in the final. The majority of our team played in the Italian league so we knew very well what sort of match it was going to be. In the game itself, Italy were perhaps not as spectacular as Spain or Portugal had been, but when it came to discipline, they were very strong. With the fact in my mind that we had so many players who played in Italy and who therefore didn't want to lose, I told myself everything would be all right. But instead, we were anything but good!

On top of everything, they were the ones who took the lead. And we all knew that when Italy scored first, you were in trouble. After the goal, I knew it was going to be tough. I won't say I thought it was over but I did tell myself that it wasn't looking good. We were struggling, to say the least. We were trying to play more direct football and it wasn't always working. And Italians know how to hold on to a lead! But in the last seconds of added-on time, Fabien cleared the ball, David Trézéguet headed it down and, in the very last second, Sylvain Wiltord thundered the ball right under keeper Toldo's arm and into the net. I think that goal completely killed them. Already, on the bench, they were starting to get up, to put the collars up on their tracksuits. They thought they had won. And Wiltord's volley was extraordinary. Thierry, who was on the bench, had felt the other guys next to him beginning to strut around a bit, to wind him up, so he told them to sit down. Suddenly, everything happened very quickly. When they had scored, we wondered 'how are we going to score?' When we scored, on the other hand, they told themselves they were dead and buried. At the end of full time, I looked at them and they looked as if their world had fallen apart. I'm sure that if you talk to those guys even today, they still don't know how on earth they managed to lose the game.

In extra time, they were running on empty. We knew that sooner or later we would score that golden goal. Then Pires did one of his runs down the side in slow motion. But Bobby is deceptively fast. One of the things he's got going for him is that he can accelerate very quickly, despite his slightly flat-footed stance. He always does those little dummies, where only his head moves. This time, he moved down the wing, crossed to the centre and David was on the end of it with a quality finish. A real striker's shot, a killer kick. A left-footer by a guy who doesn't doubt. Ever.

It wasn't as if David hadn't had some difficult moments in Euro 2000. He hadn't much appreciated the fact that he wasn't playing at all. He doesn't need to touch the ball very often but he needs to be on the pitch! His goal in the final could not have been scored by many players. Robert crossed the ball but it was a bit high, not along the ground. And it came on to David's left foot. The way in which he balanced himself to take the ball was, technically, extraordinary for a striker. That was a golden goal. David took his shirt off, Roger Lemerre went running down to the corner flag. I was so exhausted that I was starting to cramp. But I found the energy to run. It was magical. I don't know if there's anything else in life that can compare with that feeling. It's not the sort of sensation that you live through every day.

Obviously we thought about the World Cup and about the Double we had just done. We talked about it. What's amazing is the amount of time we spent together. Lizarazu said that we hadn't had time to savour the World Cup. But during Euro 2000 we did. We stayed on the pitch for a long time. Dédé, Lilian, Thierry, Robert ... we all stayed a long time to talk about it, we lay down on the grass, in order to allow what we had just done to really sink in. We kept saying 'It's amazing! We won the World Cup, now we have won the European Championships.' The trophy was right there. We wanted to stay on the pitch to savour the moment, to sear that moment into our memories for ever.

I was 24 years old and, in terms of my international career, I had won all there was to win. But you always want to do better. I have always been aware of what I have achieved and I have always wanted more, both in terms of the team and in terms of raising my own level of play. I have always had people around me who I could talk to about improving my performance.

Sometimes, you boast a bit about having won the World Cup and the European Championships. You are proud of the fact that, at twenty-three or twenty-four, you have achieved something major that very few professional players ever will. I have always been aware of my successes and have savoured them. The English showed me a lot of respect for what the France team had achieved. They congratulated me a lot because there were plenty of people out there who didn't think we were capable of doing what we did. We changed the way that people viewed the blue shirt of France. And that's perhaps the thing that makes me most proud.

8

French Blues

I was dead on my feet when I got to the World Cup in South Korea and Japan in 2002. Dead. I had not missed a single game for France, I had played a lot for Arsenal and we had just done the Double again. I was physically and mentally drained and, what was worse, I knew it. Where I went wrong, or was at least partly to blame, was to have played in all the friendly games during the season, especially the one against South Korea only a few days before the opening game of the tournament even though I could feel that I was not physically 100 per cent. That's when I should have told the coach, Roger Lemerre, that I had to have some time to recover, to rest. But I have this 'I want to play all the games' side of me. Given that the tournament was about to start, I should never have played against the South Koreans. It was a pointless game for us although our opponents gave everything they had, as if they were playing in the final.

But that's what I am like, I always want to play. I tell myself that I'm young and that I recover quickly, that as far as I am concerned, there is nothing to worry about: I don't see the downside. Also, it's the France team and naturally you want to play in all the games. After our failure in the tournament, people talked about the wisdom of going on lengthy tours of Chile and Australia. But I had wanted to go to Australia, I had never set foot there, even if, in the end, we hadn't exactly seen much of the country other than Melbourne zoo! With hindsight, I can see that these had been mistakes. I don't think I should have gone. I should have said instead that I was tired and needed to rest. I am convinced that if I had missed these trips, I would have been much fresher.

Robert's knee injury – received against Newcastle at High-bury, earlier in the season – was also a big blow for us. He had gradually earned his regular place in the team and he was in great form. The fact that he was injured was definitely a handicap for us. That said, at the time, we felt we had such strength in depth in the squad that we could overcome his absence easily enough. But once the tournament started . . . and once it was over, that's when we realised how important he was. Whether he was amongst a group of us off the pitch or on it, Bobby had a solution to everything. Zizou's injury was also a psychological blow for us because, naturally, when you have Zizou in your team, you feel much stronger. When he got injured during the South Korea match, mentally we told ourselves that we were in the shit. A lot rested on him. We all offloaded a little bit of our individual responsibility on to Zizou's shoulders. We relied on him. And when he got injured, we had no one to fall back on and we were on our own.

Our preparation for the tournament got criticised a lot as well. It lasted two weeks, no more. The problem was that, at the time, I felt the coaching staff did what they wanted to do without taking into account the physical state of each individual player. Some guys, of which I was one, had played seventy-odd games over the course of the season, whilst others had only played about twenty. And the problem was, we all trained together, at the same pace, in the same way. In my eyes, that was a real problem. Instead, the reason which was given to explain our World Cup failure was that we had excessive sponsorship obligations. That was complete rubbish from start to finish. We attended no more sponsors' events than we had done in previous years. People tried to find a reason for our failure and this business of sponsorship duties was a perfect excuse. But that's not where the real problem lay. The truth is that we did not prepare ourselves very well; some players, such as me, had arrived at the tournament already in a state of fatigue; that's why we hadn't been up to our usual level. End of story.

After Bobby's injury and then Zidane's against South Korea, the boss did not change his tactics and we were blamed for not having intervened. But Lemerre was stubborn and pigheaded when it came to doing what he wanted to do. He was not someone who could easily be persuaded to change his mind. Lemerre will go to his grave with his ideas intact. We tried to tell him a few things, just on a tactical level. Zizou was no longer playing, so the best thing would have been to play with three defensive midfielders – me, Claude Makelele and Emmanuel Petit. Emmanuel on the left, Makelele slightly on the right and me down the middle.

I don't know if Zizou went to Lemerre's room to try to talk to him but I know that some players did. I had a conversation with him on the subject. It was before the first game against Senegal. We felt that something was missing. Without Zidane and Pires, we couldn't play with the same system and we were worried that the 4–2–3–1 system wouldn't work any longer. I brought it up again after our defeat against Senegal. Thierry and I were having a coffee when the boss joined us and we had a discussion about it. We got the feeling that he had understood what we were saying but the next day it was back to the same old thing. He had his opinions and he was sticking to them.

Against Uruguay, Thierry was not flowing. You could feel it. He had been ready to play down the middle with David Trézéguet. But Lemerre put him on the left and no one understood what the hell he was doing! We were all expecting Thierry to play up front. That's what killed him. But that's Roger Lemerre for you. In everyday life, he's a delightful guy and you can talk to him about anything. But he is stubborn when it comes to tactical positioning. I know that we had won Euro 2000 with Roger as the coach but we also had Laurent Blanc and Didier Deschamps in the squad then who were able to put pressure on him. Also, that tournament, which had taken place in Belgium and the Netherlands, came on the heels of the '98 World Cup and the situation was much easier for him than in 2002. In 1998 and 2000, we had broadly the same team, the same structure. When Didier and Laurent retired, that's when those of us who were the senior squad members, the senior execs in a way, should have stood up for ourselves a bit more. Lemerre too could have been more aware of the situation.

When it came to this Far Eastern World Cup in 2002, though, we did not prepare well. Thierry's knee was not right, Robert and Zizou were both injured, and we had to play our opening game against Senegal.

Senegal . . . When I saw the draw, I was with Arsenal taking a short break at a hotel, and my first reaction was that this was unbelievable. I saw it as a gift from heaven, because I was born there and grew up there. I was barely eight years old when I left Senegal. Later, when I talked about it with my parents and with my family, it was incredible. Also, I still have family over there and I am always speaking to them on the phone. And on top of everything, it was the opening game. So for me, it was a fantastic draw. During the game itself, I pushed all that to the back of my mind. And afterwards as well, because we had not really played up to our usual standard. The absence of Zizou and Robert was really felt by the team. But we were not playing well, in any case. We were not surprised because we hadn't been up to much for some time: it was more of the same thing in fact.

Even in the last game before the start of the World Cup, against Belgium at the Stade de France in May, despite the fact that we had lost 1–0, the atmosphere had been more like that of a celebration. I had not had the feeling that this was a warm-up match, that we were working hard in order to prepare for an important event. We climbed up on to the podium, there were fireworks. It was like a charity or testimonial match.

A lot of people thought we had got big-headed and I don't think they were far wrong. We had been winning constantly, so maybe we got complacent and over-confident. We had developed a nasty habit of feeling superior to others. We thought we were going to win games before they had even begun, that all we had to do was to set foot on the pitch. Somewhere, we had left behind the values that make football great. And as a result we got a whipping.

Even after that Belgium game, we were not particularly worried about South Korea. Not enough, in any case. At the time, we told ourselves that we would be up to it when it came to the tournament, that these were purely friendly games and that it did not matter if we lost them. We told ourselves that come the big day, we would be up to the task mentally. It was only gradually, after each game came and went, that we understood our mistakes and realised that we had lost sight of what we should have been doing on the pitch.

Everything started after the game we lost against Senegal. I have to admit that my loyalties were slightly divided after that game. I was disappointed, for sure, to have lost because it was the opening game. Also, in a competition like the World Cup, everyone knows how important that first game is, how important it is to win it. On the other hand, I told myself that it was better to lose against Senegal than against Uruguay or Denmark. And deep down, I hoped that we would both qualify, ourselves as well as the Senegalese. After the game, they were totally euphoric. It was a historic moment. Even if they didn't get past the group matches, it didn't matter: they had beaten France! It was as if they had won the competition and everything else was a bonus. As for me, despite my slightly mixed feelings, I was still mad because we had lost!

Even after this inaugural defeat, we were still sure we would get through. That too was a mistake. We should have been much more concerned. The right attitude would have been to say: there are only two matches left, we have to be careful after all. But no, we were calm. The reappraisal that we should have had after the friendly games did not even take place after the defeat against Senegal. Lilian Thuram and I talked about it a lot. We were very close to one another; we could see what the problem was. But at the same time we were sure of our strength. Too sure.

Then there was that goalless draw against Uruguay where we did not have much luck. It was certainly the best game we played out there. But the bottom line was that the score was still 0—0. Against Senegal, we had created a few openings but had not managed to follow them through. Against Uruguay we had some chances too, even when we were down to ten men after the harsh sending-off of Thierry. But we never managed to score.

We had Thierry, David and Djibril, the three highest scorers in the English, Italian and French leagues. Despite that, we never found a way through. After the Uruguay match, we began to tell ourselves that it was going to be difficult. But it was already too late: we only had one point and to get through to the next stage we were going to have to beat Denmark by two goals. We were probably pretending to believe in ourselves without daring to admit that this was the case. Zidane was returning after his injury and that was going to give us wings; we really believed it. But that lasted all of half an hour. Once we conceded the goal, we understood . . .

In any case, even if we had got past the group games, we would quickly have been sent on our way. We were not right physically and we were not right mentally. There was no way we were in a fit state to win that World Cup.

We had won the previous two big international competitions, we had three in-form strikers, we had Lilian who was the best defender in the world, Zidane who was the best player in the world, and Barthez, the best goalkeeper. We thought that nothing bad could happen to us. But even with all that individual talent, if you don't have the values, it can't possibly work. Or rather, it no longer works.

This premature exit was the first big setback of my career and it was something that I found difficult to come to terms with. I asked myself a lot of questions. 'How did we manage not even to win a single game? How did we manage not even to score a single goal? How can you mess up a competition to that extent?'

On a personal level, I blamed myself in particular for not having skipped some of those friendlies. I had not rested and that had been a mistake. But then, even today, I still don't rest, even though I now feel more able to pass up the opportunity to play a friendly if I think I might worsen an existing injury.

After the World Cup, Jacques Santini was named as our new coach fairly quickly. Our first game under him took place in Tunisia. It was there that the discussion took place about who should wear the captain's armband and that was when my name came up for the first time. It was something that I had never previously thought about – it had honestly never crossed my mind. There was still Lizarazu, Thuram, Zidane ... And obviously, Marcel Desailly was still there. People had really criticised him because of his allegedly individualistic attitude during the World Cup. But Marcel has always been like that, that's his personality. In time, I have come to understand that and it's not a reason for me not to talk to Marcel or not to enjoy his company. That's simply what he's like: take it or leave it. With Marcel and Jacques Santini, we easily qualified for Euro 2004. And once more, the tournament began with an opening match that had a particular resonance to it. This time, we were playing England.

The English: that was a game we had to get right, because there is a rivalry between us and them. On top of that, because of all the French players who were doing well in the Premiership, the atmosphere in the game was very special. If we had lost that game, the whole of England would have been unbelievably proud of themselves, from the press to the fans. I had already felt the excitement mounting in England between when the draw had been made and the day of the game itself. France, despite the setback in the World Cup, was still the best team in Europe. Everyone wanted to measure themselves against us to see what their team was capable of. Because whatever they said about the French, the other countries still admired us enormously. They liked our beautiful game, the quality of our players. Sol Campbell went completely nuts at the idea of playing against Thierry, though we didn't wind each other up too much about the whole thing. They were capable of beating us, in any case, so we didn't want to mess around too much! For us, it was definitely a match we could not afford to lose. And nobody could predict which way it would go.

We were in a much better state going into the tournament. The World Cup had taught us a lot of things, we had a new coach and above all we had found out the hard way what could happen to us if we were not well prepared psychologically, mentally and physically. Individually, we had each gone away and analysed our own performances. That was why we had played well in the qualifying games. Even if we had not been up against the hottest teams on Earth, we had still won some difficult games; we had felt a real shift in attitude.

The France–England game that we were all so looking forward to finally got under way on the evening of 13 June, and everybody remembers that it was incredible! The motivation was 100 per cent there. Psychologically, I had fully prepared myself. I had been thinking about the game for quite a long time. This was against England and those of us Frenchmen who played over there had a duty to ourselves to be beyond reproach.

I can't say that the atmosphere on the pitch was particularly unusual. The English go at you physically but they don't talk to you much; that's their mentality, their culture. They might exchange a few words but it will be after the final whistle. During the game itself, you get a few knocks but that's about it. They'll try hard to intimidate you. During the match as a whole, we were not very good but the closing stages were perfect and really played us into the competition.

Things had started well for us – we forced the early pace and won a corner in the first minute. A piece of hesitant England defending soon after left an opening for me to shoot but unfortunately I was not able to capitalise and sent the ball over from 25 yards out. Play flowed and David Trézéguet narrowly failed to score when his header went just over the crossbar. But for all our passing and attempts at goal, we gradually sank into a stalemate situation with England.

Suddenly, in the 38th minute, David Beckham crossed from the right and Frank Lampard outjumped Mikaël Silvestre to open the scoring with a header at the near post. We were stunned and at that stage, left wondering how on earth we were going to score. We had possession of the ball but we couldn't seem to create the openings because up front, there was this wall of English players. They were all pushing right up against us. They wouldn't allow Thierry any space so that he could play deep. Wayne Rooney, who was to have a fantastic tournament, and Michael Owen were up front but the four midfielders and the four at the back, they never went out of position. It was difficult to find spaces, to outmanoeuvre them and to play our game. And when we conceded that goal, we became really scared.

The turning point of the match was midway through the second half when Silvestre gave away a penalty after he brought down Rooney who was making a run at goal. Barthez dived to his right and saved Beckham's penalty – the latter's second penalty miss in successive competitive internationals. We would not have come back from 2–0 down. But that's why Fabien is one of the two best keepers in the world, along with Buffon.

England were still leading 1–0 at the end of 90 minutes, but a minute into stoppage time, we were given a free kick within striking range. When Zizou got us out of jail with his wickedly curling free kick, I told myself 'Thank God, the hardest part is over!' I couldn't believe it. The whole team went crazy.

Now I have to be frank. The English goalkeeper, David James, had a disastrous game. They cannot hope to win anything with a goal-keeping performance like that. I have watched that free kick many times over now and he should never have been standing where he was. He let down his team because I honestly don't think we were capable at that stage of scoring from direct play. England have struggled to find a consistent replacement for David Seaman.

With the score at 1–1, I told myself that we would happily settle for that. But then I remember looking at the England players and noticing that they looked dead, defeated. As soon as play kicked off again, we closed them right down. Finally we were managing to push forward, whilst they looked like they had just been hit with a sledgehammer; in complete contrast we seemed to have suddenly taken on board rocket fuel. For the first time in the game, we could sense a sort of nervousness in their camp. They were disgusted by what was happening to them.

Barely a minute after the equaliser, with just seconds left on the clock, Steven Gerrard passed to his keeper. It was a terrible back pass, and we all realised that he was scared. Thierry took the ball brilliantly: he anticipated the pass perfectly and earned himself a penalty when James brought him down. That's when I knew they were dead in the water. I was sure that Zidane would stick the ball in the back of the net. It must have been a moment of extreme tension for him – he even threw up just before he took the kick – but as far as I was concerned, he was going to do the business. I watched the penalty without a trace of anxiety. Usually I watch the keeper. But this time I was sure. I was confident. Zidane scored. His second goal in injury time!

At the end of the game, the atmosphere was unbelievable. You can say what you like, the English supporters are unique. There's no one like them. During the warm-up, I looked around and it was as if I was playing back in England. The flags were all out, the fans were cheering. If the France team had fans like that, we would be even stronger. In France, people don't realise how important the supporters are. They can literally win you a game. Wherever England play, they know they can count on their fans. They follow the team everywhere and their passion is simply fantastic. I envy them for that. It's not enough to win a game, but it can really help.

When the final whistle went, I remember running around like crazy, even though it's not normally something I do. I'm more someone who keeps his emotions to himself. But when Zizou scored his second goal, I remember running practically seventy metres. I was elated. We had beaten the English with the last kick of the game! After the match and the press conferences, I had a quick chat to Ashley Cole in front of the team bus. He was mad; he still couldn't believe they had managed to lose the game. We, on the other hand, couldn't believe we had actually won it! I think we really dug as deep as it was possible to dig for this victory.

In the changing room, we were so happy, we were singing. We had wanted to win so badly. And because the changing rooms were almost next door to each other, the other team could hear. But although we were singing away, it wasn't aimed at them – it was just that we were so happy and relieved. Lampard's controversial views printed in the newspapers (claiming that we had deliberately been singing in order to taunt the English) made no difference. We hadn't wound them up because we had had no reason to do so. Thinking about it today, though, maybe it would have been better if we had drawn the game, given what happened afterwards.

I felt really good at the time. I had prepared myself well. The Real Madrid situation had surfaced but I was not letting it get to me and was managing to keep it out of my thoughts. Anyway, it concerned Real Madrid, so it wasn't exactly a bad worry to have! It did not stop me concentrating on the pitch. The next match we drew 2–2 against Croatia and even though we hadn't lost, we had conceded two goals and we started to doubt a bit and to look critically at our performance.

The press started to question Zizou's positioning, so, subconsciously I think, we started to question it ourselves in the squad. But where is the problem with Zizou's positioning? The question should not even arise. The bottom line is, he's the world's best player. But as a result of all this, he went and played on the right even though he should never go off and play there.

I think this crazy debate finally got to Zizou, even though he didn't show it. Today, with hindsight, I tell myself that we had the best player in the world and we should have left him free to play exactly where he wanted.

Naturally, as all teams do, we had some tactical discussions to try to improve the situation. We could see there was a problem because we were not defending very well. Santini was very open and we talked things through at length. But in the end, I am convinced that we discussed things too much. In the press, nobody brought up our doubts. The problems remained between us and that's as it should have been. To sum up what I think, we did too much talking and not enough playing.

During the warm-up in the Switzerland game, I felt a twinge in my thigh. I told myself that once I had warmed up, it would go away. That's what I'm like, I always think it will just go away. Then, little by little, I felt the pain getting worse. By the end of the game, I was finding it difficult to walk, it felt like something was piercing through me, like a dagger. But I had played the entire game.

We finished top of the group, scored seven goals and were happy with our overall performance. The squad really wanted to achieve something. The press was more worried about the way in which we were playing than the actual results. They were criticising the fact that our game lacked fluidity, that we weren't managing to play our game and that certain players were not at ease. It's true that Thierry had not managed to find his best form. I was aware of his Achilles tendon problem because we had talked about it. He was quietly getting treatment. But Thierry and I are similar in that respect, because we both always want to play, at whatever cost. We love playing and we feel capable of lasting the whole 90 minutes.

People talk and talk about Thierry Henry's more restricted role in the France team compared to his role at Arsenal. But you don't play for your national team like you do for your club: you play differently, with a different group of players. That was another non-problem. When I look at the stats and I see that with all the goals that Thierry has scored for France, Zizou did not once make the decisive pass, I tell myself that it's more a coincidence than anything else. I might be wrong but I do think it's a coincidence. It's true, with Arsenal, Thierry calls for the ball and it arrives at once but football is made up of too many tiny elements to be able to make a sweeping generalisation about what happens in a game.

Then we had to play Greece. At the time, we thought it was the best draw. With my thigh strain, I found myself on the bench. I was going round in circles – on the bench, in the changing room. The evening before, we were in the treatment room watching the Portugal–England game. There were at least a dozen of us and the atmosphere was unbelievable! It was a brilliant game, which went to penalties. The way we gathered together to watch it illustrates perfectly the atmosphere that existed amongst us. The treatment room has always been our meeting point, our HQ. This is no longer the case today because a new team is being built and it takes time to forge those sorts of bonds. But at the time, that was what the France team were all about – the treatment room. Although there were worries as well during that tournament the team was closer, and the atmosphere that reigned throughout the whole of Euro 2004 was fantastic. That evening, during the Portugal–England game, everybody was there. Thierry was there, Zizou got there before the end. We were falling about laughing throughout the whole game. After Portugal's victory, we all went up to our rooms. I couldn't settle though because I knew that I would not be playing in the quarter-finals. I also felt a pinch of sadness for Sol and for Ashley whilst at the same time telling myself, 'They're on the plane home, so if we are as well tomorrow, it won't feel as bad!' because we didn't want to go home before them. I had spoken to them on the phone: they were disappointed to be leaving, but that's how it was.

England will have a good team for the 2006 World Cup. It's a pity Scholes has retired from international football even if, after many long years of competing at the highest level, some players have to stop because they want to spend a bit more time with their family or be more available for their club. Even so, I couldn't understand Scholes' decision. He's so good and he still had so much to give the England team. But Beckham, Gerrard and Lampard are still there. Their midfield is very strong. Their defence as well: Sol Campbell, Rio Ferdinand, John Terry, Ashley Cole on the left, Gary Neville on the right. And of course, there is Rooney, whose skill and strength are completely incredible for someone of his age. So I think that in 2006, given how quickly they are improving, England will definitely be one of the teams to beat because they are already probably one of the best teams in Europe.

Before the Greece game, I was convinced that we were going to get through. For us, this was good opposition to have, they were easily within our reach. I was injured but I was already fast-forwarding to the semi-final, which I would have played in. It was taking place three or four days later, so I would have had time to recover. I was getting the treatment I needed. From the bench, it was a tense game to watch. We were going forward to try to take the game to them, trying to score, and were coming up against a wall. The opposition weren't coming forward, they weren't playing. When they got possession of the ball, they would chuck it towards the corner flag to gain a bit of time. They were doing everything they could to stifle us.

Time went by and straight after half time, they scored. That's when you tell yourself that things could not be worse. But I was still full of hope. It was a bit like the scenario we get in a lot of Premiership games. The opposition defend like crazy, but once they have conceded one goal, you can put three or four past them. But this time, they defended so well and they got better once they scored. I was convinced, though, that we would equalise. So when the referee blew the final whistle and it was all over, that was hard to take.

France had failed in these European Championships but in a different way from the World Cup in 2002. It was even harder for us to live with this time because we were less out of it, we were in better physical shape, and were better prepared. We had got through the group stages only to be beaten by Greece. I'm not sure if the fact that they won the tournament made the pain any more bearable. But I'm convinced that everything we felt was also felt by the Portuguese and all those teams who were beaten by Greece. The Greeks were not favourites. And when I see that most of their squad cannot command a guaranteed first-team place in their respective clubs, I tell myself that we witnessed a truly unbelievable moment in the history of football. The Greeks twice beat the Portuguese at home, as well as the Czech Republic and France. It was an incredible performance. And 'incredible' really is the right word to use here because just a few weeks later the very same Greek team was beaten in a World Cup qualifier by Albania. A major international competition offers a snapshot of where players are, at a set moment in the season. Over the course of that season, a player can go through a lean spell for a month or so. But if you hit one of those spells during a tournament, you cannot make up for it during the rest of the season. It's too late and of no use to your country's team. The other thing I conclude is that there is no longer much of a gap between the small and the large nations. Nowadays, all the teams contain players who run fast, jump high and are strong.

Aside from that, the level of technical skill will be a decider but physically, there is no longer much of a gap. Desire and determination are crucial factors at the highest level.

It's the same thing in the Champions League. Panathinaikos are as good as us, they are as well organised as us, they can jump as high, run as fast for as long. There is no longer much difference between the players. While, obviously, there are some unbelievable players in the big clubs, the mental aspect is more and more important. And that's also why a lot of the bigger nations perform disappointingly.

After Euro 2004, we were criticised a lot in the newspapers. From the outside, people imagined all sorts of things that were not true and that were systematically negative. As if we, the Arsenal players, were going to mess around plotting something against Zidane! We all love Zidane! I have always had a really good relationship with Zizou. And I think the same goes for all the others. Zidane, as far as I'm concerned, is a real star. He's the player I most admire in the game today. He's the best of the best, as a human being and as a player. He is humble, unaffected, has a big heart and you can always count on him. Yet he could really show off if he wanted to. You never hear anything about him in the media because he keeps his private life out of the spotlight and he doesn't want to share his life with the media. He is fantastic and I respect those choices so much. So I was really annoyed by everything that was said and written. Because people who don't know him will read those things and have a completely false impression of what the truth is. When Zizou reads those things, he knows it's all just a load of rubbish. Those involved in the squad know that very well too. But other people, the fans, they're going to imagine God knows what. I know Thierry very well. I know that he has never had any problems with Zidane. We all know that in every generation of the France team, as with any club, there are always some stars. Some will shine more brightly than others, that's normal. At that time, the star of the France team was Zidane. Before him it was Platini. Nowadays, it's Thierry. Stars come and go. That's the natural order of things.

I was on holiday when that story was printed in a French newspaper. In England, we're used to the press coming out with these sorts of lies, but we were all unpleasantly surprised to discover these were coming from France. They were talking about fights between Titi and Robert. How ridiculous is that? They might have had the odd disagreement about something, but that hardly means they had a fight! When it comes to sport, the French press is starting to be like the British and that's really not a good thing.

After Euro 2004, things were very up and down for me and the France team. On a personal level, I had the immense honour of being named captain but when it came to international results, the team had a difficult time. That's because it is not easy to rebuild a team after some of its main players have retired from international football. Give me one team that can start up again a few weeks after Euro 2004 as if nothing had happened, having seen the last of players such as Marcel Desailly, Lilian Thuram, Bixente Lizarazu, Zinédine Zidane and Claude Makelele – the latter showing what an exceptional player he was during the course of his season with Chelsea. A lot of things have been said and written about Raymond Domenech's new France team. The results certainly have been disappointing. And in football, the only thing that counts, when all is said and done, is scoring goals and winning. It's up to the coach, whoever he is, to pick the right players to get the results.

There was a lot of debate, particularly concerning tactics, because we twice played 3–5–2 with the new generation of players. The first time was during 45 minutes of the Bosnia-–France game in Rennes, the second was for the first World Cup 2006 qualifying game against Israel at Paris' Stade de France. Most players play 4–4–2 with their clubs but I also think you can get by with 3–5–2. To be honest, I have never been very interested in the whole debate even though, personally, the latter tactic forces me into a more lateral style of play and prevents me from going forward.

I had a thigh injury against Bosnia but the coach had insisted I should be there in order to take the pulse, as it were, of the new generation. The game against Israel was not very satisfying. Despite a 2–0 victory against the Faroe Islands, for me that game wasn't much good either because I was sent off for the first time in my international career. It was a harsh sending-off following a second yellow card that the referee gave me after he felt I had dived in the opposition's penalty area. In actual fact, one of the guys from the other team had simply knocked into me unintentionally and I had lost my balance and toppled over. That said, I accept that it's difficult for referees to judge these sorts of incidents.

Unfortunately, I was then suspended for the following game at the Stade de France, so I had to watch our 0–0 draw against the Republic of Ireland from the stands. Despite not playing, I lived through the whole week of preparations with the squad. Against the Irish, although we defended well together, we attacked less well together. The public were now starting to get impatient and the press were even worse. Everyone wanted to know why the France team was finding it so difficult to play well again. We had to try to find some reasons and come up with some answers which is not the thing I like to do most. Maybe our results over the last few years were actually at the root of our problems, because perhaps we had lost something of our edge since then.

Even so, during the preparation for the Republic of Ireland game, I stayed very close to the youngsters who were newcomers, such as Rio Mavuba, from Bordeaux. He felt the need to talk and to be reassured, which is completely normal. I tried to involve myself fully, not that that was difficult. It's just that I didn't want to be dishing out advice because, as captain, that's really not my style. Usually, I'm not one to interfere, to tell people what they should do off the pitch. I save my talking more for the matches themselves. As a result, I have always had a really good relationship with all my team-mates; there has always been a special bond between us.

After our setback in the 2002 World Cup, my name had been mentioned before Zidane was eventually chosen by Jacques Santini to lead the team but, to be truthful, I had never thought about being given the captain's role. I had always told myself that if it happened, it happened. In fact, it's more than an honour to be captain of the France team, more than a dream. When you are a kid, the idea of playing for *les Bleus* is almost unreal. So to wear the captain's armband as well was more than I could ever have dreamed of. I must say that, unconsciously, although this great honour didn't change my daily life, it nonetheless gave me a much greater sense of responsibility towards my new, young team-mates. I am not saying that I owe them anything but I do owe it to myself to set some sort of example.

It's difficult because you get the feeling that the new France team hasn't made a good start. It is undergoing a process of rebuilding, and we are going to need some more time in order for everyone, from the coach down to the players, to adapt. The problem is that time is a rare luxury in football, something we never have. Clubs often make the big mistake of being too impatient and changing things too quickly, from the president to the coach or manager, the minute they get a series of bad results. Everyone then finds themselves working with a sense of urgency. It is an incredible luxury to be able to give ourselves a bit of time, which is something that we had at Arsenal where the club is built on an atmosphere of mutual trust between the various parties. But in the France team, none of that is possible. We have to win, and to win at once, especially when we are playing the qualifying matches for a big competition, and doubly so when that competition is the World Cup. That said, although the France team's results were not great last season, we are still in the running to qualify.

If we had played against Italy or Spain, I am sure that we would have played differently. On the other hand, I don't think we deserve all the criticism that is currently levelled at us. It's not our fault if certain players have retired from international football. And we're talking, after all, about world-class football stars with a unique hunger for victory who have won everything there is to win.

As a result, during the whole of the 2004/5 season, we talked a lot about rebuilding the France team and that seemed completely normal to me. The problem now is that we have to rebuild a squad whilst getting the results necessary to qualify for the next World Cup finals. Inevitably, this situation quickly brought up various issues. Already, at the end of Euro 2004, there had been a persistent rumour that the Gunners allegedly had a supernatural hold over the international team. That had particularly irritated me. But then I remembered that at one time, a lot of people thought that the France team was run from the inside by Marcel and Zizou. I had never had that impression. That said, given our status and our past, I think it's totally logical that our coach should talk more to Titi and me. We speak anyway on behalf of the team as a whole and to say that we run the Blues is meaningless and ridiculous.

During that first game of the 2004/5 season, against Bosnia, which was Domenech's first game in charge since taking over from Jacques Santini, I was not able to play because I was injured. So the first time I actually led the team out as captain was against Israel at the Stade de France where we drew 0–0. That was the proudest moment of my career. My entire family was watching from the stands because not one of them wanted to miss this moment.

A few days before, my mother had understood that I was going to be appointed captain of France because of what the coach was saying publicly. She and my grandfather were the two happiest people on earth. All this has a personal significance as well when I think back to my arrival from the Senegal and to my dreams as a young child. There are stages that you reach step by step, day by day, game by game and when I look back at my career and where I started out from, I think what I have achieved is fantastic. I tend to forget the value of all this too easily because games follow on from each other thick and fast. I make the most of the present, that's one of my personality traits. I know that things have not always been easy and that I have waited a long time for my turn. With the Blues, when I was called up, I wasn't selected to play and I was frustrated because I felt I deserved to be. It used to eat away at me but I respected the choices that were made. I bided my time without a grumble, and I am proud to see that everything finally fell into place. Everything in my career has progressed both logically and illogically. On the one hand I started out very young, before long I played in Division One, then I was quickly transferred to AC Milan; on the other hand, I had to work hard and to fight to become what I am today and to live out my wildest dreams.

Ever since our victory over Cyprus, Robert Pires has no longer been part of Raymond Domenech's squad. He has spoken out publicly about how disappointed he is with the coach's team selection. Since then, I have learned about the line-up of the team via the newspapers and each time Robert has been left out. I have never wanted to get into an argument about whether he should have been selected or not. But having often spoken to him about it, it's clear that he misses being in the team. You can tell he is disappointed, though he is not upset, despite scoring fourteen goals for Arsenal last season. But ultimately, it's all down to the coach. I had the same attitude when it came to the times when Olivier Dacourt was left out of the team, which meant that I found myself playing next to Benoit Pedretti.

People may be surprised that the coach has never consulted me. But to be honest, I have never wanted to get involved in team selection. I didn't with Arsenal and I have no need to do it for the international team either. As far as I am concerned, it has nothing to do with my role as captain. I am consulted when it comes to tactics but that's all. My motto is 'everyone in their place'. Since becoming captain, I have never been asked for my preferences and that's completely fine with me. It doesn't mean that I am not happy with my relationship with Raymond Domenech. If I have something I need to say to him, or a message to send him, I pick up the phone and he does the same. So everything works very well on that level.

Amongst the many questions that I have been asked in relation to the many changes in the France team, there was one that kept coming up: 'Isn't it difficult to start almost from scratch with a team when it has just won everything there is to win?' I always used to reply that not only was it not difficult but that also it was very motivating. We are all top-level sportsmen and there is something in us that makes us want to improve the whole time. The aim was to qualify for the next World Cup finals and if that didn't succeed in motivating us, then there was no hope for us at all. Plus, we have to live with pressure on a daily basis.

Following a succession of draws, a sense of optimism grew because we felt that we were improving with every game. Nonetheless, we are all aware that the bottom line is we have to win. That's all that counts in qualifying matches. We were in a really tight group where all the teams had been managing to draw against each other, but our win over the Republic of Ireland at Lansdowne Road in our recent qualifier has put us right in the driving seat in our campaign to qualify for Germany. Titi scored the only goal, and it was fantastic. Our goalless draw against Switzerland left us with a crucial last game at home against Cyprus. We started a bit nervously because we knew that it was essential for us to win to avoid going into the play-offs. I had to go off injured after twenty-five minutes but we were all relieved when four minutes later, Zizou opened up the scoring, and Wiltord shot past the Cyprus keeper three minutes later to give us a good 2–0 lead. That said, although we ended up winning 4–0, and finished top of our group, if Switzerland had won by even one goal against Ireland (whom they were playing at the same time), we would have had to win by an enormous margin to stay ahead on goal difference. So the result was in doubt until the 92nd minute when suddenly the cheers rang out all around the Stade de France indicating that the result from Dublin had just come through.

It was not a very comfortable way for us to qualify but maybe that will make us focus properly during the tournament in Germany.

So I am still optimistic for the France team's chances, as well as for Arsenal's. In any case, I am fundamentally someone who thinks positively. I so hate losing that I only ever want to think about winning.

9

A Double Double: 1997/8 and 2001/2

I began my first full season with the Gunners — which was Arsène Wenger's first as well — full of confidence that we could improve on our third-place finish in the Premiership the previous season. Over the summer, the club had signed Marc Overmars and Emmanuel Petit, amongst others, and I knew that my international team-mate Emmanuel, with his physical style of play in midfield, would have a big influence on the way the team performed. As it turned out, Marc did as well.

The season was barely a couple of weeks old when we went to Filbert Street to play Leicester City. Ian Wright was just one goal away from equalling the club's goal-scoring record of 178 set by Cliff Bastin but in the end it was Dennis Bergkamp who got all the attention that evening with a hat-trick so fantastic that it was the only time that the three best goals in the BBC's *Match of the Day* competition went to the same player. For his first, scored in the 9th minute, Dennis simply curled in a beautiful ball from 25 yards out, then added a second after an hour's play. It looked all over for Martin O'Neill's team. Suddenly, though, England's muscular striker Emile Heskey got one back with seven minutes left to play, and Matt Elliott equalised in the 90th with the help of a deflection. It was 2–2 at the end of normal time but there were more goals to come in what became a nail-biting end to the game for us. Dennis completed his hat-trick three minutes into injury time by effortlessly controlling a long ball from David Platt and beating their keeper. Surely that would be the final kick of the match? But the referee, Graham Barber, had other ideas and he decided there was still more playing to be done. Corner to Leicester, and the next thing we knew, their captain Steve Walsh had headed home to equalise just seconds before the final whistle after a massive four minutes of stoppage time. We weren't too pleased with the draw and we didn't think there should have been so much injury time – Wright and I had words with the referee after the final whistle – but no one could argue about Dennis' goals: they were simply unforgettable.

Ian finally broke Cliff Bastin's record a couple of weeks later – on 13th September, to be precise – when we beat Bolton 4–1 at home. The game began in a strange way because Bolton actually took the lead in the first quarter of an hour. Maybe that woke us up because we certainly had a couple of near misses soon after, but halfway through the first half, Dennis sent a through ball to Wright who ran on to it, took it down the right and with a low angled shot from about fifteen yards out, rifled it into the far corner of the goal. Wright went crazy; he had done it; he had equalled an incredible fifty-one-year-old record. He ripped off his shirt, knelt down before his fans and celebrated. But the day was going to get even better for him – and very soon. Just five minutes later, a shot by Dennis left the Bolton keeper Branagan sprawling and the ball loose in the goal-mouth. I scrambled for it, but it was destiny that, two yards out, in front of an empty net, Ian should be there to tap it in. Cue more celebrations. This time, Ian ran down the East Stand touchline, Arsenal shirt over his head, revealing the specially made Nike T-shirt he had been wearing underneath which said, quite simply: 179. And below, the words 'just done it'. Afterwards, Ian said of his second goal, 'I was happy even before I put it in. I'll never score an easier one.'

Ray Parlour gave us a 3–1 lead just before half time and Ian, just to prove the point that he was now the most prolific goalscorer in the club's history, bagged his hat-trick with ten minutes to go when David Platt chipped one just behind the Bolton defence. Wright was on the end of it and hit a fantastic side-footed volley into the net, right in front of the North Bank. What more was there to say? The fans went crazy, and Wright went off, to leave the stage for Nicolas Anelka to get a taste of the game that day. Needless to say, Ian was given the sort of standing ovation that players rarely experience in their careers.

I'm sure he must have been moved. Afterwards, he spoke of his relief at having broken the record, because for some time, it had been preying on his mind, as well as on that of all the Arsenal supporters and the British media who kept going on about it. He had felt some pressure to perform and when he had failed to score in the last few games before this Bolton one, he had started to become a bit anxious. Plus, he'd been wearing that Nike T-shirt now for a while, so it was beginning to need a wash. 'I'm glad it's out the way,' he admitted, 'but at 33, there's so much more I want to achieve. I want to take it past 200.' It's a shame he was never quite able to do that. A shame also that all those T-shirts being sold outside Highbury that day with the number 179 on them were already out of date.

Our next big match was away to Chelsea. Like us, they were already championship contenders and a London derby is always a big game. At half time the score was 1–1, with Dennis equalising after Ian had set the goal up for him. Although Chelsea were probably more dominant in the first half, we created more of the chances in the second. Dennis – again – blasted one in from fifteen yards out after Chelsea made a defensive error but this time it was Chelsea's turn to equalise almost immediately when substitute Mark Hughes curled one to Gianfranco Zola who ran it into the net, after Seaman had been left stranded. Our international team-mate Frank Leboeuf then got himself sent off for tripping up Dennis when he was making a surge towards goal – Dennis was having one of those incredible days when he was playing out of his skin – and in the end it was Nigel Winterburn who, in completely unlikely fashion, got hold of the ball on the halfway line, ran to within striking distance of the Chelsea goal and blitzed it in from twenty yards out to give us the winning goal. He didn't often do that, I can say! It was a great finish to an exciting game and the three precious points moved us to second place in the Premier-ship. If we could beat West Ham at Highbury a few days later, we knew we could go top of the League. The whole team was very upbeat as we left Stamford Bridge that afternoon.

Sure enough, the game against West Ham could not have been

better scripted if we had tried. First of all, just to fire us up a bit more, there was a presentation before kick-off to Ian Wright for his goal-scoring record. It was brilliantly done: children ran on to the pitch and formed a circle, with each one wearing the kit from all of the different clubs that Ian had scored against. That was a lot of children! The guy making the announcements over the tannoy then pointed out that somewhere there was a kid wearing a Spurs kit which certainly made the crowd react even more loudly! Then Ian ran on to the pitch between the West Ham and Arsenal teams who had both formed a corridor and the fans went wild. Finally, they watched a replay on the giant screens of some of Wright's best goals.

After that start, it wasn't surprising we were motivated to show the fans what we could do. Dennis put us ahead, Marc Overmars scored his first goal for Arsenal and got himself a huge ovation, then, to complete Ian's dream evening, he converted a penalty. Finally, just before half time, Marc scored his second – in a perfect end to the script – to kill off West Ham's chances. Actually, although we thought we might go on to score a few more in the second half, the scoreline remained that way, 4–0 to the Gunners. A good evening's work and all the more satisfying because it put us top of the League after Manchester United were held to a 2–2 draw at Chelsea.

We had an easy 5–0 win against Barnsley, who I think everyone considered to be the worst team in the Premiership that season, but it was still good to score so many. Dennis scored two, with Wright, Platt and Parlour getting the others. Dennis was going through an incredible time – he was voted Man of the Match in the Chelsea game with over 90 per cent of the vote, which is exceptional – and his contribution in all areas of the game was enormous. But the big game, our home match against Manchester United in November, was still to come. In terms of the final outcome of the season, this was one of the key games and we all knew it.

Luckily, it produced a tight 3–2 win for us. As I say later, all my games against United have been special, for good or bad reasons, but this one was all the better because it gave me my first goal against them – and a good one too. This was a very important psychological victory for us because we had been 2–0 up at half time, United had pulled two back before David Platt finally headed home the winner from a Ray Parlour corner with five minutes left to play. Incredibly, given how things went over the next few years, this was our first victory over United in five years. Unfortunately, because of their consistency, they were back at the top of the League, although we were just one point behind them.

The next few weeks produced some bad results for us and some good ones for them. We lost to Sheffield Wednesday, Liverpool and Blackburn Rovers (the last two were home defeats), so many people thought that our season was now over and that we had no chance of catching United. I had been out for those games with an injury picked up in the United game (I had gone off at half time, just after I had scored) and Dennis had also been out for a while. Wright suddenly seemed to have lost his form and the team as a whole had maybe lost its momentum after those great wins against Chelsea, West Ham and United. In any case, by the start of 1998, we were down to fifth place in the table and fifteen points behind leaders Manchester United. Many in the press had written off our chances, especially after our December loss to Blackburn when we had squandered a 1–0 half-time lead and conceded three goals in the second half. However, deep down, we still believed in ourselves and we still felt there were plenty of opportunities to pull things back.

Sure enough, by mid-March, following wins over Leeds, Chelsea, Crystal Palace and Wimbledon, we were nine points behind League leaders Manchester United which sounds a lot but, crucially, we had three games in hand. It was now time for the all-important Old Trafford game.

We came out determined to attack and were the better team in both halves, even though United came close to scoring on a few occasions. But often, Emmanuel and I would break them down in midfield and would stifle any attacking moves. They were beginning to look vulnerable, whereas we were looking in command. With the score 0–0 and twenty minutes to go, Marc

Overmars beat their defence and sent a low shot from inside the penalty area past Schmeichel who had come off his line. 1–0. The question was, could we hold on to our lead? United never gave up, to the extent that a corner in extra time saw Peter Schmeichel run the length of the pitch to try to help his teammates score the equaliser, a high-risk tactic he sometimes employed. To be honest, it was something that happened so quickly that I didn't even have time to notice and to register fully what he was doing. The only thing we were madly concentrating on was not to concede a goal from the corner; that was the only thing that mattered at that stage of the game. We could see they had all their men forward, so the fact that Schmeichel was there didn't really change anything. In any case, his plan backfired because the ball was soon cleared by us and, in his struggle to run back to his end, he tore a hamstring. His injury was costly because it meant he was out for the next few games which was not something United would have wanted at that stage of the season. It was a fantastic victory for us and the first time in many years that we had won both home and away games against our arch enemy. The papers said that the last time we had won at Old Trafford, we had gone on to win the title. It remained to be seen what we could do this time. All we knew at that stage was that we had a good chance, we had reached a consistently high level of play, and we knew we were still in the FA Cup. The odds, though, were still against us achieving the Double.

Those odds lengthened a few days later when we nearly lost our FA Cup quarter-final replay at West Ham. Already, in the 3rd round, we had had two 90-minute periods against Port Vale where we had failed to score. Extra time in the replay had produced a tense 1–1 draw and the whole thing had finally been decided on penalties which we had won with the final kick by the narrowest of margins, 4–3. That's the truly fantastic and unique thing about the FA Cup and the reason I used to love it as a competition: you cannot take any team for granted, it doesn't matter what division they are in. You have to prepare for each game in exactly the same way, and with exactly the same attitude mentally and physically, whether you are playing Port Vale or Manchester United.

Having escaped against Port Vale, it looked as if we were about to go out to West Ham, even though I had created a great opening goal that Anelka went on to fizz past the West Ham keeper, our fellow Frenchman Bernard Lama. But the Hammers had equalised with a few minutes left to play and, at the end of extra time, we were still level at 1–1. So once again, it was time for those do-or-die penalties. You can't recreate in practice sessions the tension and atmosphere of a penalty shoot-out. On the whole, I can't say I practise penalties much. In the match, though, I pick a spot – which obviously varies from one time to the next – and then I just stay very focused. I concentrate hard and aim for that spot, without once looking at what the keeper is doing. It's true that nowadays they move around more and more. You only have to see how much Liverpool's Jerzy Dudek was leaping around, waving his arms in the air, in the 2005 Champions League Final penalty shoot-out to realise how much keepers bend the rules. Referees rarely stop them, even though it's all part of the keeper's attempt at intimidation. That's why I never look at them when I prepare to take a penalty. The two other factors that count in a penalty shoot-out – apart from a certain amount of luck, of course – are how much the importance of the occasion gets to you, and how fresh your legs are. There's no doubt that if you are physically exhausted, you are more likely to miss.

In the West Ham game, things could not have been tighter. After all five penalties had been taken, both teams stood at 3–3; we had both missed or had saved two kicks, and it was now down to sudden death. The first team to miss was out. Captain Tony Adams, appropriately, was the one to take our next penalty. He hit it hard and low, right down the centre of the goalmouth. He gambled that Bernard Lama would dive one way or the other and that's exactly what he did, diving to his right. Next in line was Samassi Abou for West Ham. He hit an angled shot, and it hit the post. With one kick, he had put his team out of the Cup, and us through. We were jumping all over the place with joy, our fans were as well, while he and the West Ham fans were in tears. That's how harsh things can get in football and I have certainly known the reverse situation where I was on the receiving end of those moments of total despair and bad luck.

In early April, we met Wolves who were in the then First Division at Villa Park. This was the semi-final of the FA Cup and, if we were to win, we would be through to our first final since 1993. We were confident, even though we were missing Ian Wright through injury and Dennis through suspension, because we had gone eight successive games without conceding a single goal. I had a great game, not least because I created the only goal that afternoon, the one that took us through to the final. It happened early on in the first half. Hans Segers, Wolves' Dutch goalkeeper, who had been instrumental in getting his team to that stage of the competition, made a bad clearance and the ball fell to my feet on the halfway line. From there, I picked it up and ran with it, beating one of their defenders on my way to the penalty area, by which time I had been joined by Christopher Wreh, George Weah's 22-year-old Liberian cousin, who was having a good first season with us. Christopher, who had escaped the troubles in his country and arrived in France as a fourteen-year-old, had been bought for just £300,000 at the start of the season from AS Monaco and, now that Dennis and Ian were not playing, he was relishing his first-team success. I saw Christopher alongside me in the box, slipped the ball sideways to him and he just coolly slammed it past Segers, as if he was the most experienced striker in the world. Thanks to him, and despite a Wolves comeback in the second half, we earned our ticket to Wembley, where we would meet Newcastle, who had beaten another First Division side, Sheffield United. I was named Man of the Match which is always a good feeling, although I have to say that I never take it as a personal recognition because, as far as I'm concerned, football is totally a team effort. If I play well, it's thanks to my team-mates who have enabled me to play well because they have done so too. It's as simple as that. So whenever I was Man of the Match, it was never a case of me patting myself on the back and thinking 'Great, everyone noticed just how well I played' – more a question of thinking I had had a good game because ten other guys helped me to.

The following week, we met our future FA Cup Final opponents at home in the League. It was a very satisfying afternoon because we beat them 3–1 and I scored one of my most memorable goals. Nicolas Anelka had scored the first two when, in the second half, I collected the ball from around the halfway line, ran towards the Newcastle box, with apparently no defenders coming near me, before deciding to shoot from about 30 yards out. I hit the ball and it was a beautiful, curling shot that sent their goalkeeper, Shay Given, diving through the air but unable to stop the shot. In fact, nothing was going to stop it that day. It just went flying into the top right-hand corner. A real beauty, total pleasure on my part and a memory I'll treasure for a long while. Newcastle pulled one back before the end of play but we ended that day just four points behind United and with three games in hand. Things were now looking very good for the Gunners. As for me, I was having a fantastic run of matches, I was on good form, I was 100 per cent fit, and I was not only winning the ball but also distributing it at just the right time, creating the chances and even scoring some great goals myself. This was my first full season and I was certainly happy with the result.

The next two league games were further confirmation for us of our increasing superiority and confidence. I'm not sure even we thought those games would go as well as they did. First of all, we had to play Blackburn Rovers at Ewood Park, never an easy game, and, having lost to them so badly at Highbury in December (our last defeat, as it turned out, and the start of our revival), we had some old scores to settle. And they had a win to defend. And yet, incredibly, we were 4–0 up at half time. Yes, 4–0. Even we were surprised. This could be our biggest away win in years. It had happened so effortlessly that the first three goals had gone in before the game was fifteen minutes old. Dennis had put us in the lead within just two minutes, Ray Parlour had got the second and Emmanuel had created the third for Dennis to fire past the keeper. Anelka, for good measure, had added to the goal tally just before half time. Even a freak snowstorm in the second half (during which time the ball had had to be changed from white to orange because we could not see a thing) had not changed things in our opponents' favour and, although they got one back to save face, the 4–1 final score showed just how far we had come since our December defeat by them.

On 18th April, a week after playing Blackburn, we demolished Wimbledon 5–0 at Highbury. We had often had problems with Wimbledon who combine a very physical, defensive style of football with a long-ball game and we had failed to beat them at home for the last seven years. This time though, we were all over them. We were 3–0 up at half time (with goals from Adams, Overmars and Bergkamp) and Petit and Wreh scored in the second half just in case there were any doubters left in the crowd. After that win, and for the first time that season, we went top of the League by one point and still had an all-important two games in hand. We weren't going to be complacent and think the title was ours, but given the form we were in, let's just say that we were confident and determined to keep winning.

Things didn't change when we beat Barnsley away 2–0, giving us our eighth consecutive victory and a maximum 24 points. The title race was still on between us and Manchester United, who could still mathematically win, even though, with one game in hand and a three-point margin, we were now the favourites. We each won our next game: United beat Palace and we beat Derby County 1–0 at Highbury in a tight, physical game where we managed to stay calm despite the non-stop, hard, aggressive tackling coming from our opponents. We knew the game would be like that and that we had to keep our heads, because otherwise we risked ruining our season with bookings and, worse, sendings-off. The one bad thing that did happen, though, was that Dennis had to go off with a thigh injury which made him very doubtful for the FA Cup Final, along with Ian who was already injured.

So we had to wait until we beat Everton on Sunday 3rd May to finally become champions. To make it even better, we were crowned at Highbury. Actually, at first, it was not an easy game to play. Everybody was desperate to win, including Everton; both teams knew how much was at stake. Appropriately, it was skipper Tony Adams who got us off to a good start within a few minutes when he headed in Petit's corner. More chances came our way, I almost scored, then Marc Overmars got numbers two and three. Both of these came after fantastic runs that took him almost the length of the pitch. In between these great goals, however, we almost lost Emmanuel (who had already been elbowed in the face) after a terrible two-footed tackle by Don Hutchinson left him with a bad cut right down his shin. As Manu limped off the pitch – I thought at first he might have broken his leg because the injury looked so serious and he seemed to be in real pain – he threw his shin pads in the direction of the referee who, along with the nearby linesman, had stood by and done nothing, despite the fact that Hutchinson was already on one yellow card and, as far as most people were concerned, deserved to go off.

By the time Tony Adams hit the fourth goal from inside the box, the atmosphere was incredible. 4–0 to Arsenal. Premiership title to Arsenal. What was unbelievable was that for guys like David Seaman, Martin Keown and Ian Wright, who was 34 by then, this was actually their first ever championship medal. For me, it was different, because this was only my first full season with the Gunners, so I was really happy, but I maybe didn't appreciate what a huge deal this was for those players who had been there for so long and yet had never won the League. I think the reason we did win, though, was that every player, whether he had just arrived at the club or had been there for years, had that incredible Arsenal spirit, the one that says 'you must never give up'. We were full of really experienced players, such as Dixon, Adams, Seaman, Winterburn, who would never let themselves get down or give up. In fact, they didn't know the meaning of those words. And because we were so good defensively, we managed to turn our season around after our bad spell in December and begin to carve out victories week in, week out. It didn't matter that some of them were tough games and were simply 1–0 wins. On the contrary, that gave us confidence, knowing that we could grind out that sort of result. What mattered was our inner conviction that if we managed to score first, then we would be unlikely to lose because our defence was so watertight. That in itself gave us tremendous self-belief, made us feel stronger and stronger mentally and that's what made the difference in the second half of the season. And the fact was that, from 31 January up to the Everton game in May, we conceded just two goals and kept clean sheets in 12 out of the 14 matches. That's how good we were in defence! And that's why it wasn't surprising that when he joined the club, the manager soon realised that there was no need to change that back four, however old they might have been! It wasn't broke, so there was no need to fix it.

When the final whistle went, everybody went completely crazy. Even the boss threw his arms up in to the air and shouted out loud, which is saying something! The trophy was wheeled out and placed on a little stage on the pitch for the official presentation ceremony. Tony went up to collect it and, when he raised it up into the air, the noise at Highbury became completely deafening. Everyone had warned me about how incredible things would be but I was still unprepared for the reality: I had quite simply never seen anything like it. It was an indescribable scene. I swear I saw the upper tier of the North Bank move, thanks to the numbers of fans leaping around, waving their banners, scarves, anything they could to show their joy. In one moment, the whole stadium became red and white, everyone was jumping around, dancing, singing, and we were all so happy: happy for ourselves, and for the fans who had waited seven years to see this day again. For Arsenal, this was their eleventh league title but, importantly, it was the first time in English football history that their league had been won by a foreign manager. And what was more, in his first full season in charge!

The atmosphere once we got back to the changing room after the presentation, and after we had run right round the pitch saluting all our fans, was fantastic. We drank champagne, we sang, we hugged. We stood and danced on the massage table, we jumped around. It was a total release after such a hard season. The way in which we had won, after having come from so far behind, was what made us so happy. We had believed in ourselves all along, we had kept on fighting in every game, for every point and, in the end, all that hard graft, all that work, all that spirit had paid off. Without doubt, that Premiership title remains one of the best moments of my career.

That evening, though, there was no party, no night on the town. We still had a lot of work to do, notably the FA Cup Final just under two weeks later. So after a long time celebrating in the changing room, it was back home for everybody, and a good night's sleep. It was normal that we would have had a bit of a dip in form after the elation of winning the League and, sure enough, we did lose our final two games of the season. In everyone's mind, including Arsène Wenger's, the hardest part had been done: we had won the Premiership. That had been our number 1 aim at the start of the season, more than winning the Cup, and we had achieved that. But throughout the next two weeks, the boss never let us lose sight of one thing: we still had one important game to play, one that would put us even more firmly in the history books than winning the League. Our FA Cup Final against Newcastle was important and he made sure that we kept our momentum up and stayed focused for that game as well. Because we knew that, however big the Everton game had been, in a way this next one was even bigger. We were desperate to win because, although it was great to be Premiership champions, it would have felt like unfinished business if we had not also won the Cup and done the Double. It would have felt good, but not satisfying.

Our preparation for the game was the same as for any other. We changed nothing, so that it should not feel any more special and different. On the Friday morning, we did some light training before going, as usual, to spend the night at a hotel – though this time the hotel was near Wembley, not the normal one near our training ground. That morning, we went for a short walk, and did some loosening-up exercises before having a final tactical talk to sort out a last few little details.

Then it was on to the coach and on to Wembley. This was the first time I had played there and it lived up to its reputation: it definitely had an awe and a magic about it, largely because of all the history that had been made there. The pitch itself was big. That made a change from Highbury which is the smallest pitch in the Premiership, and it allowed us to play a more open game.

The moment when I waited in the tunnel seemed like an eternity. I was vaguely conscious of the TV cameras but I was so used to them – they are present now at every game – that they didn't bother me. I just couldn't wait to get out there on to the pitch. I was desperate to run out in front of the fans, to taste the Wembley atmosphere I had heard so much about, and of course to play the biggest game of my career so far.

When the signal was finally given, we all ran on into the blazing hot sunshine, led by Tony. The blast of noise that greeted me was like nothing I had ever heard before. That second when the noise hit me as I emerged on to the pitch was like being slapped across the face. It sent a shock wave and a huge surge of adrenaline throughout my body. 'Let's get on with the game,' I was thinking to myself. At that precise moment, I think I could have run all afternoon if necessary, such was the energy I had. But first, we had to go through all the preliminaries. As with international matches, there were anthems to be played. This time of course, being the FA Cup Final, it was 'Abide With Me', not a hymn I knew but one that I soon learned to recognise and love and totally associate with Cup Finals. And by the time I left Arsenal, believe me, I had heard it a few times! Although I couldn't make out the words that first time and could barely make out the tune, I could hear 80,000 people chanting it; and all I could see was a mass of red and white and black and white covering every inch of the stands. That too had been an unforgettable sight as I had emerged from the tunnel – the way that the stadium was so clearly divided into two equal parts, one red and white, one black and white, each chanting away, each waving banners and each demonstrating a similar passion for its team. Not surprisingly that scene had sent shivers down my spine. During moments like those, I love to look around, to listen, to soak up the atmosphere as much as possible. That's when I remind myself that I really am incredibly lucky to have such a fantastic job. And that's what fires me up even more, so that when the game begins, I'm really ready to go for it!

When it came to the game itself, we were fielding a very strong team, even though we were without Dennis who had still not recovered from the hamstring injury he had got during the Derby County game. We had all been hoping it would heal in time, particularly as Ian Wright was not quite fully fit either (he had a similar injury) and would be unlikely to start, maybe even play at all. Arsène had stayed positive throughout the previous few days and had insisted that despite the absence of those two players, we still had what it took to win the trophy. The loss of Dennis, though, was really disappointing for him. He had had an incredible season, possibly his best ever, as it turned out. He had just been voted the players' Player of the Year, the Football Writers' Association Player of the Year and, to cap it all, one of his hat-trick of fantastic goals against Leicester City back in August had been voted goal of the season in the *Match of Day* competition. Which is why it would have been great if he had been playing, if only for him to feel he had contributed to the result that day. Ian Wright must have felt the same way after the season he had had, because he didn't play either, even though he was named as a substitute and spent almost the entire 90 minutes warming up on the touchline in the hope that he would at least get to make an appearance. In the end, it was not to be for him and in fact he never played for Arsenal again. That summer, he signed for West Ham, having notched up 185 goals, a total that many people thought would not be equalled for many years. But that was before a certain Thierry Henry joined . . .

Our starting line-up on that Saturday 16th May was, therefore, Christopher Wreh and Nicolas Anelka up front; Ray Parlour, who eventually picked up the Man-of-the-Match award, Marc Overmars and Manu Petit formed the midfield with me; whilst our experienced back four was Dixon, Keown, Adams and Winterburn. David Seaman, of course, was in goal.

We outplayed Newcastle from the moment the whistle went.

Alan Shearer, their lone striker, was marked so tightly by Tony that he barely got the ball in the entire first half, whilst Manu and I pounced on every stray ball in midfield and prevented Newcastle from mounting any sort of attack. At the other end of the pitch, we were putting the pressure on and came close on several occasions, and we felt it would just be a question of time before we scored. Finally, in the 23rd minute, Manu floated a ball over the Newcastle defence to Marc who headed it down before thundering it past the opposing keeper Shay Given. 1–0 at half time, a lead we were determined to build on in the second half. With Platt now on for Wreh, we kept searching for that second goal. Kenny Dalglish's men had just one real chance when Shearer's left-foot shot beat Seaman and rebounded off the post. That was as close as Newcastle got all afternoon. A few minutes later, midway through the second half, Nicolas picked up one of Ray Parlour's high passes, sprinted rather than ran with it, and ripped it low across the diving Shay Given who didn't stand a chance, such was the strength and accuracy of the shot. It was already a hot afternoon but Nicolas had just made it a blazing one.

Even with a two-goal lead, we didn't give up. We kept attacking. Ray kept surging forward – he even hit the post, such was his determination to get a goal and to seal the game for us. At last the final whistle went and we realised that we had done it: we had done the Double. The first Arsenal team to have done it since 1971 – that's a long time! Once again, Arsène Wenger let slip his usually reserved mask, leaped off the bench and ran on to the pitch to celebrate with us, his faithful army of warriors who had done everything he had asked of us and more. Did he really think, at the start of the season, that we would be that successful? Only he would know, but I have to confess that I myself never thought, when I arrived in London a year before, that so much would come to me so quickly.

We climbed those thirty-nine steps to receive our medals, led by Tony. The moment when he held that famous trophy up in the air for all the fans to see was fantastic. I couldn't quite see the expression on his face from where I was standing in the line, but I could certainly guess what he was feeling. Pure ecstasy!

Back in the changing room, it was time for more champagne, and more singing and dancing. Of course we were elated but, more than anything, what we really felt was pride in what we had achieved. We knew that what we had done was rare and special and that was a fantastic feeling.

As far as I was concerned, I had never known success like it and, coming at the end of my first full season with the club, it had all happened so quickly. So my first thoughts were that, out of the various clubs that had contacted me when I was with AC Milan, I had certainly picked the right one. But I also hoped that this would be just the beginning. I knew I would not be satisfied with only that in terms of trophies and medals. I wanted more, much more.

It was already early evening when we finally left Wembley and were taken back to the Sopwell House Hotel where we had left our cars. There, a celebration dinner had been organised and we were joined by all the Arsenal staff who had worked with us all season to make the Double possible, as well as by our wives and girlfriends. But it was not a mad, drunken affair, more a really happy, relaxed evening, and afterwards, we all went home to sleep off our incredible day. Because the next morning, we had an appointment to keep on the top deck of a London bus; we had a victory parade planned that would take us from Highbury to Islington Town Hall near by and we knew that that was going to be the highlight of the celebration.

Again, I had been warned to expect the unexpected, but even that didn't prepare me. I had never seen people hanging out of trees in the way that I saw them do that day, not to mention people hanging out of windows, standing on rooftops, and lining every square centimetre of the route. It felt as if half of London had turned out, not just half of North London. Everyone was dressed in red and white, babies were being held up for us to kiss, just like politicians do, it was all completely crazy! Eventually, it was time for us to say our goodbyes. For some of us, that meant meeting up soon after to prepare for our World Cup campaigns in our home countries, but for others it meant saying goodbye for longer. Some of course, such as Ian Wright, were never to return to the club, so it was particularly emotional. We had gone through an unforgettable, highly charged season, we had bonded as I never thought it was possible for team-mates to do (this was, after all, before France '98), so it was tough to say goodbye. But when we went our separate ways, we took with us memories which we will always share and that bind me for ever to an exceptional group of players.

The 2001/2 season when we did the Double again was very different. For a start, the team had changed quite a lot from the one that had won in 1998. Ian Wright was gone, as were Emmanuel Petit and Marc Overmars, both sold for a total of £32m to Barcelona in the summer of 2000 – something which I hadn't been too happy about at the time. If they had stayed, they would have combined with the new players to make up an even stronger first-team squad than we had. Instead, the top-quality players we bought replaced those who left and meant that we treaded water in terms of strength. First, Freddie Ljungberg joined in the summer of 1998 for £3m from Swedish club Halmstad, even though at that stage, the boss had actually only seen him play on TV. Once Manu and Marc left, though, he became an automatic first choice in midfield and the 2001/2 season saw him hit his best form. After him, Thierry Henry was signed from Juventus in August 1999 for £10.5m and was immediately switched from playing on the right wing (which had not worked out for him at the Italian club) to a centre-forward role, even though he had said 'But boss, I don't score goals.' Arsène, who Thierry had played for at Monaco, knew exactly what he was doing when he made this change and Thierry soon started to show his true potential. Then, a year later, in the summer of 2000, Robert Pires arrived from Olympique de Marseille. Again, the vision he has for the game and the pace he shows in midfield, plus his technical and goal-scoring abilities, soon made him an essential part of the line-up. Finally, in the summer of 2001, with the back four who had anchored the team for so long coming to the end of their careers, the manager signed Sol Campbell on a free transfer from Spurs, of all clubs. At the time, Sol got a lot of stick and the fans at White Hart Lane have never really forgiven him for what they see as his 'betrayal', but he bravely decided that it was the best thing for his career. And he turned out to be correct, because he timed his move to perfection, arriving just in time for what turned out to be our next Double-winning season.

The first half of the season, however, was an up and down affair for us. We would play well one game, then drop points at home. We weren't getting the consistency we needed in order to be top of the table. The season before, we had been runners-up in the League (to United) and FA Cup (losing, disappointingly, against Liverpool to a Michael Owen goal in the final minutes of the game). We were determined not to have another season like that because, to be honest, 2nd place is for losers. As is 3rd or 4th, for that matter. For me, the only place to finish is 1st.

It took us a few months before we got into our stride and before we could believe that we could be winners again. I remember there was one period in December, for example, when we came back from 2–0 down after 45 minutes against Aston Villa at Highbury to snatch a last-minute victory 3–2. Sylvain Wiltord, who had been signed from Bordeaux in the summer of 2000 for a then record fee of £13m, pulled one back with his first touch seconds into the second half and that seemed to liberate us. Eventually, almost half an hour later, I retrieved the ball on the left, crossed it over to Thierry on the right who skilfully went past their keeper Enckelman to score. We would have settled for a draw, even though we needed all the points we could get at that stage but suddenly, an injury-time goal-kick by Villa found its way to Robert. He passed to Thierry who was advancing fast and who then slotted it low past the keeper's left. That fifteenth goal of the season for Titi, scored in the 92nd minute, put us back up to 2nd in the Premiership behind Liverpool.

However, just over a week later, we had a terrible home game against Newcastle that resulted in a 3–1 defeat. The worst thing about that game was that Graham Poll, the referee, lost control and started booking and sending off players for offences they hadn't committed. Ray Parlour and Newcastle's Craig Bellamy were sent off first. Then, with the score standing at 1–1 five minutes from the end, the referee thought that Sol Campbell's tackle on Laurent Robert deserved a red card, even though subsequent video footage showed that it was a perfectly good, sliding tackle. Alan Shearer converted the penalty and that turned the entire match. Sure enough, within a couple of minutes, Robert had added a third goal to kill the game off once and for all.

When the final whistle went, Thierry, who doesn't normally get involved in this sort of thing, went crazy at the referee and had to be restrained by various people including Martin Keown and even Alan Shearer. Police officers eventually came on to escort Poll off the pitch because Thierry was finding it impossible to calm down. Bobby Robson, the Newcastle manager, agreed afterwards that 'Championships were won and lost on situations like that. There was a lot on that match.' That was certainly true but it was also true that we should never have lost it in that way and were feeling totally cheated. For Thierry to lose his temper in the way he did was proof that something had gone very wrong with the refereeing that night.

At the beginning of March, we got our revenge at St James' Park with a 2–0 away win, despite fielding a team that was not at full strength, due to injury. We were missing Thierry and Freddie, as well as Ray Parlour, Ashley Cole, Martin Keown and Tony Adams. Despite that, the fans were right to chant 'We've got Dennis Bergkamp' after he scored the goal of the season after just 10 minutes. I dispossessed Laurent Robert in midfield and sent the ball on to Robert Pires. He in turn threaded the ball through to Dennis who controlled it with his left foot just inside the penalty area. At that stage, with his back to goal, and surrounded by defenders, not many would have given Dennis much of a chance of making something of the ball. But he suddenly turned, leaving his marker Dabizas standing, and calmly ripped one past keeper Shay Given with his right foot. It was an unbelievable piece of skill, timing and vision and the manager couldn't help but exclaim afterwards that 'He only scores great goals'. Not content with scoring the first goal, Dennis then created the second by hoisting a free kick up for Man of the Match Sol to head in shortly before the end of the first half.

We had had a fantastic game and it was a crucial one for us to win. Before the start, we had been lying a clear second to Manchester United in the table. Afterwards, we were level on points, separated by goal difference only. As with the previous Double-winning season when we had turned things around after a terrible December defeat, we had gone on to have a really good run after Christmas. This was a pattern that we repeated over several seasons when I was at Arsenal and every time it happened, we would ask ourselves, 'What is the reason? What can we do to stop this early winter dip?' But we were never able to come up with a clear-cut answer. Every time, there were different factors: players who were injured, one or two bad performances, enough in fact to make the difference in the first half of the season. In any event, since December, we had beaten Liverpool away (and with ten men) and Chelsea at home, both by two goals to one, I had scored in a 4–1 hammering of Fulham, and enjoyed a 4–1 demolition of Bayer Leverkusen in the Champions League (during which Dennis had again scored an unbelievable goal), with Robert in particular playing brilliantly in all the games and scoring in most. Our only setback was that, despite Champions League wins at home against Leverkusen and, most satisfyingly, against Juventus back in December, we had not done quite enough in the remaining group matches to qualify for the knock-out stage of the competition. So once again, we had produced good football in Europe, but not consistently good enough.

Still, after that 2–0 Newcastle win, our fans couldn't help chanting 'Same time next week' to the opposition's, because that's when we were due to travel back up north to play Bobby Robson's men in the FA Cup quarter-final. That game ended in a 1–1 draw, so it was back to Highbury at the end of March for the replay. That time, we nailed them 3–0. Robert kicked off our winning night after just 62 seconds when Dennis' through-ball sent him running down the left before cutting back inside and slotting his shot almost nonchalantly past Shay Given's outstretched left hand. Before the match was ten minutes old, Dennis and Robert swapped roles when the latter again escaped down the left and crossed the ball right to Dennis' feet, so that all he had to do was match Robert's previous coolness and side-kick the ball into the net. Cue more chants of 'We've got Dennis Bergkamp' from the crowd. The way we were playing, there was no reason why we couldn't have added a good few more to that number (Sol headed in one more in the second half) but midway through the first half, Robert was carried off with a serious injury. When we went in at the interval, we were told that it was looking really bad, that he had damaged medial knee ligaments and that he was being flown that evening to Cannes to consult a specialist. In all likelihood, he would be out for most – if not all – of the rest of the season. That was terrible for us but especially bad for Robert who was having such an amazing season that he went on to receive the Football Writers' Player of the Year award. The diagnosis of torn knee ligaments was soon confirmed from France, as was the fact that Robert would now miss not only the rest of the English season but also the forthcoming World Cup in Seoul in which he had been expected to play a major part.

The final stages of the Premiership brought us more victories, including two 3–0 victories against Sunderland (with a goal by me) and Charlton, plus a 2–1 home win in the local derby against Spurs, as well as qualification for the FA Cup Final by beating Middlesbrough 1–0. With Manchester United now out of the Cup, it looked as if they were going to be handing us the Premiership crown and were going to finish their season without a trophy to their name. They had had an even more up and down start to the season than us and that had been enough, once our run of victories had begun, to badly damage their title hopes. Unlike our previous Double, however, the order in which we had to win our trophies was reversed this time: the FA Cup Final was scheduled for Saturday 4th May, with the final two Premiership games of the season taking place after that date. And who was the first of those two games against? Yes, that's right, Manchester United.

First, though, we had to win the FA Cup. In our minds, it was definitely harder to win the Double this way round. We would have preferred to have sewn up the Premiership – the hard bit and always our number 1 objective, as far as we were concerned – before trying to win the Cup. But that's the way the season had panned out. So we flew down to Cardiff the night before in a privately chartered plane, as this was quicker than driving all the way down the M4. Most of us had already been the previous year to the Millennium Stadium with its brand-new, palatial changing rooms, when we had lost our Cup Final to Liverpool. As a stadium, it feels more enclosed than Wembley and it holds in the noise. The crowd also are closer to the players, so because we were facing our big London rivals, Claudio Ranieri's Chelsea (who went on to finish 6th in the Premiership), the atmosphere was particularly electric. As the media needlessly kept reminding us beforehand, the midfield battle would be played out between me and my friend Emmanuel Petit, now flourishing at Stamford Bridge. I would also be facing my fellow international and former AC Milan team-mate, Marcel Desailly.

Despite his injury, Robert Pires had accompanied us there for the game and, as he's not the sort of guy to show his feelings much (on the contrary, he tends to bottle them up), he had avoided talking about how difficult it was for him to sit in the stands, whilst the rest of us were playing for our FA Cup medals. He completely hid his emotions on the day and I decided, along with the rest of the team, that it was better not to rub it in by showing sympathy. After all, what on earth could any of us say that would make him feel any better?

The game itself was not that great from our point of view. I can't honestly say that we produced a classic, but then I think it's rare for these big occasions to produce great matches. Rarely do they produce many opportunities for scoring and the play often remains uninspiring. As a result, I'm always a realist when it comes to these games because I believe that the main thing is to be on the winning side. For example, I'm sure we had played better in the previous year's final. But who cares, and who remembers? The end result, the one that goes down in the history books, was that we lost. All I can say this time round is that we desperately wanted to win; partly because we had finished runners-up the season before in both the League and the Cup, and partly because we felt we had such a good chance of winning the Double and of making history again that it simply wasn't an option to let that opportunity slip by. We knew what was at stake and we were determined to do everything we could to get the result we wanted.

The first half was evenly matched, with neither team coming close to scoring. In the second, it was Chelsea who started off more positively. But we felt we just had to hang in and hope that we would get an opportunity to score. In the end, it was Ray Parlour who broke through after 70 minutes, before shooting from about 20 yards out with such accuracy that Carlo Cudicini could not get close enough to stop the ball going in. Ten minutes later, Ljungberg settled the matter with another one of his great goals: he collected the ball around the halfway line, and strode through virtually unchallenged towards the Chelsea goal before curling his shot in from 20 yards out as well.

That two-goal margin was the final score in a match that maybe we had wanted to win just a bit more than Chelsea. It was tough for players like Emmanuel and he, in particular, looked really upset to have lost. I had purposefully avoided all eye-contact with him during the entire game, and I'm sure he had done the same as well, and shut out anything that might signal the affection I still had for him. It had been bizarre for us that afternoon because when we had been team-mates, we had been very close. Of course, we had already faced each other that season in straightforward Premiership games but we both knew that the Cup Final was a completely different situation. So at the end, we shook hands as neutrally as possible, as if it had been just any other match. I knew there was nothing I could say to Manu at that stage that would console him, and I didn't want to put him in a situation where he had to congratulate me. The next day, though, when our emotions were a bit less raw, we spoke on the phone about the match and it was good to be able to clear the air and have a calm conversation with him.

This was our first FA Cup since 1998, so even though we were hoping to do the Double later in the week, it was still fantastic to win our first major trophy in such a long time. But we didn't have long to celebrate. Our biggest challenge lay just four days ahead: an away match at Old Trafford. If we won, the biggest prize – the Premiership – was ours.

This was the climax of what had turned out to be a really close title race, one of the tightest in recent years, and all the United fans were hoping we would trip up on their home territory, particularly as we were missing Thierry, Dennis and skipper Tony Adams through injury. Several of their players, including Paul Scholes, Phil Neville and Roy Keane, did their best to intimidate us with hard tackles but we had so much self-belief that evening that nothing they threw at us could make us lose our composure. Our defence was made up of Lauren who that season had become a vital first-team player after a difficult, injury-disrupted start the previous year, the veteran Keown, Arsenal born-and-bred Ashley Cole and Sol Campbell and, together with Seaman, they were rock solid. The Brazilian Edu, who had been signed for £6m in January 2001, combined well with me in midfield; those two key elements gave us the platform to attack, so that, not long into the second half, with the score still 0–0, Wiltord broke away and slotted the ball through to Ljungberg who was alongside him. Freddie escaped from the on-coming Laurent Blanc and fired a low shot at goal that Fabien Barthez could only half stop. The ball bounced back off him to his fellow Frenchman Wiltord who hit the ball home from just outside the box.

That win, which clinched the second Double for me at Arsenal, remains one of my all-time most precious memories. Arsenal's current rivalry with United is bigger than their rivalry with any other club in the League and I think it will stay like that for some time. For their supporters, the evening was a disaster, and even

Sir Alex Ferguson had to admit that he held his hands up to our achievement.

The way in which we had won this second Double had been very different from the way we had done it in 1998. First of all, the team was very different. Slowly but surely, players had been brought in who would revolutionise the way in which we played. Under Arsène Wenger, our football had taken on a more continental style of play. Gone was the long-ball game; in came quick, accurate passing to players' feet. We were now mounting carefully constructed series of attacks at a speed that some other Premiership teams maybe found surprising. Not only our manager, but also much of our team was now foreign so it was probably inevitable that a passing style of play would dominate. In any case, it certainly seemed to be working. Also, crucially, we were playing for each other, not for ourselves. We had a great team spirit and there was no question of the team being made up of a series of 'star' players. We were a unit and we played as one. That was undoubtedly one of our great strengths.

When Arsène Wenger had arrived, he had also started to change the way in which we approached our lives, our diet, the way we looked after ourselves physically. An osteopath would be at the club twice a week to sort out any problems, a doctor was permanently available to us, our meals were designed for maximum nutritional impact and we no longer had any choice in what we ate: we were now given much more pasta, rice, complex carbohydrates, lean proteins such as white meat and fish. Previously, when we were together, we could eat whatever we wanted, which left some guys free to indulge in nutritionally empty dishes. All this meant that Wenger brought in an approach that had already been adopted by other continental clubs (including, I have to say, AC Milan) but that had yet to become the norm in England. Certainly, things had not been like that at Arsenal until then. The manager's approach to sport was more all-round, professional and thorough, and it helped to give us that extra edge that season.

In any event, we probably had the strongest Arsenal team ever that season. We continued to defend well – as we had in the

97/98 season – but now we were an attacking team as well, and that was reflected in our results. We were the only team in all four divisions not to have lost an away game all season, plus we scored in all 38 of our Premiership matches. That, to me, said it all about our all-round strength. Thierry Henry ended up as our top scorer with 24 goals and we were unbeaten in the final twenty games of the season, in fact since that home defeat to Newcastle back in mid-December.

What is fantastic for me is that not only did I win two Doubles with Arsenal – something I now realise very few footballers will ever do, whoever they play for – but each one was also totally special in a very different way. And on both occasions, we had to work so hard for every one of our successes that the final glory definitely tasted all the sweeter.

10

49 And Other Magic Numbers

When I started thinking back to my years at Highbury, I realised how difficult it was going to be to pick out some of my favourite memories — and some of my less favourite ones as well. After nine years, and some real highs and lows, I had almost too much choice. Some of my best and worst memories revolve around Manchester United, which is why I have devoted a whole chapter to the Red Devils. Some of my greatest memories, of course, revolve around the two Double-winning seasons that I was lucky enough to contribute to, but others came in the course of our incredible run of 49 unbeaten matches that allowed us to dominate the 2003/4 season.

The end of the previous season had been bittersweet for us. We had surrendered our Premiership title to Manchester United in early May when we had lost at home to Leeds 3–2, despite leading the title race by eight points at the beginning of March. The fact that the Premiership had been decided so late in the season, that we had been so close to retaining our title, and that, worst of all, the crown had finally gone to United of all teams, had left a bitter taste in my mouth. I have to confess that one of my greatest regrets during my years at Arsenal was the fact that we never managed to win the Premiership two years in a row. That had always been one of my goals and I'm sad that I was never able to achieve it. That's why the way in which we relinquished the Premiership in 2003 hurt all the more.

That said, we knew at the start of the season that if we did not win the title, then United almost certainly would. It was really a case of us or them. For me, though, the most frustrating thing about the last few weeks of the 2002/03 season was that in mid-March I had picked up a knee injury which took time to heal and it meant that I was unable to take part in those last few all-important games. In the FA Cup semi-final replay against Chelsea at the end of March, my knee had swollen up and was in bad shape. I had tried to play through the injury but in the end I had limped off before the end of the game. It turned out to be the end of my first season as captain, and I felt really bad about missing out on the crucial, championship-deciding matches coming up. When things are not going well for a team, it's a case of all hands on deck. A team needs to be at full strength to haul itself out of a bad phase and the fact that in the end I had to admit defeat and not play the last five Premiership games of the season was incredibly frustrating for me. It felt as if I was not shouldering my responsibilities as I should have been. And the fact remains, as far as I'm concerned, that it wasn't United who won the championship, it was us who lost it. We handled those last few games badly, we weren't up to the level required to be Premiership champions.

As it turned out, I was also forced to miss the FA Cup Final against Southampton. After our Premiership disappointment, we had one last chance to take home at least one trophy that season. I had to sit the game out on the bench, which, as Robert Pires knew from the year before, is always a terrible place to watch such an important game from. Sol was also missing from the starting line-up, due to suspension. Actually, it makes no difference for me whether I miss out on a game because of injury or suspension because they are both equally frustrating situations to be in. Luckily for the Gunners, it didn't matter in the end that Sol and I didn't play because we still won.

We had already beaten Southampton at home just ten days before when Robert, announcing his intentions for the final, had scored a hat-trick. This time round, the Saints started off positively. They closed us down, they chased after every ball, they tried to build on some set-pieces to attack our goal. They even came close once or twice but were stopped by some great Seaman dives. But we were feeling confident that day, and Thierry had two shots on target within the first ten minutes. Then, in the 38th minute, Thierry picked just the right moment to release the ball to Dennis who had made a dash down the line. Dennis held on to the pass and, with a fantastic reverse ball, crossed it to Freddie who was ready and waiting just inside the box to fire it home. The shot was blocked by the Southampton defence, denying Freddie a third goal in a row in successive FA Cup Finals, but the rebound came to Robert who took a split second to set himself up and drive the ball into the net from five yards out. That was to be the game's only goal and it was particularly good that Robert should have been the one to score it, given that he had missed out on last year's win because of his knee ligament injury. Sometimes there is justice in sport, after all!

The result was in doubt until the very end, though, with Southampton never giving up. They even came very close to equalising with barely ten minutes left of the game, when a brilliant turn and shot at goal from striker Brett Ormerod needed all of Seaman's agility and experience to be kept out of the net. Minutes later, Ashley Cole was forced to clear a James Beattie header off the line. Who knows what would have happened if either of those efforts had gone in and we had had to recover from such a late equaliser? Although Thierry was named Man of the Match afterwards, it was David Seaman, thanks to a few crucial saves that afternoon, who really made sure we won that trophy. As it turned out, it was also David's final appearance for Arsenal, because over the summer he was transferred to Manchester City. We certainly weren't aware that this might be his last game and he maybe thought he would sign another contract with the club but, for whatever reason, after over 1,000 first-class appearances, he bowed out on a high with Arsenal. He did a really fantastic thing, though, when it was time to go and collect the trophy: he insisted that we lift it up together. I had simply thought that I would come on to the pitch and lift it up after him but, no, he insisted that we do it together. That meant so much to me and it was typical of David – generous, modest and thoughtful to the end.

There was so much relief and happiness when we won. At least we would end the season with a trophy. We felt we deserved to: even though we had just lost out on the Premiership, we had played some great football over the course of the season and worked really hard. Our victory – our 9th FA Cup and our second in a row – was a vindication of all that effort. We had won a double of sorts, after all. The celebrations went on in the dressing room afterwards but I have to confess that, as with the whole build-up to the game, I had slightly mixed feelings about the victory. When you are injured like I was, you are never part of the team in quite the same way. Your team-mates prepare and train for the game, they live and breathe it on the day, then, when they win, they are ecstatic. If you are injured, however much you have played your part in getting the team to that stage, you are not actually part of that final victory. You are slightly outside the loop, not exactly excluded from the celebrations but an outsider nonetheless. That feeling definitely hurts and it made that particular win harder for me to enjoy.

The FA Cup victory set us up for the following season. It certainly allowed us to go away on our summer break full of new-found confidence, after our dip in form in the previous weeks. That, plus our determination to avenge our loss of the Premiership crown, meant that when we returned, we were totally ready for business. And we immediately got into our stride. Jens Lehmann had been signed over the summer from 2002 Bundesliga champions Borussia Dortmund to replace David Seaman, and I had found a great midfield partner in the Brazilian World Cup winner Gilberto who had joined in the summer of 2002. Also, Arsène Wenger had decided to move Kolo Touré to a centre half position, rather than the right back one that he had been used to when he had first joined the club the year before. Immediately, he settled into his new role and in fact he never looked back, becoming a first-team regular, something he had not been up until the switch.

By the second game of the season, we had announced our intentions by overwhelming Middlesbrough 4–0 away, with Gilberto scoring his first Premiership goal. It was especially good to have such a big win away because it sent out a strong message to all teams: we would be looking to attack both at home and away. Even when we had a comfortable 3–0 lead, we had kept trying to increase it: we were determined not to let the opposition back into the game. All too often, particularly towards the end of the previous season, we had let teams sneak a goal back and then squeeze out a draw when in fact we should have won the game. So that 4–0 win did us a power of good and strengthened our team spirit.

Our good away form continued when we travelled up to play Manchester City where we had the uncomfortable experience of having to get the ball past David Seaman in order to win. However bizarre it had been to face Fabien Barthez in goal when he was at United, that didn't compare with the difficulty I now had of facing David who I had played hundreds of games with, and who I had seen almost every day of every year since I had joined the club. David also happened to be one of the guys I was closest to at Arsenal and today is one of the two ex-team-mates that I am still in regular touch with (Martin Keown is the other). I adore him and to see him on the opposing team was not easy. Before the start of the game, our eyes met, he gave me that little smile of his, but then we both had to forget all that and forget our friendship for 90 minutes. I just stayed very focused on the game, on what we were trying to achieve and, when the goals went in (we beat them 2–1), I was of course pleased for the team. I was able to set aside the fact that it was David who had let them in. When the whistle went at the end, we even had a little chat for a couple of minutes. That was nice, although it obviously wasn't the same as having an end-of-game chat with someone who is your team-mate. You can't recreate that sort of relationship when a guy is now your opponent.

After that match, it was back up to Manchester for that infamous game against United which ended 0–0 but created enough newspaper column inches to wipe out several forests (I have saved my memories of that game for the chapter on United). Despite everything that happened that evening, we still took the view that we came away with a good result for us – a draw. Further away wins at Liverpool (2–1), Leeds (4–1) and Birming- ham (3–0), all while I was out with a thigh injury, further strengthened our position at the top of the League, because in the meantime, we had been getting good home results.

Confidence breeds confidence and there's no doubt that a gradual feeling of invincibility was spreading to all members of our squad, even the youngest ones. Which was why the boss decided to field what was almost a junior team to play Wolves in the Carling Cup in December. My French team-mate Sylvain Wiltord and I were the oldest players by some years, but we gelled really well as a team and demolished the opposition 5–1. A great result, given the inexperience of the side. It was in that game that Cesc Fabregas, our new young midfield signing from Barcelona, tapped the ball in from in front of an open goal to become the club's youngest-ever scorer at 16 years and not quite 7 months, giving the fans a clear sign of things to come. Two of the other goals came from my young compatriot Jérémie Aliadière, one of which was an incredible solo effort that started from the halfway line. He too has a great future with the Gunners.

We were also finally having some good results in the Champions League, winning our last three group stage matches against Lokomotiv Moscow, Dynamo Kiev and Inter Milan. That last game, in November, had resulted in an incredible 5–1 away win for us and, because I was still injured, I remember sitting in the stands watching with joy as we played one of the best European games I think we ever played during my years at Arsenal. The fact that we won our group as a result of those last three games led us to think that this could be our year in the Champions League, as well as the Premiership and, why not, the FA Cup as well. If Manchester United could do it, why couldn't we?

February saw landmarks for two of our key players: first, Thierry scored his 100th Premiership goal against Southampton, then Robert reached his 50th for Arsenal against Charlton. Sandwiched between that, José Antonio Reyes, who at twenty years old had just been signed in the January transfer window from Seville for a club record fee of £17.5m, announced his arrival big-time by notching up his first two goals for the club and, in so doing, knocking Chelsea out of the FA Cup. That was a sweet moment for him, especially after his terrible first game a week before against Middlesbrough in the Carling Cup when he had scored an own goal that had given our opponents the victory.

March saw us striding on in all three big competitions – the FA Cup, the Champions League and the Premiership. We destroyed Portsmouth 5–1 away in the FA Cup quarter-final, we beat Celta Vigo in both legs in the Champions League and we had two wins and a draw in the Premiership (against Blackburn, Bolton and Manchester United, respectively). We were looking impressive in all areas of our game: we were playing a really good, collective game, we were defending solidly, passing well and scoring lots of goals.

Then, at the beginning of April, something happened. In the space of just four days, we were eliminated from the two Cup competitions by our two fiercest English rivals. First, Manchester United beat us by a slender 1–0 at Villa Park in the FA Cup semi-final, then in the quarter-final of the Champions League, Chelsea beat us 2–1 at Highbury to knock us out, after we had managed a 1–1 draw at Stamford Bridge. Even today, I still can't understand how we managed to lose that home game. Some of the blame goes to the fact that we should have made sure of victory in the away leg. We played too defensively, too cagily, as if we were happy to settle for a draw. That was our big mistake in my mind, because when I think back to the four periods of 45 minutes, we were the better team during the first three of those; only in the last 45 did we not play as well as our opponents. Maybe we had got a bit tired precisely because we had played so well in the first half, and that was enough to concede the second-half goal that killed off our Champions League chances that year? I don't know. In any case, that defeat still sticks in my throat every time I think about it, particularly as, in all my years at Arsenal, I had yet to lose to Chelsea. Actually, I firmly believe that if we had beaten United in the FA Cup semi-final four days before, we would have gone on to win that return leg against Chelsea. But losing in the FA Cup shook us a bit, even though we didn't necessarily realise it at the time. I think it dented our confidence and made us doubt ourselves just enough to make the difference against Chelsea.

Some people thought that the reason for those two costly defeats was that we had simply played too many big games in quick succession. Personally I don't think so, although it's true that, if you look at the relative lack of success of English teams in Europe and consider that they don't have a mid-winter break like other European countries, there is perhaps something in that argument. I have always taken the view, though, that if you agree to play for one of the big English clubs, you have to accept that you are going to play maybe 60 or 70 games a year. If you don't think you can handle that, then don't go and play for the Arsenals and Chelseas of this world. And if you think you can't live with the media criticism if and when your results in those big competitions fall short of expectations, then again, don't go and play for those clubs. You have to learn to take it.

In any event, after those two defeats, we had two options: we could either let those slaps in the face make us crumble and give up on the rest of our season, or we could decide to show people that we had a strength of character which enabled us to battle on. We had to prove to the world that we were not finished and, what was more, that we were now going all out to win the League. That's why our next match against Liverpool at home is one that I look back to with real pleasure because it revealed the true Arsenal spirit, the one that never gives up.

Liverpool went ahead within five minutes with a Sami Hyypia header from a corner but on the half hour Pires chipped the ball through to Henry who controlled it and slotted it home on the edge of the box. Just before half time, though, Gerrard slid a ball through to Owen who managed to evade our defence long enough to score. Trailing by one goal at half time, that's when we told ourselves to fight. We couldn't envisage a situation where we would lose three games in a row. Sure enough, within a few minutes of the start of the second half, we had scored twice, which was the best possible response. First, Thierry came inside from the wing, passed it to Freddie who laid it on to Robert for him to direct the ball into the net. Then, a minute later, Thierry went off on a brilliant solo run which left the Liverpool defence stranded, before firing the ball past Dudek into the right-hand corner. He hadn't finished for the day either: with just over ten minutes left, Dennis Bergkamp floated a beautiful ball into the box for Thierry to run on to and complete a fantastic hat-trick.

That was a great result for us for all sorts of reasons and, in our next home game, against Leeds, we notched up one more goal than against Liverpool, to come through 5–0. As for Thierry, not content with his previous hat-trick, he managed to score four (Pires scored the other), which made a total of seven goals in eight days for him. All the goals were classic Henry: from the first and the third that were both the result of Gilberto through balls, via the second, a penalty that was almost chipped down the middle, to the fourth that again left defenders stranded as he headed for goal from just inside the Leeds half, before scoring as he fell when one of the opposition finally caught up with him and clipped his ankles. That final goal meant he had now scored 37 that season, and 150 for Arsenal in 250 appearances, which was incredible, considering what he thought of his goal-scoring capabilities when he had first arrived at the club. It was also appropriate that the last player to have scored four goals at Highbury was Ian Wright back in 1991.

By that stage of the season, we were red-hot favourites to win the Premiership. But we had been caught before – the previous season, in fact – after a seemingly unassailable lead, so the priority for us was to keep going as if we still had a lot of work to do. The fact that we were unbeaten that season was not something that was of particular interest to us. It was more a landmark that was being built up by the media. For us, the main objective was to win the League. If we stayed unbeaten, all the better, but we weren't thinking about that too much. The only pressure we felt was the pressure to bring the Premiership trophy back to Highbury, rather than to create any sort of record.

In the end, we won the Premiership at White Hart Lane on 25 April. We still had four games to play, so it was fantastic to be able to seal the title so early. And of course it was doubly fantastic that we did so against Spurs, at their ground. The fact that I scored the opening goal on the way to a 2–2 draw was also nice for me, particularly as the goal was a beauty! It happened in the first three minutes. Thierry got the ball from around our penalty area and took it to beyond the halfway line. From there, he passed it to Dennis on the edge of the box who then hit the ball across for me to finish with my right foot, at full stretch in front of goal. We had produced the sort of quick, flowing football that had now become the norm for us and, on days like that, it was leaving our opponents standing. I was really pleased to round off my afternoon by creating the second goal for Robert Pires. I suppose it was a nice symbol that the team captain should have scored one goal and made the other on the day that the team won the Premiership. Although, as it happens, I'm not bothered about that sort of thing, nor about whether the goal I score is a good one or not. What interests me is whether we win, not whether I have been instrumental in that victory. Football is a team sport, above all.

There was a fantastic coincidence though to us winning the Premiership at White Hart Lane. In 1971, when Arsenal had won their first-ever Double, they had also sealed the First Division title (as it was then) at White Hart Lane. I'm sure many Spurs fans were well aware of this irony of history that had repeated itself in such a terrible way.

It was also fitting that that evening Thierry Henry collected the PFA Player of the Year trophy for the second year in a row. In addition, he had been voted the Football Writers' Player of the Year for the second successive year and had been runner-up in FIFA's World Player of the Year and European Footballer of the Year awards. Thierry was having a good year, that was for sure!

As it turned out, the day that the Premiership trophy was actually presented to us at Highbury – which was after the final game of the season against relegated Leicester City – I also scored the winning goal in our 2–1 victory. That was a satisfyingly symbolic moment for me. But the day was memorable for more important things than my final goal. Firstly, as well as holding up the trophy in front of our fans (the first I had lifted as the club captain, incidentally), we had also ended the season unbeaten after 38 games, breaking the previous record set, incredibly, back in 1888/9 by Preston North End. We had won the title with 90 points, eleven points clear of second-placed Chelsea, which was a big margin and something that we were very pleased about. Secondly, that game was also the last in Arsenal colours for Martin Keown who was finally retiring after so many years at the club. Rightly, he got a fantastic ovation from all the supporters when he came on as substitute with a few minutes left of the game.

At the final whistle, Highbury literally exploded into noisy celebration. The presentation ceremony, the moment when I lifted up the trophy, the singing and dancing on the pitch, and afterwards in the dressing room, are all forever etched on my mind as some of the happiest moments of my life. The season had ended on a real high. The parade the next morning through the streets of Islington was every bit as crazy as the one in 1998 or in 2002 but being the captain of the team made it even more special for me.

When I look back at the season and ask myself what it was that made us so dominant in the League that year, I can't put my finger on one single thing. What I do know is, that season, we had several players in the team who were absolutely at their peak, players such as Thierry, Robert, Dennis, Sol. I also felt that I had had possibly my best season of the last three years. We also had a fantastic team spirit, we all worked well together and, crucially, we all enjoyed our football so much. There were so many matches that we won from which we got sheer pleasure, and I can honestly say that that feeling alone contributes a lot to a team's success.

Whenever I am asked whether I can rank one Premiership title over another, one Double over another, or one FA Cup Final win over another, I always reply that it's impossible to choose between them. All the trophies I have won at Arsenal have meant different things to me. They were all won in very different circumstances, after long battles, after highs and lows, and after a lot of hard work. I can't rank them in order of importance. And that's why each one gives me unique but equally precious memories.

11

Being Captain

One day, a journalist asked me, 'Patrick, what makes a good captain?' and I replied 'I'll tell you at the end of my career!'

I have always thought that before I could know what made a good captain, I had to analyse what this role consisted of, both in simple terms and in more complex ones as well. A captain has to think positively, even in the most difficult moments, he has to make the team aim ever higher, he has to have a close relationship with the coach or with the manager and he has to look out constantly for the well-being of his team-mates. He also has to be able to look after others without his game suffering, so he either has to be experienced or very mature.

Becoming first the Arsenal captain, then the captain of the French team did not just transform me, it totally left everything else behind. But generally, responsibilities don't frighten me. In fact, I like them, I go in search of them. I didn't feel any extra pressure, even though I still needed a bit of time to get used to the idea that I was the captain of *les Bleus*, that I would be the first one out of the dressing room, the one who would lead the team out. It gives me enormous pride and pleasure to wear the captain's armband of one of the most famous teams in the world. It's more than a dream come true, because although you dream about one day playing for your national team, you never dream you might captain them as well. You either do or you don't. It's something that happens naturally or it doesn't. My family were especially proud of me and it's a great feeling to look into their eyes and to see that I have not been a disappointment to them. When I look back at where I started out from, I realise that it's not bad to have got to where I have! I read somewhere that when his club coach at the time named Didier Deschamps as captain of

Nantes, when he was barely twenty years old, he saw Didier visibly grow in height. Well, I puffed out a bit, because I was already tall enough as it was! I was so happy to have been rewarded for all my hard work and patience in all situations. And if I am where I am today, it's because I'm not a bad man either, for relationships are also very important to me.

You either have what it takes to be a leader or you don't, it's not something you can go and work on. To be a captain in England is the ultimate recognition because it's a role that carries enormous symbolism as well as responsibility – especially off the pitch because it's the captain who makes all the decisions. For example, I was the one who decided if we played in short sleeves or long sleeves. Even if there were twenty guys who wanted to play in short sleeves, if I was cold, I was the one who made the final choice.

I had an entire page devoted to me in every club programme. My word carried weight and I could say anything I wanted. Usually, I liked to analyse the upcoming game, look back at how we had played against that team in the past, what we needed to do to win, and talk about any other current issue concerning the club or the team. All in all, the captain's role in England is much more important than it is in France. I didn't just limit myself to what happened on the pitch – I had the power to make decisions about all aspects of the sport. I also had a privileged relationship with the coach.

On top of that, I could not forget that at Highbury I followed in the footsteps of a captain with a towering personality. In terms of the image of a captain, Tony Adams is still everyone's idol. The fans will never forget him and that reputation is totally deserved. That's what's good about England. People have long memories and respect for those who went before, who contributed to making their club bigger and better. Tony left a permanent mark in people's hearts and I still respect him enormously. In England, fans learn to respect the old players, never forgetting what they brought to their club or to their national team. It would be good if we could learn from that in France.

That said, I never drew inspiration from Tony when I took over his role, even during his last season at the club in 2001/2 when he was often injured and I was effectively much more than a vice-captain. I could never have become a second Tony Adams because our personalities are diametrically opposed. I am not somebody who talks much in the dressing room. I am calm and low-key. Tony was a dominant figure, partly because he had a large physical presence. He used to shout a lot in order to motivate people, telling the players when there was a problem that they had to get their heads down and fight if they wanted to win, that's how he built the strong team spirit that existed under his captaincy. But that was not my style. I preferred to lead by example on the pitch rather than by raising my voice off it. I knew a good tackle or managing to get forward would lift the team, so I led by what I did more than by what I said. And I like to think that under me, the same togetherness continued within the team.

Now that I have gone to Juventus, I have obviously lost that special status. During my last few seasons at Arsenal, the fact that I was captain was a big element in my decision to stay there for as long as I did. In fact, it was a key factor. I knew very well that I would never find anywhere else what I had there. I don't think people understand what I felt by having this level of responsibility in a club of such importance: it went way beyond just being a player.

At Arsenal, we developed a very strong bond between us. There was a real team spirit throughout the whole club; I'm not just saying it, it really did exist. There was – and still is, I'm sure – a real *joie de vivre*, a desire to work together. And above all, we got the results. In my years at the club, we were permanently in one of the top slots of the Premier League and won the FA Cup several times, which was enough to make other people jealous of our success.

Some people have suggested that the France team was made up of various cliques, and even that there was an Arsenal one, which was very hurtful for me – for us, I should say – because it simply wasn't true. The Arsenal internationals are very open, sociable guys. We are also keen to give something back, just as the previous generation gave back to us. So, yes, I did mind when I heard about these so-called cliques. On top of that, the rumours came at a time when things weren't going great, and some people were happy to criticise, to put their finger just where it hurt, even though they didn't know what they were talking about.

As for me, I could never have seen myself captaining all those players who have since retired – the likes of Zidane, Thuram, Lizarazu, Desailly. Nowadays, I feel I deserve it more than I did then. My appointment as captain of the France team was talked about once those senior players announced their retirement, but it was only once the manager Raymond Domenech talked to me about it, a bit before the first international of the season (against Bosnia Herzegovina in Rennes at the start of the 2004/5 season) that I was officially informed of the news. I was totally on-board with the idea, so much so that although the game, being played in August, was only a friendly and I was injured, I still came to the squad gathering. I had intended to anyway so the boss never needed to convince me. From my point of view, I was sending a clear and powerful message that demonstrated my total desire to live up to the trust that had been placed in me and the honour that had been conferred on me.

Raymond Domenech is someone who encourages players to take responsibility, rather than imposing it on them. In fact, he continues to teach me about the various aspects of leadership as well as the importance it has in everyday life. He encourages me to get involved a little more every day when it comes to him and the players. Above all, being the captain is a role that requires me to be clear in everything I ask others to do and, in a short space of time, he has taught me a lot.

Consequently, I found myself in the same situation within the France team as I had been when Arsène gave me the captain's armband at Arsenal. I had to learn to change my nature a little, and to speak a lot more. On the pitch, for example, I intervene more than I used to, both at club and international level. In quite a lot of situations, for example free kicks, penalties or corners, I don't hold back, even if I know the player has understood, because I think you have to keep repeating the same things over and over again. On the other hand, I'm not someone who barks out instructions the whole time, so the extra workload does not have any repercussions on my own game. I get involved without getting annoyed. I am not untouchable either; I accept my team-mates' criticisms. Finally, I also have to make sure that I don't spend time on extra tasks just because I am captain: I have to know my place.

My first task when I took over as captain of the France team was to ensure that everyone felt good within the group that we were trying to rebuild. I went out to the others, I took the first steps, just as the older guys had done with me. I did not have to force myself to do it. It's not against my nature because, fundamentally, I am someone who is open, albeit reserved as well. Either way, I managed to have a conversation with everyone. In any case, I owed it to myself to do it.

The situation was therefore quite complex and very different compared to the early days of my Arsenal captaincy, although I have to say it was equally enriching. With the Gunners, although I was wearing the captain's armband, the team had a lot of established players such as Bergkamp, Henry, Pires, Keown, Seaman and many others. I was also following directly on from what I had known when I was Tony Adams' vice-captain. The transition was simpler because we had complete continuity and that was obviously not the case with the France team.

With the new internationals, in particular, I first had to get to know them a little by talking to their mates and those who knew them already. In general, I could feel the youngsters were quite reserved towards me, which is completely normal; now, our relationship is different, even if it is still not totally free. In the space of three days, we rarely have time to establish any rapport, whereas over a ten-day period we do.

I have never tried to imitate someone in my role as captain. I want to be myself, because that's enough anyway. Didier Deschamps was by general consensus a great captain. He was open-minded, and he loved to listen, to exchange opinions. He spoke in exactly the same way to Zizou and to the new kid who had just arrived. He chatted easily and he always said the right thing. He spoke sense and knew the right moment to speak. You would very quickly feel close to him. He was also someone who did not beat about the bush, he quickly got straight to the point, and never let a situation fester. He would intervene as soon as a problem reared its head, whether it was a tactical problem or one that concerned the group of players as a whole. I have more of a tendency initially to let time sort things out, to push people less, to give time the opportunity to work.

You also had the feeling that Didier knew exactly what was happening and wanted to know everything. I am honestly not in that mould! I'm also not sure that this expanded role is really what I want. The atmosphere in the team and the matches are my main preoccupations but perhaps, with time, I'll expand my horizons. It will either happen naturally or it won't happen at all.

Marcel Desailly was a very different captain of *les Bleus*. He had another way of embracing the role: he was able to stand back from everything, he was really calm. I think he took things less seriously than Dédé. For Deschamps, it was all or nothing, at once. Marcel was more relaxed. If I can borrow a bit from both, then I'll be happy!

Zizou had the captain's armband during Euro 2004. Did he really want to be captain? I don't know . . . I don't actually think so. He did it for the good of the team, which is perfectly laudable. I'm not so sure though that he coped with the situation very well, especially as a load of ridiculous stories started surfacing as a result, which, however wide of the mark, must have affected him nonetheless.

I have always been told I am a leader. Consequently, I only had one final step to take when I was made captain of both Arsenal and of France. On the pitch, I have always carried my team-mates along with me; my game predisposes me to that anyway, my temperament as well; it's a part of me, and it is not therefore an obligation or a part that I am playing.

Off the pitch, I have to learn that a bit more. Everyone has his or her personality and not everyone reacts to events the same. You therefore have to learn to communicate, to not upset who you are talking to, to find the right words. One game that summed up how I viewed my role as Arsenal captain was the FA Cup 5th round replay we played in March 2004 against Sheffield United at their ground. We had not lost an FA Cup match to a lower-division side since the days when Bruce Rioch was in charge, in the mid-nineties, so we were desperate to keep that record. But our team was missing nine of its usual first-team players, either through injury or suspension, so we were forced to field a very young side: five of them were under twenty years old. Some, like the 17-year-old Italian forward Arturo Lupoli, had hardly had more than a couple of first-team outings since he had been signed from Parma on a scholarship contract the summer before. The same went for striker Quincy Owusu-Abeyie, who had been part of the Arsenal development scheme for youngsters, who has come up through the ranks, and who has so much talent. I had to keep these young guys calm beforehand and focused on what they were about to do. But more importantly, I had to lead by example on the pitch, and keep everyone disciplined. The game went to extra time and was still 0–0 after 120 minutes, so things were very tense by the time we went to penalties. I stayed very composed, I had a fantastic game and I think all the youngsters followed my example and produced an unbelievably mature performance on the night.

It's an honour as well as an immense responsibility to have the captain's armband, but it's also something that makes the player who wears it grow in stature. Becoming Arsenal skipper allowed my attitude to progress and allowed me to feel responsible not only for my own performances but also for those of my team-mates, as well as for their well-being. I had to learn from my mistakes and, over the years, analyse what went wrong and then try to improve it. I gained a lot from being captain, both on the playing and on the personal front. It definitely made me into a better player and a better person because I was always wanting to improve my game and to improve the team both on and off the pitch. I hope that, in the same way that I learned a lot from Tony Adams and some of the other great players who were at the club when I arrived, I have managed to pass on something of my experience and attitude to the game to the younger ones who are still there now that I have left. That would make me feel very proud. I am incredibly honoured to have led this historic club but I think I will only truly recognise how lucky I was to captain Arsenal once I have finished playing and start to look back at what I have achieved in my career.

12

United: My Favourite Enemy

From the moment I arrived in England in the summer of 1996, I understood that Manchester United were the team to beat. They had just won the League title. They were the benchmark, the best team at the time. There was a tangible rivalry between Arsenal and United and tensions between the players. I remember that the atmosphere was very heated between Schmeichel and Wright throughout the whole season. It had first flared up in the November fixture that year at Old Trafford, then again at the Highbury one the following February. On both occasions, the players had clashed, both physically and verbally and, at one stage at Highbury, Wright had had to be restrained firstly by the police when the final whistle blew, then by the club physio, Gary Lewin, as the players entered the tunnel after the game. Everyone assumed that Wright would get charged with misconduct by the FA but in the end it was Schmeichel whose behaviour led to the Crown Prosecution Service investigating Wright's allegations that the Danish goalkeeper had racially abused him, allegations which he denied. In the end, no charges were brought. That whole incident certainly gave me an indication that there was — and is — no love lost between the two clubs.

Ever since, whenever I have played against United, some incident has always taken place. It might be something unusual, extraordinary, tough, unjust or fantastic, but something has always happened. I always felt the pressure off the pitch . . . and even on it, amongst the players. We might respect each other a lot but there is an additional something there as well. When I first played for the Gunners, everyone wanted to beat Manchester United because they were the best team, whereas we were still improving. Nowadays, I would say that it's the other teams which play differently against both us and United. The two teams have been swapping trophies for the last ten years. Now Chelsea is also going to experience this situation, which is a nice one to find yourself in, because it means that your team is the one against which all the others in the Premiership measure themselves.

One of my first goals in England was in fact at Highbury against Man U in November 1997. My fellow Frenchman Nicolas Anelka had opened up the scoring early in the first half. Anelka had been signed a year before, as an exciting 17-year-old prospect, soon after Arsène Wenger had arrived at the club. He had recently broken into the first team and he became a key player for us that year, which was one of our Double-winning seasons. He has exceptional pace and ability and he scored some great goals in his time at Arsenal but, by 1999, he had been sold to Real Madrid. Since then, he has found it difficult to settle at the various clubs he has played for which is a pity because he has unbelievable talent. After Anelka had scored, I then went on to score myself. I have to say, it was a great goal, possibly one of the best of my entire career. I hit the ball on the half volley from about twenty yards out, and it went in just under Schmeichel's crossbar. I was slightly off-centre and struck the ball absolutely perfectly! So much so, that Schmeichel looked stunned to see the ball in the back of his net. To celebrate my goal, I threw myself on the ground with the aim of sliding forwards on my knees, a bit like Titi sometimes does. Except that I stayed put on the grass and managed to stretch my knee ligaments. I had to go off and United then pulled two back before half time. Luckily, late into the second half, David Platt scored our third goal from a corner to give us victory. I was a bit disappointed to have to limp off with an injury and not to be able to celebrate with my team-mates. But ever since that day, I no longer slide on my knees to celebrate my goals! And especially not when the pitch is dry!

Actually, I have always enjoyed playing against Manchester United because they are always big games. I love the atmosphere that builds up beforehand. That's when you see who the great players are, the ones who are made of steel. These games are always very revealing. There is nowhere to hide when you play against United, you can't be half-hearted in the way you play. You have to commit 100 per cent and in the end, that's what I love. I have never needed to motivate myself for those Old Trafford encounters; I have never needed the manager to give me a pep talk. The burning desire was already there because I knew I was playing against the best in the country. That was more than enough.

On top of that, there are some individual rivalries. On my part of the pitch, there's Roy Keane. And that gives rise to some great duels. I was young when I played against Roy for the first time; I knew about his reputation and had watched a lot of his matches. But I have never been afraid of him. There were times when I could see he was late in his tackles and I could feel him coming. He's been bad on the pitch. But it is done more to unsettle than anything else.

In fact, since I have been in England, only one player has frightened me: Vinnie Jones, who I played against when he was at Aston Villa. It was enough for me just to look at him to feel afraid. He didn't speak. But there was pure nastiness in his eyes and in the vibes he gave off. You could feel that you were not safe when you were playing against him. With Keane, it's different. He tries to get a psychological edge over his opponent. He wants to put pressure on him, and place him in a situation where he gets all steamed up. The fiercer the midfield battle is, the more at ease he becomes. I soon cottoned on to his game and after that it didn't bother me. On the contrary, I loved it.

I have good memories of the games against Manchester United because above all they were football matches, even if there were also a lot of clashes along the way. Despite the respect we had for each other, we also had a pride that meant we did not want to be on the losing side. During my nine years in England, we lived through every emotion against United: joy, disappointment at controversial moments when we were robbed, delight at other moments when things went in our favour.

If I look back to the game that gave me the most joy against United, it has to be the one in May 2002, when we secured the

Premiership title at Old Trafford, in front of the Manchester United fans. That was an incredible, unforgettable moment for us because not only had we won the title, we had also done the Double (we had won the FA Cup against Chelsea just a few days before), and we had done it at United's ground, on the 'enemy's' patch. It doesn't get any better than that. We had become only the second English side to win the league championship and FA Cup double three times. I think all this really stuck in their throats because we won 1–0 despite not having several of our key players such as Thierry Henry, Dennis Bergkamp and Tony Adams who were all injured. Celebrating at Old Trafford was a great memory for me, even though the first half had been brutal and they had tried to make us buckle under, both physically and mentally. There had been several bookings, including one for Keane when he tackled me heavily, but we had all kept totally calm. Then Sylvain Wiltord scored the 57th-minute goal that gave us the title. For that goal alone, he will go down in Highbury history. We had won the League after winning our last twelve games, plus we had won the FA Cup, so afterwards, even United's manager, Alex Ferguson, confessed that we deserved the Double. 'I certainly hold up my hands to their achievements,' he admitted, which, coming from him, was certainly satisfying to hear.

Nine months later, in February 2003, we had won there once again. That time, it had been in the 5th round of the FA Cup and we had won 2–0 after dominating most of the game. That was the day of the Beckham business with Ferguson and the shoe. Ferguson had admitted, afterwards, kicking a football boot in an angry tirade and it had left a gash needing several stitches above Beckham's left eye. We had had a good laugh when we read about it in the papers. Ferguson throwing a shoe at Beckham . . . At the time, we knew that something had happened in their dressing room but there had been so many rumours that we hadn't really discovered the truth. We heard that a scuffle had broken out between Beckham and Ferguson, that Keane had broken it up and that a few punches had been thrown. After that, we followed the story in the papers. It was so funny!

When I look back at the game that gave me the most disappointment against United, it was probably the FA Cup semi-final that we lost in 1999. The game itself was a replay, at Villa Park. United took the lead in the 17th minute after Beckham drove the ball past Seaman, but we fought back and equalised halfway through the second half with a fantastic Bergkamp right-foot shot. Keane then got sent off for a second yellow card and we were looking good, even having a goal disallowed soon after. Suddenly, deep into injury time, Ray Parlour was brought down in the box by a late Phil Neville tackle and we were awarded a penalty. We were seconds away from almost definite victory and a second trip to Wembley in successive years. Dennis lined up to take the penalty. He was desperate to get to the final because he had missed out on it the previous year through injury. He ran up to the ball, kicked it low and hard, Schmeichel leaped to his left and saved it. Thirty seconds later, when we could have been celebrating our road to Wembley, we were having to play extra time. Again, Schmeichel saved a Bergkamp shot at full stretch. He had injured his thigh and was finding it difficult to move properly but still we just couldn't manage to put the ball past him. In the 108th minute, I got the ball halfway inside our half. I was on the left and wanted to cross it to the right but I messed up my pass and sent it straight to Ryan Giggs' feet. Before I knew it, he had started on a run towards goal, beating not just one or two but five of our players, before reaching the penalty box and shooting the ball just under the crossbar past Seaman to score the deciding goal. Afterwards, I felt incredibly responsible for our defeat. As far as I was concerned, it was my fault that we weren't in the final. It was the first time they had beaten us in seven attempts and, when the final whistle blew, their fans went crazy, whilst we were left to think about how close we had come to victory. The result was made even more painful by the fact that United went on to achieve a unique treble of league title, FA Cup and European Cup wins whilst we ended the season without a trophy. After that, whenever we went to Old Trafford, their fans would sing

'Vieira, Ohohoh, Vieira, he gives Giggs the ball,
And Arsenal fuck all.'

Every time, 60,000 fans took the piss out of me – that was a pretty big number. But what all those people didn't realise was that I actually loved playing at Old Trafford. The stadium is fantastic and the atmosphere is incredible. So whenever I heard that song, it made me laugh, but the first time, I can tell you, I didn't find it funny at all!

As for controversial moments against United, there have been plenty. In September of the 2003/4 season, I was sent off after a second yellow card as a result of an incident with van Nistelrooy. I got a red card, but even just thinking about it today makes my blood boil. It annoys me because although this is all in the past, I still can't forget it. I got shafted. He tried to stamp on me and then he made more of the challenge than he should have done. I'm not blaming the referee because he too got shafted. I never intended to touch van Nistelrooy. It was not a violent gesture that deserved a red card. The way in which he laid it on with a trowel annoyed me even more.

Personally, I can't stand the sight of van Nistelrooy. Everything about him annoys me. He's always complaining, whingeing. To me, he's deceitful as well as being a nasty piece of work. There are some players that I respect, despite the fact that they'll stick the boot in, because I can sense that there's no malice behind their actions; they are not hiding what they are doing. Paul Scholes, for example, gives as good as he gets in terms of knocks. He won't complain, though, he won't moan and roll around on the ground. He gives, he takes, end of story. Van Nistelrooy, on the other hand, is someone I dislike. He's a great player, I can't deny it; he's a great striker who has proved himself time and time again. But, for me, the man is a cheat and a thief.

The crazy thing was, when I was sent off, Keane came over to calm me down because deep down he knew that van Nistelrooy had cheated once again. He came up to me and said 'Let it go, it's not worth it.' He saw I was really upset and, as far as I was concerned, that said it all about what he thought of his teammate's attitude. I think he knows that I didn't deserve to be sent off and that's why he reacted as he did. So I think he's quite honest as a human being. I don't think any other Manchester United player could have done it. That's the bond between us. And I respect him for it. I got back to the changing room and showered. I was trying to calm down but I just couldn't swallow what had been done to me. It stuck in my throat.

At the end of the game, I was standing chatting to a friend in the tunnel that leads to the exit where the coach waits for us when van Nistelrooy walked in front of me. We looked at each other. He tried to talk to me. I told him that it was finished and that I had nothing more to say to him. But he persisted. So I asked if I had touched him. He simply replied, 'You have no class.' And that was the icing on the cake. In fact, he had been trying to convince himself that he had not cheated, which just went to show that he did not have a clear conscience. So I added, 'Watch it, because I'm going to land one on you.' We were on the verge of fisticuffs but Mikaël Silvestre, Fabien Barthez and Robert Pires got there just in time and intervened, so we went our separate ways. The English papers had a field day with the story even though, in the end, nothing had actually happened. But this little altercation confirmed my view of him that not only is van Nistelrooy a cheat, but he lacks courage as well.

The match itself was full of incidents. The penalty that the Dutchman had missed; Parlour, Lauren and Keown jumping on him. We were really criticised for that. When you watch the replays on television, it's true that it doesn't make for pretty viewing. The way in which the game finished and the way in which the Arsenal players reacted when the final whistle went. As professional players, given our status, there are some things that we should not allow ourselves to do. But people must not forget that we are also human and that we each have our own way of reacting to situations, depending on our feelings and our emotions at the time. It was the injustice that made us behave as we did. And that's a feeling that we have experienced all too often when we have played against Manchester United.

It is at times like these, in the heat of the moment, that we forget we are professional players and we react like any normal human being would. When an injustice has been committed, we all tend to react instinctively. The way in which some Arsenal players showed their true feelings that day projected a very negative image of the club and all the general public could do was to judge what they saw on TV. But I still think van Nistelrooy is a coward who is sneaky in the way he goes about fouling other players. Everyone thinks he's a nice guy but in fact he's a son of a bitch. He has a history of incidents that all too often have gone unnoticed. We hate him and have real reason to do so.

The boss was not pleased either after that September 2003 game and he was quoted as saying 'You cannot tell me that Vieira is the devil and that van Nistelrooy is an angel. If Patrick was sent off, van Nistelrooy had to go too. Patrick is 100 per cent sure that van Nistelrooy caught him and I saw it from the bench. We saw van Nistelrooy went for him. I think it is cheating. Patrick should not have reacted, but again we are punishing the consequence rather than the source of the problem.' After that game, we were severely criticised and it took us a long time to forget that, especially because during the FA Cup semi-final in April 2004 that we lost 1–0 at Villa Park, José Antonio Reyes and Freddie Ljungberg were injured as a result of two unacceptably harsh tackles.

Even the last two matches I played against Manchester United gave rise to some bad memories. First, of course, there was that notorious game in November 2004. We were unbeaten in 49 matches and we were well and truly robbed. Having played in Italy, I know that the big teams are given the benefit of the doubt. Referees are more willing to overlook things with the big clubs. When Arsenal play against United, the referee gives the latter the benefit of the doubt, or that's how it seems to me, but when Arsenal play against Spurs, the former tend to get it. That's how it works. Even so, that doesn't account for events that night.

We were going to Old Trafford with our unbeaten record and nobody was talking about anything else. Are Man U capable of stopping Arsenal?' Alex Ferguson had already been quoted as saying that in the previous year's game, we had 'got away with murder'. So the stakes were high. Despite that, when I think about everything that happened during the game, I find it hard to believe. If we had conducted ourselves like the United players had, we would have been down to eight men by the end of the ninety minutes, no doubt about it. Reyes seemed to be the target once again of intimidation by several United players. Rio Ferdinand fouled Freddie Ljungberg at one point and I think he should have been sent off. Instead, he did not even get a yellow card. On top of that, there should never have been a penalty in the 72nd minute given for a tackle on Rooney because he quite clearly dived and, in so doing, cheated blatantly and pathetically. Everyone knew that the referee had given United a penalty in each of his last eight visits to Old Trafford. There was huge pressure on him during this game and I felt that he was not able to cope with it, but I never imagined that such unfairness could occur in such a crucial game, one that was being shown to millions on TV throughout the world. Either way, that penalty was the turning point because up until then, we had been the better team.

We were also sickened by the way in which the United players spoke to the referee during the game. I'm thinking in particular of Wayne Rooney. It was revolting and I find it hard to understand why some referees and officials react so inconsistently, depending on who they're dealing with. Those are the sort of things that really affect you when you are on the pitch.

That defeat was enormously disappointing and frustrating for us. The problem was not only that we lost that feeling of invincibility; it was also that we felt a huge sense of injustice.

That game changed everything for us because up until then we had lost the habit of losing. We did everything we could to put the words 'turning point' out of our minds. We could not believe what had happened and maybe also thought that the unfair way in which we had been beaten at Old Trafford did not therefore mean that our run had come to an end. Unfortunately, we did not win again straight away, we were not able to bounce back. In fact, the bad run began right then. We had trouble winning matches after that, even though we did not talk much about the loss amongst ourselves. We more or less convinced ourselves that after 49 unbeaten games 'it wasn't because we have lost one game that we won't win any more'. We stayed positive. But I think that game did us more damage than we realised at the time. We didn't take the loss or its consequences seriously enough. We had lost against Manchester United, not against a bunch of monkeys! In the following games, we drew, we lost, we drew. Slowly but surely, we lost confidence in ourselves. There had been times, previously, when we had been losing 1–0, 2–0 even, but we had known that, in the end, we were going to pull it back. That had been our strength – we knew we would score. And little by little we lost that feeling. Our confidence was much more fragile than we had thought.

I had not forgotten any of this when the return match came round on 1st February 2005. Every time we play against United, Gary Neville is the one who acts like the tough guy. I don't know him personally but we're always on the receiving end of his knocks when it comes to us. During the Old Trafford game in October, his behaviour towards Jose had been unacceptable. Yet whenever I watched him on TV, I never saw him fouling the other players. I used to ask myself, 'Why is he so terrible against us and not against the other teams?' So I went up to him and said, 'You, every time you foul the guys, I'm going to be watching you, and if you do it, I'm going to sort you out.' Yes, it was intimidation, pure and simple. I hadn't planned in advance to say it, there was no premeditation. I just saw him and it occurred to me to say it. Anyway, Gary Neville is a big boy and he can handle himself. Then Keane got involved, which did not surprise me: he's the captain, his job is to defend his players, that's normal. He told me to leave Neville alone and that if I had a problem I should come and talk to him. Keane told me that he thought it was unacceptable for me to talk to Neville and tell him these things. He also said that I was not a nice guy.

Actually, I don't have a problem with Keane, even though, frankly, we have often wound each other up. I'm not talking about the man because I don't know him personally, but he's someone I respect in terms of the image he has created for himself and the way in which he captains his team on the pitch. He has charisma on and off it as well; he's the sort to stand up for his rights. He fights for what he believes in and is not one to be afraid. He's a winner, he wants to win for the team. He's quite similar to me, in that respect, except he's older! For him still to be playing at the top of the game is a great achievement and it's because he has a very strong mind. That's why, out of all the midfielders I have done battle with in England over the years, Roy Keane was the toughest, and for that, I really respect him. When you compare behaviour and courage on the pitch between him and Neville, or him and van Nistelrooy, it's like night and day. If he wants to tell a player to go screw himself, he'll go up to him and tell him face to face. He will never duck saying what he thinks: he'll look his opponent straight in the eyes and tell him what he has to say. He expects a high level of play not only of himself but also of the others in his team. 'They are paid to play well,' he says, so he doesn't accept anything other than maximum effort and results from them. He doesn't care if he has to shout at players to get what he wants out of them. On the other hand, I have been disappointed by some of the opinions he has expressed about me. He has said it wasn't right that I should be playing for France because I was actually from Senegal. He also said that the reason I had not gone to Real Madrid was that Real had not really wanted me; also that I was doing things for Senegal with my charity even though I was playing for France.

Actually, none of that had any effect on me. It's pathetic, and I wonder where it all came from. I don't see that there's any link between that and our problems in the tunnel. After all, he's the one who quit from the Ireland squad during the 2002 World Cup and who then came back with his tail between his legs. If anybody should avoid commenting on who should play for a national team, it's him.

After the tunnel incident, which, when all was said and done, was a storm in a teacup, we were beaten 4–2 by Man U. Like so many of our recent games, this one was highly charged. After just eight minutes, I had opened the score with a header from a

Henry corner, only to see Giggs equalise not long after. Bergkamp's goal before half time came after a fantastic series of passes involving myself, the young Frenchman Mathieu Flamini and Henry before Bergkamp finished the move off by sending his shot through goalkeeper Roy Carroll's legs. But we were unable to capitalise on this 2–1 lead in the second half. We so wanted to beat them, to dominate them, that we allowed ourselves to play too much with our hearts and, sadly, not enough with our heads and United took advantage of that and counter-attacked. But they also lost a man when Mikaël Silvestre was sent off in the second half for headbutting Ljungberg and Rooney was lucky to stay on after repeatedly hurling bad language at the referee Graham Poll. In the end, two goals by Cristiano Ronaldo, the Portuguese international who was still two days short of his 20th birthday, did the damage and we never recovered from it. The fourth, chipped in by John O'Shea, simply sealed a disastrous night for us. We had a strong team so we were really disappointed with the way we had played.

It might surprise a lot of people to know that, although I don't know him personally, whenever I see Sir Alex Ferguson on TV, I like what I see. I like the way he is with his players. Beyond that, whatever he says about Arsenal and Arsène can just be put down to the rivalry between the two teams. When Ferguson said, for example, following the September 2003 game at Old Trafford when I got sent off after my problem with van Nistelrooy, 'The worst thing I've seen on a football pitch. They conveniently forget things, that mob,' did he really believe everything he said? I'm not sure that it isn't part of one massive act on his part. The rivalry is huge, of course, and each manager defends his club and his players. That's what Arsène Wenger was doing when he said before the October 2004 Old Trafford game, 'Alex has a good sense of humour. I hope he calms down before the match. This is not a game for resentment and aggression and, on my side, I can guarantee that what has happened in the past will not influence us at all.' As for knowing whether they are both telling the whole truth, I'm not so sure.

At one stage, some time back, I heard the first murmurings of an approach by Manchester United. I had been at Arsenal for approximately a couple of years, I don't remember exactly how long. I had signed another contract with them and United at one point had been very interested in me and had approached me. Today, it would be completely impossible for me to move to United, but even at the time, my presence with the Gunners was already sufficiently well established that everyone would have thought this was the ultimate betrayal. Even then, to have left Arsenal to go to another English club would have been really, really tough. Not impossible, but tough.

United made me an offer, a very good one in fact. I don't think Ferguson took my refusal badly. I think he understood, even though I never met him in person. The big misunderstanding in this whole business was caused by an alleged interview I was supposed to have given a newspaper. The article stated that I said I wanted to go to Man U, even though I never actually gave that interview. In fact I was on holiday in the States at the time. I never did find out who had published such a web of lies and, more importantly, who had had a vested interest in doing such a thing. But it's water under the bridge now.

At one time, there were a lot of Frenchmen at Manchester United. Barthez, Blanc, Silvestre, who is still up there. I remember the match at Highbury in November 2001 which we won 3–1. Fabien was in goal and he made two terrible mistakes that Thierry seized upon to score two goals. For the first one, Fabien was clearing a Beckham back pass when his shot went straight to Thierry who was standing on the edge of the area. All he had to do was slip it past him to score. The second time, I had sent a high pass to Thierry, over the heads of the defenders, and Fabien had come running off his line to collect the ball. He caught it, then immediately dropped it, leaving Thierry free to tap it into goal. At the time, it didn't matter whether it was Fabien in goal or someone else, it was the same thing. Once it was over, though, I thought that it would have been better if it had been someone else in goal, because it wasn't great that it had been Fabien, of all people, who had just had his fellow-countryman put two past him in such a humiliating way.

If I had to pick out one player from United, though, who I really admire above all others, I would choose Paul Scholes. There's a real lack of recognition for him when you consider everything he has done for them, although he's fine about that. He's someone who is very reserved, who keeps himself to himself, who keeps his private life out of the newspapers, who is very calm. Yet what he does on the pitch, the goals he scores, that's impressive. He can do everything. I love to watch him play. He is what I call 'a big player'. And that is why, as far as I'm concerned, there's a big gulf between what he does and the recognition he gets in return and I think that's terrible.

It was ironic, therefore, that it was Scholes' miss in the penalty shoot-out that in effect gave us the FA Cup in 2005. We had been looking forward to playing our old 'enemy' in the final and, for me, it was going to be my fifth and, as it turned out, my last for Arsenal. I love everything about those games; getting the suits fitted, the build-up to the match in the hotel and on the coach, then walking out on to the pitch before the game, seeing all the supporters, and soaking up the atmosphere. It's a fantastic feeling. We all know what a big day it is for us players and for the fans as well. You can't get a better final than Arsenal versus Manchester United, so I couldn't wait. Defeat for us would have meant a trophyless season, so we were determined to avoid that. Even the players who were playing in their first final and who some people thought might be intimidated by the occasion, were ready for the challenge and for the incredible experience that is an FA Cup Final.

To be honest, everyone agrees that United were the better team for long phases of the game. We were missing Henry who had aggravated his Achilles tendon injury and that meant we had less attacking potential than usual. Although Robin van Persie went close with a free kick in extra time, Manchester United came very close on a number of occasions. Rooney, who was named Man of the Match, had three shots on goal, whilst van Nistelrooy had a late header from a few yards out that was heart-stoppingly nodded out on the line by Ljungberg who headed it against the bar, then out to safety. It's true that there were times when we were lucky but in the end, we kept to our task and, if we couldn't score, it was crucial at least that we prevented United from scoring themselves.

In extra time, the game was incredibly tight. We were being cautious, as we knew it would be catastrophic to give away a goal at that stage. We worked very hard for each other, and our spirit was fantastic, so it didn't matter when, just as the 120 minutes came to an end, Reyes got a second yellow card for bringing down Ronaldo and was sent off.

When it came to the penalties, we lined up Lauren, Ljungberg, van Persie, Cole, then me to take the final one. I agreed with the order and with the fact that my penalty might well decide our fate one way or the other.

United's first penalty-taker was van Nistelrooy. He took a very short run-up and sent Jens Lehmann the wrong way. 1–0. Lauren then calmly side-footed his into the top corner. 1–1. Scholes was next. He drove the ball towards the corner but Jens dived to the same side and saved it. From then on, United were playing catch-up. Freddie remained calm and chipped his kick down the middle, just after Roy Carroll had moved to one side. 2–1 to us. Ronaldo scored with no problem, as did van Persie, Rooney and Cole. 4–3 to us. That left the two skippers to fight it out. If Roy Keane scored, it was all down to me. He did his job, sending the ball to the corner of the net with his right foot. Then I had what turned out to be my last kick for Arsenal. Roy Carroll actually moved in the right direction but my shot still found the back of the net. The Cup was ours, we all went crazy and the celebrations were incredible.

Penalties are all about keeping your nerve and having a bit of luck. It was a tough game for us and I have to give credit to Manchester United who created so many chances and who were just unlucky. It was the first time in history that the FA Cup had been decided on penalties and it gave everybody a final to remember.

In every country there are one or two teams who are the best and when those teams meet, you know how important the result is. When you win a game against United, you know it will be important in deciding either the Premiership or something like the FA Cup. Every game is crucial. That's why, in the end, Manchester United were always my favourite enemy. I experienced everything against them, every emotion: the joy of victory, the sadness of defeat. And there were great tensions between us as well. I have known injustice, incredible matches. And when we won, we really celebrated. In fact, the games had everything that football can throw at you. Manchester United is probably one of the teams against which I have experienced the most emotion. I felt hate towards them, but also love. Because without United, my memories would not be as powerful. And that is a priceless feeling.

13

Red Cards and Refs

I don't need to be reminded of the fact that, in my nine years at Arsenal, I got sent off precisely ten times and had a few run-ins with referees and officials. I think I need to explain how some of those incidents felt from my point of view and what effect they had on me personally and professionally.

One of my first red cards, for example, was against Charlton Athletic in December 1998 when a bad foul by one of their players had really angered me. Although I had just about controlled myself at the time, I raised my elbow unwisely later on in the game which earned me a red card. Fair enough, but I had been brought to boiling point as the game had progressed and in the end had retaliated. I had not gone out to attack the player concerned, because I have never done that. I was just overreacting in the heat of the moment to the situation on the pitch.

I was already the focus of attention for the opposition because, two weeks before that game, I had been fined £20,000 for making a V-sign at Sheffield Wednesday supporters at the end of our game at Hillsborough earlier in the season. But the reality was that the gesture had been made in response to racial abuse from the fans that I had had to suffer for much of the game.

The first two games of the 2000/1 season were amongst the worst moments of my years at Arsenal. The first, away at Sunderland, was a game which was going really well for me until an incident in the 90th minute. Throughout, Darren Williams had been unsuccessfully doing all he could to hold me back. Right at the end of the match, he had one final go, pulling my shirt back in such a way that I tried to break loose and, in so doing, I put a forearm to his face. I wasn't intentionally aiming to injure him – like I have said, that's not what I am about. But the referee was having none of it: he instantly dismissed me. After the game, both Williams himself and the Sunderland boss, Peter Reid, who knows a thing or two about physical players having been one himself, came to my defence. Williams said, 'I was pulling him back and I thought the ref was going to book me. Patrick only brushed me with his forearm. It wasn't as bad as it must have looked.' Peter Reid backed him by adding, 'I thought he was desperately unlucky to be sent off. I don't think his arm was raised maliciously.' It was nice to have been vindicated by them, but it came all too late, of course, to change the situation.

The next game, three days later, was at home to Liverpool. Graham Poll, the referee, somehow lost control of the game: Liverpool were reduced to nine men and my departure sent us down to ten. Already in the first half, perhaps because of my Sunderland game, I had come under the unwanted attention of Jamie Carragher, who caught me in a late tackle. Then, in the 38th minute, it was Gary McAllister's turn to lunge at me with what at first appeared to be both feet. Off he went, while I lay on the ground for a few minutes in agony before having to go off temporarily to get treatment on the sidelines. Halfway through the second half, Carragher went for me again with yet another crude tackle. This time, I couldn't stop myself, the anger that had been bubbling up inside me came to the surface and I was booked for retaliation. Soon after, a clash with Dietmar Hamann saw me receive my second yellow card and I was straight off for an early bath, my game prematurely over for the second time in successive games. The fact that Hamann came off at the same time (for his own second yellow card) made no difference. Nor did the fact that Liverpool manager Gérard Houllier again vindicated me by saying after the game, 'I didn't think any of the red cards were right, not Patrick Vieira's either.' The reality was that I had once again let a difficult situation get to me and had acted in retaliation. I had not, however, been the instigator.

It goes without saying that the media went to town. The 'hot-headed Frenchman', they called me. The media love to pigeon-hole people and in many ways I was Arsenal's answer to Eric

Cantona who had regretfully (as far as they were concerned) left England and retired from the game. I fitted the bill perfectly, and provided them with lots of wonderful column inches.

After those two dismissals, however, I was in despair. Immediately after the incidents, I even thought that I might give up on England and go back to the Continent to play my football. I was that upset with what had happened and the way in which I seemed to be targeted both by opponents and by referees. My friend Manu Petit, who had just left for Barcelona, had even publicly stated that his own move that summer had in part been influenced by the sort of problems I was now experiencing. He feared I might end up joining him in Spain for the same reason. Frank Leboeuf, my French team-mate who was at Chelsea, had also been quoted as saying that 'English fair play is a myth. I have never seen as much violence on the pitch as in England.'

I had a long talk with Arsène Wenger who was quite honest with me: however unfair or unjustified each of the incidents might have been, I had to face up to my responsibilities and learn to control myself. He supported me in public but he told me that I had to accept the reality of playing in the English League. I had a long think about what he told me and, though I found it hard to swallow, I eventually accepted that he was right.

I knew that I had the sort of temperament that could flare up easily on the pitch. Whereas off it, I am generally someone who is fairly laid-back and calm, in a match situation, I can get wound up quite quickly. I am human after all, I have weaknesses, and, because of the position I play on the field, I have to play a physical game. Playing in midfield as I do, I have to get stuck in, I can't avoid confrontations with players, I have to commit to balls and be 100 per cent involved. I can't be frightened of sticking my foot in, and in fact nobody can ever accuse me of not going for the ball, in whatever situation. Inevitably, therefore, I risk getting yellow-carded maybe more than some of my team-mates in other positions.

What I had to accept, though, was not just that my physical style of play might land me in trouble more than some other players but that, as a result of getting a certain reputation, I might attract the attention of opponents and match officials. The fact that I was a foreigner probably didn't help either. What I was slowly realising was that I had to learn to control myself better, not to get carried away in the heat of the moment, however hard that was. Until I did so, I would continue to be on the receiving end of trouble.

There is one incident, though, which even after all these years, I remain ashamed of. Whatever the rights and wrongs of the situation, I know I should not have done what I did. I am talking about the game against West Ham at Upton Park in October 1999. The bottom line was that, after a lot of verbal abuse from Neil Ruddock, I finally lost control completely and ended up spitting at him which obviously earned me an instant red card. Afterwards, he was quoted as saying 'I can still smell the garlic' which brought him a charge of misconduct by the FA and nearly one of racism, although, frankly, that was not the worst that he had come out with that afternoon. But that made no difference to my punishment: a six-match ban and a £45,000 fine. It doesn't actually matter what he had said to me; I know that I was wrong to have reacted like that. Even the boss couldn't support me on that one, and I have to say, that incident is without doubt the lowest point of my Arsenal career. I guess Ruddock was pleased with the result: he had got what he wanted, he had got the Frenchman sent off. If I were to see him now though – and I have never had occasion to come across him since – I know that I wouldn't bother talking to him about the incident. Neil Ruddock is not someone I'm interested in talking to.

The double sending-off at the start of the 2000/1 season, and in particular the discussion I had had with the boss afterwards, caused me to think and made me determined to try to calm down on the pitch. Obviously I was never going to change my personality completely but since that time, there has been a reduction in the number of incidents I have been involved with. I only got sent off once in the following season, in our 4–0 early-season win against Leicester City. A year later, we played Chelsea at Stamford Bridge. The referee in both matches was Andy d'Urso. In the first half, I was booked for a tackle on

Gianfranco Zola, then in the second, I got another yellow card and my marching orders for apparently catching Gronkjaer's foot. I think I was unlucky to be booked on both occasions, because with Gianfranco, I went for the ball and he jumped over the tackle. The referee in my opinion got it wrong. It looked spectacular more than anything else, that was all. For the second one, I could understand why the referee thought Gronkjaer was hurt. When he fell to the floor, he was screaming. But Jesper is a good guy. After the match he was quoted as saying that it was more a case of him catching my foot rather than the other way round: 'As I kicked through, I hit the bottom of Patrick's boot. I don't think it was deliberate.' So I think the referee was wrong on both counts and that the sending-off was therefore harsh.

In the past, I might have got really angry about the injustice of the red card, but by then I had come round to accepting that these mistakes do happen. Referees are human as well, after all. I'm not saying I was pleased when errors were made at my expense, and I was very angry at the time when Andy d'Urso sent me off, but once I had calmed down off the pitch, I learned to tolerate them better. Equally, the fact that it was the same referee who had sent me off the previous season was, I believe, a coincidence. In any case, I had decided I wasn't going to get steamed up about whether or not my reputation was now going before me and affecting a referee's judgement. I know my conscience was clear in that I had never gone on the pitch with the intention of hurting anyone. If referees felt that they needed to be harsher to me than to others, that was their problem. I couldn't afford it to be mine.

If I worried about what refs thought of me and if I thought I might be unfairly treated by them, then I might as well not go on the pitch that day. I have noticed over the years that sometimes I would be booked for shouting out 'F*** off' or some other very Anglo-Saxon word, whereas another player, using exactly the same language, might get off without even a word of warning. And of course, between us, we would discuss certain referees and some of my team-mates might say to me, 'This ref, he obviously can't stand you,' and we would all agree. But again, you can't let that sort of thing affect the way you play. I decided that, no matter what, I would never change the way I played. I am a physical player, in a midfield position requiring a lot of physical commitment. All I had to try to do was learn to retaliate less if a player got to me. I had to learn to control my temper if it was in danger of erupting. I couldn't do more than that. And I believe that, over the years, I genuinely made that effort and it did pay off. Since being made Arsenal captain in the summer of 2002, I was only sent off twice in Premiership or Cup matches, each time as a result of collecting two yellow cards.

Another thing I realised over the nine years I spent in England is that football there is a passion, both for the fans and for the players. The former support their club with a passion that is unknown on the Continent, and the players play with a passion that is also rare abroad. English players are perhaps less technical, less into a tactical, passing style of play than those from other European countries but they make up for these shortcomings by playing with real intensity. I have to say that I love that about the English game: nowhere else do players and fans get as emotionally involved in a game. But that's why, in England, the game is more physical and why, as a result, it can sometimes overheat. In other countries, a player might get red-carded for something that in England doesn't even get a free kick. In the heat of the moment, it's sometimes difficult not to react, but in the end, I understood that that was how the game was played.

What I do think is a shame, though, is that there used to be greater communication between players and referees than there is now. In the past, a referee might have a quick chat with me about an incident on the pitch and we would be able to sort it out sensibly, without resorting to anything official. I got to know some of the referees over the years, my relationship with them improved, they saw me as a human being that they could talk to. Recently, though, there have been so many rulings from on high, either from FIFA or the FA, that I think referees feel pressure to follow the letter of the law. There are too many rules and regulations, in my opinion, and referees resort too quickly to handing out yellow cards, instead of trying to sort the situation out in another way. They have lost the 'feel' of the game, they have lost contact with players and as a result the relationship between match officials and players is now much more impersonal, much more 'us and them'. I think that is unfortunate because it doesn't help good relations and I'm not sure there is any way back.

My problems with referees had definitely been lessening by the time I left Arsenal. I think with age and maturity, I had come to understand certain things. I had realised that I was a certain type of player, and that referees had a job to do. Sometimes my aims on the pitch did not coincide with theirs. It took me a while to understand this and to adapt to how things are in England. Already, I have collected a sending-off playing for Juventus in the opening game of the 2005/6 Champions League against Bruges, receiving a straight red card for a late tackle. I know all about the pressure of progressing in the Champions League and hope that the result – we lost the game 2–1 – won't prevent us from qualifying for the later stages of the competition. Now, I will see whether I have to adapt once more to how things are in Italy. If I do, let's hope it doesn't take me nine years.

14

Real Madrid

The story with Real goes back to the 2004 European Championships. We had just played our first match against England and I took a phone call from the agent of a friend of mine at Real who is in regular contact with the Madrid club. He told me that Real were hot, they really wanted to sign me. Some contact had already been made in previous seasons but never anything very concrete.

The first time that he spoke to me on the phone, the conversation was very brief.

'Real want you very much. Are you interested?'

'Listen, I've always heard that Real were keen on me but I'm fine at Arsenal, I don't want to leave just for the sake of leaving.'

A few hours later, I got another phone call from him.

'I've just spoken to the president of Real, he wants to speak to Arsenal about you. But before he begins negotiations with your club, he wants to know if you are ready to consider a transfer.'

That was when I realised things were getting serious and I gave him my permission for contact to be made between the two clubs. After that, I immediately called the manager. I told him that Real had been in touch with me and that I would like to have talks with them, that I had a genuine desire to embark on a new adventure. Arsène was surprised; in fact he was lost for words. On top of everything, we were right in the middle of the European Championships.

The situation was a bit bizarre for me. I was completely focused on the tournament, but as soon as I got back to my room, the phone would start to ring and discussions would begin again.

After the third match, against the Swiss, I bumped into Arsène in the players' car park. He was with David Dein, Arsenal's vice-president. We exchanged a few words and he told me to call him the next day. At that stage, their position was very clear. It was out of the question that I might leave to go to Real or anywhere else for that matter. I completely understood their point of view but for me to go to Real Madrid would have been a progression, the next stage in my career. At the time, it was the only club for which I would have left Arsenal. Arsène and David were surprised because it came at a bad time. We had just won the Premiership title and had been unbeaten all season. They were at a loss as to how to react to my decision.

At that point, some people might think that my desire was driven by money considerations. Stories started coming out in the press about how much Beckham and Zidane were getting paid and how much I was supposedly being offered. It goes without saying that all the rumours about me wanting to be paid the same as them were false. At Arsenal, I was very well paid. In terms of salary, in fact, Real Madrid were offering more or less what I was earning at Arsenal. The issue, given what was on offer, was never one of money.

I had reached a point where I had to take stock of where I was professionally. I had just finished my seventh season with the Gunners. I had won practically everything there was to win and now I had the opportunity to play with Figo, Zidane, Ronaldo, who all embodied everything Real Madrid stood for. It was one of the most glamorous clubs in the world. Perhaps even *the* most.

Of course, I talked to Zizou about it at once. In fact, as soon as I received that first phone call. He was well placed to discuss things with me. I went to see him because I needed to have him confirm certain things for me. I needed to know if all this was really serious or if they were only messing me around, like in the previous years. Zizou obviously wanted me to come. He knew that the club needed a player like me, with my particular skills. He knew that my arrival would strengthen Real's defence and give them greater possession of the ball. But Zidane is a man of few words; he doesn't talk much. So he had his own way of making me understand the situation.

During this time, I didn't speak to anyone else about this initial contact because I didn't yet know what was going to happen. I knew very well what went on with agents and I was far from sure that negotiations were really going to take place. In the end, it was Zizou who brought me the confirmation I was waiting for. Once he told me that it was certain, then for me, it was definitely true: Real were on board. Even though this was something of massive importance, and surely my biggest career decision to date, I didn't let it get to me. I managed to keep cool about it, and not let it take over my every thought. I'm quite strong mentally so I didn't let it stop me playing my game. But it's also true that I spent whatever free time I had at the Championships on the phone to check what was going on. I was only in touch with Alain, though, and I never talked directly to anyone from Real Madrid.

The European Championships came to an end and the story started to leak out into the papers. The media got on to it after Real's president got re-elected. He then let slip something like 'I want the best team in the world and I want the best defensive midfielder in the world'. Then he said my name. Predictably, the whole of the English media sprung into action. 'Vieira is leaving; Real want him; the president of Real has always had the players he wanted, Figo, Zidane, Ronaldo, Beckham. Now he'll have Vieira.'

I didn't take too much notice of all this speculation because I was used to it. After our elimination by the Greeks from the European Championships, I decided to leave at once for the Caribbean. I passed through London very briefly. The holiday would be only a short one, so I didn't want to hang around. During the holiday, I stayed in touch with Alain. After the Caribbean, I flew off to Miami. Things hotted up by the day and became increasingly certain right up to the day we were due back. But even during my holiday, I never once spoke to anyone from Real Madrid itself.

The person I did often speak to during those weeks over the summer was my mother. I'm very close to her, she was always there for me when I was young, guiding me. She is such a strong woman. When we first moved to France she worked during the day and studied in the evenings, and we didn't see much of her, but I knew she was fighting very hard for us, to give us what we wanted and what we needed. I knew she had my best interests at heart, so I turned to her to help me. That's what I had wanted to do nine years before when I had signed for AC Milan and had not even been allowed to call her to discuss with her the fact that I was about to sign the contract. This time, I was determined that the situation should not repeat itself. I asked her whether she thought I should leave or stay at Arsenal, the club at which I had achieved so many dreams. Not surprisingly, I suppose, she couldn't give me an answer. Instead, she gave me the confidence to think that I was able to make the right decision, that I was now old enough and experienced enough to know what would be in my best interests. I knew she was right, but I still could not make up my mind.

The first time that happened was once I got back to London. The phone call took place at David Dein's house. A few days later, we left to go for pre-season training in Austria. The last time I had seen the manager was in the car park in Portugal after the France–Switzerland match. Since then, I had only spoken to him on the phone. I would tell him that I wanted to think about this opportunity. He would reply that I should wait until I saw him during the pre-season training.

Once we reached Austria, Arsène and I arranged to have a couple of informal meetings between just the two of us. The atmosphere was one of calm. The rest of the time, we went about our training in the same way. Afterwards, slowly but surely, we started to get to the heart of the matter. At first, the discussion with Arsène focused on my objectives, and on the questions I was asking myself. I told him that I was twenty-eight, that I was wondering if it was not time for me to experience life at another club and that that club could only be Real Madrid. I had always been very clear in my head that if I did not leave after these negotiations, then I would never, ever leave.

This talk did me a lot of good because I felt that Arsène understood my aspirations. That's why he left the door open for me. I could leave if I really wanted to. I really appreciated his attitude. He didn't get all entrenched, saying, 'You're not leaving, you're under contract and you'll stay here until the very end in 2007.' There was no negotiating an extension of my contract at that stage, there was no bidding war going on between me and Arsenal and I never had the intention of obtaining anything extra from them.

At that stage, I was sure I wanted to leave. Yes, I was sure . . . Because I could feel that my departure for Real was becoming ever more definite. Everything was in place for me to leave. That's what I had told David Dein and the manager when we were in Austria. After a while, they told me that they were leaving me to make up my own mind. The door was staying wide open but I had to inform them of my final decision by Thursday 12 August, because they had to be clear where things stood by the eve of the start of the new season on the 14th, which was completely understandable.

I wasn't at all surprised by their reaction. David Dein, the manager and I have always had a very good relationship. We have always been frank with one another. I told them exactly what I was feeling. They talked about the services I had given to the club over the last seven years, about how the team had progressed thanks to my skills, and how much I had given of myself. I took that to mean that they were grateful for what I had done. It was during the pre-season training in Austria and the subsequent tournament in the Amsterdam Arena that I once again injured my thigh. I had been plagued with this injury since the European Championships; that was why I had been forced to miss our quarter-final against Greece.

Psychologically, also, I was not up to it. I had one foot in Arsenal and the other already on the road to Madrid. That was when I really started to ask myself some serious questions. I was nearer the end of my career than the beginning. My last experience of a club could well be at Real Madrid. To leave . . . or not to leave . . . that was the question.

The pre-season training camp was a psychologically difficult time for me. I didn't say anything but the other players knew what was going on. They read the papers and it was all over the back pages. Even though I had not been quoted, the players weren't fooled; they knew there was no smoke without fire. I decided not to speak to the press. With hindsight, I'm glad I didn't. But occasionally I would tell myself that I should say something for the benefit of all the Arsenal fans because I would read things in the papers that were simply not true. Really stupid things. For example, that I had fallen out with Thierry and Robert during Euro 2004 and that was why I wanted to leave. Or else that I was leaving for financial reasons, that Real were offering me a better contract than Arsenal, even that my house was up for sale ... Loads of things were written that were complete lies. In the end, I decided that it was better for me not to say anything. If I started to talk, I would never stop. I preferred to let people say what they wanted, and for things to sort themselves out. But there were times when it was really hard to stick to my decision.

That period was unpleasant to live through because lies were being told about me. Luckily, my relationships with David Dein and with Arsène allowed me to stay relatively calm. They were always aware of what was going on, from the very beginning through to the very end. Things have always been totally out in the open between the three of us.

In fact, I was more concerned about my relationship with the fans. I had always had a fantastic bond with them, so I didn't want the image they had of me to be tarnished by everything that was being said. I told myself that the day I left Arsenal, I would like them to think that I had served the club right up until the end with determination and with no regrets.

I don't think that my image was affected after my decision to stay but people looked at my performances with a different eye. The general public and the press watched my games more closely because they wondered why I hadn't gone to Real Madrid. In their minds, I hadn't left because I chose the easy option of staying at Arsenal. I'm convinced that's what people thought. And that's why I felt under a certain amount of pressure during the 2004/5 season. Much more so than the season before that. Mind you, I could handle it. What's more, I liked it . . .

As crazy as it might seem, I only spoke once to Florentino Perez, the president of Real Madrid. In fact, I spoke to him the day that I decided not to leave and to stay instead at Arsenal.

David Dein had called me into his room one day when we were in Austria so that we could talk. As we had always been very honest with each other, he told me that, together with the manager, they had struck an agreement with Real and would let me go. As for me, I never got involved in any discussions concerning the transfer fee. Once, an agent had approached David Dein and had offered to sell me for £7m. He was taking the piss. I was really surprised by that completely absurd offer. I knew very well that I was worth more than that. After the pre-season training in Austria where I asked David Dein to begin negotiations, we set off for Amsterdam. Then we returned to London.

I didn't play in the Community Shield game on 8 August because I was still carrying my thigh injury. In fact, I didn't go to the game, preferring to watch it on TV at home. After the final whistle, with my younger team-mates having played really well against Manchester United, Arsène gave me a sort of ultimatum, saying that I needed to make my mind up because we were almost at the start of the new season. Our first match was on a Sunday and I had to make my decision by the Thursday before, which was 12 August. Pressure was mounting and I could feel it was starting to have a stronger and stronger hold on me. I think that at that stage Arsène had abandoned all hope of keeping me because whenever I spoke to him, I would reiterate my continuing desire to leave.

The deadline had not yet been reached and I still had a little bit of time left to think. Forty-eight hours before I had to tell the club what I had decided, I went to the final training session. Throughout this whole time, I had carried on training and, more importantly, looking after myself, as if nothing was going to change. I still smiled in the same way. So two days before the actual day, I was just leaving the training ground. David Dein was in the manager's office. He told me that everything now rested on me because he had spoken on the phone to the Real president, Perez, and the two clubs had agreed a transfer fee. This was now the Wednesday before the start of the Premiership. Then he looked at me and said 'You know, as long as nothing has been signed, we can always change our minds.' I told him that I was aware of that but that my position had not changed. But because he knew me well, he looked me squarely in the eyes and said 'I sense that you're a lot less calm about things, what's going on?' It was as if the nearer my departure date got, the more I was starting to change my mind. I even wonder if that is a bit what happened to Steven Gerrard at the end of the 2004/5 season when he decided to stay at Liverpool after all, despite the fact that everyone thought he was about to go to Chelsea.

In any case, after my latest meeting with David Dein, I went home. I spoke to Cheryl that evening. I don't like to talk about my private life because I don't want to play the celebrity game – I have seen where that gets people. So all I will say is that I met Cheryl at a Destiny's Child concert a few years back and she has been with me ever since. She is originally from Trinidad but she has lived in England for over fifteen years. Because her first language is English, she helped me a lot to learn the language and to adapt to the English way of living. What I love about her is that she's an independent woman. She likes to do her own thing. As far as she was concerned, her position was always quite clear: she would have preferred to stay because we were happy here, we had a fantastic house in Hampstead, a nice lifestyle and we didn't know what we would find in Madrid. So it was difficult for her to give her opinion, and for her to know whether we should go or we should stay. She didn't want to interfere with my decision. She preferred me to make this important choice on my own and I was grateful to her for that. She never put any pressure on me one way or the other. She didn't with my move to Juventus either.

I spent Wednesday evening at home knowing that I had to give my reply by the following evening. I decided I needed some advice, so I called Dennis Bergkamp. He's probably the person I know best at the club. He arrived there a year before me, and were sort of the two 'survivors'. By now, I was completely confused in my head. I kept asking myself a thousand questions. In fact, I no longer had any idea what I should do: I felt like I was divided into two. I was completely unsettled – but partly in a positive way. I wasn't exactly out on the streets, after all. There are worse things in life than having to choose between Arsenal and Real Madrid. I was in a quandary but not in despair. I just wanted to be certain that I was making the right decision. I have been lucky that I have always made the right choices throughout my career. This could be the last one I would have to make but it was without doubt the most difficult one so far.

So Wednesday evening I called Dennis. I told him that I was really stuck between two stools and I asked him what he thought. He told me that, as far as he was concerned, Real Madrid represented the ultimate dream for all players but that on the other hand it was tough to let go of everything that I had here. In the end, he couldn't tell me whether to go or to stay because things were so evenly balanced. We talked for a full half-hour then, when I hung up, I called Thierry, because I knew he would tell me what he really thought. And it was the same as with Dennis. I hadn't said a word to Titi beforehand but when I talked to him that evening, he couldn't tell me either whether to leave or to stay because of all the respect we had for each other. Thierry obviously wanted me to stay, as he was to tell me some time later, but that evening, he didn't want to influence me. In the end, after having spoken to the two of them, I was no clearer in my head, quite the reverse. And I still hadn't decided what to do.

I was left alone with Cheryl. I thought about all the good things that I had here at Arsenal. About the relationship that I had with the fans, that I felt I would never find anywhere else, or at least not at Real Madrid. About the recognition I received from my team-mates, my manager, the fans and everyone who worked at the club, from the guys in the club shop right through to the secretaries. That relationship was extraordinary on a daily basis. I have never once got up in the morning and thought I didn't want to go to training. I was very happy with my contract, I earned a very good living. On top of that, my everyday life in London was pretty laid back. I went out, wandered around and lived life to the full. I was always hanging out with some of my team-mates at our favourite café right in the middle of Hampstead, surrounded by shoppers, and no one ever bothered us, they barely gave us a second glance, even if they recognised us. I used to love going there after training with Robert or Thierry just watching the world go by. I never questioned where I could go here or if there would be too many people who might bother me. I could do my own thing. I could see that at Madrid, it was a pain in the arse for some of the guys just to go out and have dinner; I could see that when we went to play against Valencia, we would have all those problems with racism which are still going on to this day, especially, sadly, in Madrid – as we saw with Ashley Cole and the other black England players during the Spain–England match in the autumn of 2004. That was unbelievably bad and it has been happening in Spain for a while now. All these things obviously carried some weight and influenced my decision.

Perhaps I would have been fulfilled and happy professionally. I spoke to Claude (Makelele) and Zizou. The club itself was huge and Zizou is very happy there. Claude, before he transferred to Chelsea, was also very happy there. But outside that framework, the players could not do anything. They could not go out to eat, to shop. Everything was complicated. Here, in London, either during the week or on a Saturday, Cheryl and I could go shopping, we could push our trolley round the supermarket aisles. Not to mention the fact that I had come to really enjoy my Sundays, relaxing reading the papers and sometimes even having an English breakfast! In Madrid, all that would simply be impossible. These little things might seem like a minor problem set against the wider background of a career but, in reality, they were the sort of details that could truly become a problem.

Because to be good on the pitch, it certainly helped to be relaxed off it.

When it came to the football, I was also asking myself lots of questions. Here at Arsenal, I could express myself fully. I could attack, defend, really get stuck into the match. I loved getting the ball, even if it was just to make little passes. I knew Real, since losing Claude, were really looking for someone in defence; someone who could play just in front of the defenders and who, in the end, would not move around much. And if I was honest, that was not really the sort of position I was looking for. I would have kept it up for a couple of matches but after that I would have found it 'balls-aching'.

I thought long and hard about all of that because I had to think absolutely everything through before I made my decision. But on the day, when you have to choose and you're at home going 'Arsenal's got this, Real's got that', then everything seems very complicated. I also had to think of the future. I could not deny that I was twenty-eight and that I was nearer the end of my career than the beginning. At Arsenal, we had a younger team than at Real, which was getting to the end of a generation of players, more so than we were.

So that Wednesday evening, sitting on my sofa, I made my final decision. Before going to bed that night, I told myself, 'Tomorrow, I'm clear about it now, I'll tell them that I don't want to leave any more.' There wasn't really a turning point. It's just that I had thought it through. It was a global decision. I'm incredibly grateful to the manager and to David Dein because they did not put pressure on me, even though it must have been tough for them because I had told them about it all at the last moment. They would not have had time to prepare for my departure. Who would they have bought to replace me, for example? Despite that, they had never insisted that I gave them a reply any sooner.

I told Cheryl on Wednesday evening that I had decided to stay. She was happy for me especially because I had finally made my choice. Thursday morning, I bumped into Titi and told him that I no longer wanted to leave, that I had had a good think. He was happy too because we were really building something good together. He told me much later on that if I'd left, it would have broken up all sorts of things. After training, I went home. I didn't even see Arsène that morning. At about 5 pm, I called David Dein. 'Listen, I don't want to leave any more. I'm staying put,' I said. He seemed surprised. I'm sure he had assumed that I was about to confirm to him that I was leaving. That evening, I had planned to go to the cinema with Cheryl and her brother to take my mind off things because my head was about to explode. But when he heard my news, David Dein immediately said to me, 'I'm at Arsène's house, come over!'

So I jumped in my car and drove over to Arsène's home in Totteridge, which is in North London. They were both there, grinning. I settled down, calmly. With his wry smile, the manager teased me gently. 'So, what's going wrong, what's happening, you don't want to leave? But only a short while ago, you seemed determined to go, what made you change your mind?'

I then went through with them my train of reasoning and all the thoughts and feelings that I had had on the way to making my decision. I told them what my worries were about going to Madrid. Arsène interrupted me. 'I hope you're not choosing the easy option.'

I completely understood his concerns and I thought they were totally natural. I therefore had no difficulty in reassuring him and confirming that in no way had I chosen Arsenal because it was the easy way out. I wanted to stay because I felt we could win a lot together, because I was happy there and because I thought I still had something to contribute to the team. I wanted to win the Champions League with Arsenal because that was something that was close to my heart.

I also thanked him for allowing me the time to make a decision. I knew that it must have been a really difficult time for him and for the club whilst they waited for me to make my mind up, especially since the season was about to start again and they had to plan how they would have built the team without me. I told him he could help me to improve, that we had a great squad with Henry, Campbell, Cole and the rest. I was very emotional when I told him all this. The boss had always been fantastic to me and I wanted him to know all the reasons why I had decided to remain at Arsenal in the end.

Arsène told me he was very happy that I was staying because I was captain of the team and the team would be stronger with me in it. The whole of the conversation took place in French. David Dein was next to us but he understands our language very well. 'The club is very pleased you are staying but we have to call the president of Real so that you can tell him yourself about your decision.'

David Dein then called the club president, Florentino Perez. It was the first time since the start of negotiations that I had spoken to him. 'Listen, sir, I'm really sorry to let you know at the last minute, but in the end I'm not coming. It's very difficult for me to leave Arsenal. I'm going to stay here because I feel good here and because that's where I want to finish my career.' Mr Perez wished me good luck, he told me that it was no problem, that it was just a shame for Real Madrid. He thanked me for having called him personally in order to tell him. A real gentleman.

Later, I still managed to go to the cinema because I needed to think of something else. I can't remember what I saw, because my head was full to bursting with everything that had been going on over the last few days. Thoughts and emotions had been swirling around inside me and making the final decision had obviously been a huge step for me. So to this day, I still cannot remember what on earth I sat through at the cinema! Of course, it didn't matter anyway.

The next day, there was a press conference. The same questions kept coming up. 'Why didn't you say anything beforehand?' 'Why did you take so long to explain your situation?' 'What happened with Real?' 'Why didn't you leave?' 'The fans blame you for not saying anything.' I wasn't thrown at all by the questions because I was ready for them. In fact, I had been mentally preparing the press conference from the moment I had left the boss's house the evening before. I knew that it would be ... not exactly difficult, well, maybe yes, a bit.

Above all, I was very aware that at that precise point in the season, people were split into two camps; there were those who were in favour of me going, and those who wanted me to stay. Some would no doubt say, 'With Vieira, it's always the same. One day it's "yes", the next day it's "no",' or else 'He's going, he's not going, he's not saying anything, that's not right.' Then there were the others, luckily, who would simply say, 'We're pleased that he's staying.'

In the end, everything went very well. The Arsenal fans that I met or the people who worked for the club were all very happy about my decision. That was the most important thing for me. I was worried that the fans would bear a grudge against me after the whole saga.

I need to be very clear: since my arrival all those years ago, it was the first time that a transfer rumour was in the least bit based on truth. Since the summer of 2001, there have been stories every summer in the press that I was about to leave and go to clubs such as Manchester United, Juventus or Real Madrid. In the past, all those pieces of gossip had come from agents or other clubs. In any case, this was my first real contact with Real. Two years before, a photo of me in Madrid had been published but that day I was there because I'd flown over to see Claude Makelele who had just become the father of a baby girl. I had not been in touch with anyone. The front-page photo, the alleged negotiations, the whole story was a complete fabrication. I'm convinced that the length of time it was taking for my thigh injury to heal was linked to the constant pressure surrounding the Real Madrid situation. It didn't speed up the healing process. During that time, I was on edge and very tense.

Having said that, why shouldn't I consider going somewhere else? It is like anyone, even someone working in a normal office. Another company can come in and offer a better contract and that person has the responsibility of deciding whether to go or stay. The decision might be made for their family and not for themselves. It might be made because they like to work with particular people. But they certainly have the right to consider going elsewhere.

In any event, once I had made my decision, and announced it publicly, I immediately felt a sense of relief, as if a huge weight had been lifted from my shoulders. My head felt lighter too. I got back down to work at once with the idea that I had a lot to prove. I was 100 per cent committed to the club because I felt that I could reach my own personal goals as part of a team, surrounded by friends.

My first game was away to Fulham on 11 September. It went really well and we won 3–0, even though we had been 0–0 at half time. I was really happy to be back in an Arsenal shirt, despite the fact that I didn't play as well as I knew I could. I was still a bit tense because reading so many things in the papers had left me wondering what sort of welcome the fans would give me. I was worried that our relationship had been irretrievably damaged, that the love that existed between the supporters and me would never recover. But the fans gave me a brilliant reception when I ran on to the pitch and they sang my song (V-I-E-I-R-A, to the tune of the Italian song 'Volare' for anyone who hasn't yet heard it) during the warm-up. During the first few games when I was missing from the team because of my thigh injury, I used to watch Arsenal play and hear my song. It was a truly fantastic feeling. It proved something. And that's why I was frightened that the spell might have been broken. It was important for me, it fired me up, it motivated me. As far as I was concerned, if that flow between me and the fans had been interrupted, I would have lost everything. The first game at Highbury itself was in the Champions League against PSV Eindhoven and it too was quite incredible. We didn't play fantastic football, but we defended well, we were patient, and we won by a slender 1–0 which gave us a good start to our Champions League campaign. Best of all, though, the song was still there. That home game was a real psychological turning point for me. I had been reassured by the welcome I had received at Fulham, but Highbury was different: it was our home for all of us. So the relief was all the more enormous.

People can't possibly understand that sort of feeling without having been in my position. If you had stopped somebody in the street and asked him or her, 'Can you understand why Patrick didn't go to Real Madrid?' that person would have replied 'Well, he bottled it.' Even my mates back in France said to me 'What? You didn't go with Zidane, Figo ... You're crazy, this is Real Madrid!' However much I tried to explain, they couldn't understand. Only those who had come to Highbury got it.

Scoring against Spurs in mid-November, in our incredible 5—4 away win, was an amazingly powerful feeling. It was only one goal but it cemented the relationship between the fans and me. And all the questions I had been asking myself over the previous few weeks were swept away in one go. It was really symbolic for them that I scored at White Hart Lane. In fact, it was even more than symbolic: it was the strongest message I could send. The Tottenham game is like no other for the fans. It's the one you have to get right at all cost and I always love playing against them. You can feel the tension between the two clubs, the hate. It's a derby, an age-old rivalry. As Arsène Wenger said afterwards, 'They [derbies] are either completely locked with no chances created, or completely crazy. And this was the crazy version.' Against Manchester United, the tension is based purely on sport and, however strong the rivalry, it's only been going for a decade or so anyway.

In the Tottenham game, we went 1—0 down but Thierry equalised just seconds before half time which gave us just the lift we needed and meant we went into the dressing room in a positive frame of mind. The second half, though, produced an avalanche of goals. First Lauren scored with a penalty, then I did on the stroke of the hour when I dispossessed Naybet and managed to run through the middle for a very satisfying solo effort. We were 3—1 up and looking good but Spurs pulled one back. Freddie then put us 4—2 up, which should have meant we were safe with 70 minutes played. But Spurs never gave up, they kept fighting, and they scored five minutes later. Robert Pires who, earlier, had come on for Reyes then scored the winning goal, although Fredi Kanoute still managed to pull one back for Spurs with two minutes to go. It had been an incredible afternoon, and a derby that will go down in history because it was the first time that there had been nine different scorers in a Premiership game.

As for me, I'm sure I had a greater sense of expectation in respect of the Spurs game than my team-mates did, given what had gone on over the summer. The fans saw that my heart still beat as strongly as ever for the Gunners. This game meant a lot to me because I was emerging from a difficult time. I was playing with a bad ankle which had swollen right up after I had sprained it. The injury took time to mend and some days my ankle had been so swollen that I could not even wear a shoe. I was therefore not 100 per cent fit and the press immediately started to say that I was no longer the same player as before, and that my personal commitment to Arsenal was no longer on the same level: all ridiculous things which were an insult to my professionalism. That's why my goal against Tottenham gave me such enormous joy and why I wanted to share my happiness so much with the fans.

In the end, I'm practically the only player to have turned down the Spanish club. Maybe that's also why they find it hard to understand my decision. To be honest, though, it's not by finishing my career at Real with two or three million pounds more in the bank that I will be any happier. So I was really proud of the decision I made because it wasn't motivated by money. Maybe in football, people are not used to players saying, 'I'm happy, I don't need to go for more money.' But that was the reality with me.

It's impossible to define my relationship with the fans. When we celebrated our Premiership title at the Town Hall in 2004 and all the supporters were there waiting for us, the boss went to speak to them first, followed by me because I was the captain. When I went to address them, they were all chanting my name, and I couldn't make myself heard. That sent shivers down my spine, it really hit me hard. In England, beyond Arsenal Football Club itself, there's a recognition for the work you do, whatever position you play in. You don't have that in other countries, where it's rare to have a defender or a defensive midfielder who is as fêted and loved as a striker. It happens but it's rare. In Europe, all the Golden Boot or other awards are always for the strikers. Over the last twenty years, strikers must have won them eighteen or nineteen times, apart from when Matthias Sämmer won after Euro '96 in England. But that's football, it's the strikers who get the limelight.

That's another reason why, at the time I made my decision to stay, I felt I had everything here when it came to my style of play, my temperament and my everyday life. In the end, it would have been out of the question for me to leave, although it seemed logical that I should at least consider the possibility. If I had said 'No, I don't want to leave, I don't even want to talk to Real,' that would have shown a lack of judgement on my part. Now, when I watch Real play, I tell myself that I was right to stay because they really struggle in midfield. If I watch the defensive midfielders play, I can see that they have an incredibly difficult task.

I obviously spoke to Claude Makelele. He has always said to me that he really liked his time at Real. But I still ask myself questions because when I see a player like Makelele leave because he had not got what he wanted – knowing as I do the importance he had in Real's tactical set-up I have trouble understanding. Especially when I know how rich the club is. If it was not a question of money, though, what was the problem? Was it one of colour? I won't go as far as saying that, but it is difficult to know. In the end, I told myself that they only liked the best, and that colour was not an issue.

I also left a message with Zizou to tell him about my decision. Since then, the subject has never come up for discussion.

Since I made my decision, I have not regretted it for a single moment. I have never told myself 'I should have gone.' Not once. I felt I had nothing to prove to anybody and I made my decision to stay for purely personal reasons, not because I felt I owed it to the club or anything. I was 28, I had been at Arsenal for eight years, and been loyal throughout. The way I felt at the time, I honestly saw myself finishing my career at the club, even if subsequent events have not turned out that way. In any event, that August evening, I made my choice and moved on straight away. Because I never look back.

15

2004/5: My Final Season

The short walk from the centre circle to the penalty spot where I was due to face both Roy Carroll and the Manchester United fans felt like a mile. I was careful to walk very slowly and carefully, and really took my time. It's true that I was under pressure but it was good pressure. It was a positive feeling because I was going to score the goal that would win the FA Cup for my club. The boss had told me that I would be the fifth penalty-taker. I had replied that I had no problem with that at all.

When I saw Paul Scholes miss his shot, or rather when I saw Jens save it, I told myself that all we had to do to win was for us all to score. That might seem like a slightly simplistic way of thinking but in a penalty shoot-out, the situation is a simple one and there are not that many possible scenarios. Slowly but surely, though, the pressure started to get to me. As soon as Ashley scored his penalty to put us 4–3 ahead, I started to fast-forward to my own kick because I had to assume that Roy Keane would score his. Ashley was really tough mentally because he could have buckled, given everything that had been happening to him regarding Chelsea. But he too showed just how much he loved the club that he has been with since he was a boy.

After Keane, their fifth penalty-taker, had scored, levelling the score at 4–4, it was my turn. I really felt that I had miles to walk to the white spot where I had to place the ball. When we had played our UEFA Cup Final against Galatasaray in 2000, I had missed my penalty and, together with team-mate Davor Suker's similar miss, that had lost us the game, but I had since scored several for Arsenal. It was pointless to think about any of that or to think about everything that this final kick symbolised for me in terms of the fans. If I had started to think about my aborted transfer to Real and about the difficult season that had just finished, then I was done for. I did everything I could to stay positive. While I was walking back, I decided to strike the ball with the side of my foot and to the right of the keeper. I just tried to concentrate on the task in hand and to aim for the side netting. The most important thing was to take my time. And I scored! 5–4 to us. After that, it was like a total release. I immediately turned towards Jens because it was thanks to him that we had just won the Cup. That Saturday in May, under the grey drizzly skies of Cardiff, it was the great Lehmann that we all had to congratulate.

Jens is a complex character. He doesn't talk much but sometimes he speaks without saying anything in particular. Above all, though, he's a winner. He was signed in July 2003 from Borussia Dortmund and his arrival coincided with the 2003/4 season during which we were unbeaten. He's German and a professional from another world. He has a bold, aggressive style of play, and he quite often likes coming off his goal-line to intercept passes. Unfortunately, he made a few mistakes over the autumn, and was dropped after the Liverpool match at Anfield at the end of November after he had failed to keep a clean sheet during the previous 11 games. The 2–1 defeat left us 5 points adrift of Chelsea. That game was lost in the 90th minute when Neil Mellor fizzed the winner in from 20 yards out. Mellor, nicknamed Gerd (as in Müller!), was on loan from West Ham, had only scored twice in 21 games and was only playing because all the other Reds' strikers were injured so it was a doubly bitter blow to let one in like that. When Jens lost his place in the team to Manuel Almunia, though, he was obviously not happy because that's what he's like but that's also when he showed what a fighter he was. He was impressive because he fought hard to get his place back and that is exactly what he managed to do two months later, at the end of January. During the FA Cup Final, he displayed those very same fighting qualities and that's why I wanted to salute him in particular.

I therefore found myself lifting the Cup in front of all our supporters. Obviously, I realise what the symbolic significance of my penalty was in terms of my relationship with the fans. After everything that had gone on before and everything that had been said, this victory and this penalty had enormous importance. People cannot possibly understand, though: only at Arsenal can I have such a close relationship with the fans. That's precisely why it was so difficult to leave this club. Almost too difficult, in fact. I had a status, an image that I had created over the seasons. In terms of everything I represent and everything I am, I know full well that things will probably never be the same anywhere else.

I went over to where the fans were. They were singing my song. I was looking out at a sea of red, yet I still managed to pick out some faces, some smiles, some tears, and some rage as well. Beating Manchester United was something our fans would particularly relish; by the same token, I imagine the Red Devils' fans could not think of a more nightmarish scenario. The important thing for us, though, was to bring back the Cup. Whether it was against Man U, Chelsea, Newcastle or Liverpool, the objective was the same. The joy was as well, particularly as we hadn't won the Premiership title, nor the Champions League. The FA Cup was therefore the only trophy we could win, just like Manchester United, in fact. The important thing for us had therefore been to keep our mind on the game and nothing else. It's true, though, that we had expected it to be a really hard game.

The match itself was very tough for us because we didn't play well at all. United were better than us during the entirety of the game, even though we finished stronger during extra time. In fact, the longer time went on, the more we were convinced that we had every chance of winning as long as we didn't concede a goal. We had to go to penalties.

I remember our 2–1 FA Cup Final defeat against Liverpool in 2001. That day, it had been our turn to completely dominate the Reds. Henchoz should have been sent off in the first few minutes for a deliberate handball which should also have earned us a penalty. We had had a good half-dozen clear chances, Freddie had opened the scoring but we had then been punished by a

Michael Owen double in the last ten minutes. So sometimes, we play well and things don't come right for us at the end. Those are tough losses to swallow. At times like that, you tell yourself that that's both the magic and the cruelty of football and that the tide will turn. Against United, it turned in our favour. Equally, Manchester United have also had things turn to their advantage: I think even they would agree that they won the European Champions League at Barcelona's Nou Camp in 1999 against Bayern Munich despite being outplayed until the 89th minute Trailing 1–0, with the trophy already brought out in Bayern colours and referee Pierluigi Collina signalling 3 minutes of stoppage time, United threw everyone forward in desperation and scored twice in two minutes to win. So all teams know that the old cliché, 'the game's not over until the final whistle has gone', is true. We have to accept that but we also have to embrace victory when it is handed to us even when we don't play well. It's obviously much easier to do that.

As it turned out, the FA Cup Final was played in a very good atmosphere, even though Alex Ferguson couldn't stop himself from declaring afterwards that I should have been sent off during the game. To be honest, that little dig didn't affect me at all. Paul Scholes and a few other United players could have got red-carded as well. That sort of statement seems completely pointless to me. I have never made a habit of attacking people through the pages of the press. There's no point, because you don't gain anything by doing it. Not in terms of football, in any case.

On an individual level, I wasn't expecting to be provoked particularly, not like I had been against Blackburn in the semi-final, where we had won 3–0 despite a really physical game involving lots of hard challenges on the part of some of the Blackburn players. We held on and, when we were already 1–0 up, van Persie came on in the last five minutes for Dennis and scored two fantastic goals that will be remembered for a long time to come. First, with his back to goal, he turned defender Lucas Neill, raced towards goal and finished with a low left-foot shot that stormed past the keeper. Then, as if that wasn't enough, in the last minute of the match, he curled home a great shot high into the far side of the net. Unfortunately, as he turned to celebrate, he caught captain Andy Todd's elbow right in the face and had to go off, bloodied and in pain. In that game, I was subjected to endless ugly tackles but I kept my cool which I was proud about. 'We knew Blackburn would be very physical,' said Freddie afterwards. The boss put it even more straightforwardly: 'Can you imagine how the Vieira of six years ago would have reacted?' Ever since I had been at Arsenal, I had got used to taking the knocks but, now that I was captain, I was much more careful about how I reacted.

When it came to the final, then, although we suffered a lot because the game was so long, we also showed a lot of spirit. We never gave up. Given the quality of our play at the tail end of the season and especially during the last few months, I believe we deserved to finish the season with a trophy.

Not surprisingly, after the final, and even before, people started asking me questions about my future. The press wanted to know whether I was going to stay at Arsenal or whether I was going to metaphorically star in yet another summer soap opera, even though I still had two more years to run on my contract.

Arsenal's aim at the end of the season was to keep hold of its young players. I'm convinced that the squad, with talented players such as Philippe Senderos, who replaced the injured Sol Campbell so effectively for the last few months of the season, Gael Clichy, Flamini, Fabregas or van Persie, has a great future ahead. Arsenal has the talent and if you add to it the fighting spirit and the solidarity that we displayed during that final, I believe that great things await them in the years to come.

We finished 2nd in the Premiership at the end of the 2004/5 season and so qualified for the Champions League. It was not so much an achievement as a sign of our fantastic consistency over the years, and of regular good performances. I think that point is worth underlining. We also won the FA Cup for the third time in four seasons.

Overall, therefore, we had a good season, even though we had had higher objectives at the start. But that's how it is at Arsenal.

Every year, we were very ambitious and wanted to win all the competitions that we took part in. Even though we had hoped for better, we still came away with something good at the end. We twice outperformed Manchester United. Firstly in the Premiership where we finished three points ahead of them despite trailing by five with ten games to go. And of course we also beat them in Cardiff.

Nonetheless, over the three games we had against them during the season – I'm deliberately not counting either the Community Shield game in August or our defeat in the Carling Cup where both clubs had chosen to field their youngsters – I think they were better than us. But this Cup Final result shows that our state of mind was stronger than in the other games. Both teams also had a lot of injuries during the season. Van Nistelrooy missed a lot of matches whilst we had Sol Campbell, Edu and especially Gilberto, absent for long periods of time.

Chelsea had the good fortune not to have as many injuries as us or United. Obviously, Damien Duff had some problems, as well as Arjen Robben with his ankle but Petr Cech, John Terry, Frank Lampard and Claude Makelele, their four key players, played in virtually all the games, and when you add it all up, that helped them a lot in the end.

Ever since Chelsea won the Premiership, fifty years after their last title, a lot of experts have stated that the Blues are now set for a period of domination. I don't agree. Obviously, Chelsea's coffers are virtually bottomless, thanks to Roman Abramovich, but Arsenal can compete with them because its players have something else: a passion for their club. In the 2004/5 season, we drew both our games with Chelsea. The first, an exciting 2–2 draw at home in December saw Thierry twice score to put us ahead. His second goal caused a lot of controversy because it came from a quickly taken free kick. The Chelsea defence were still forming a wall when Thierry asked referee Graham Poll what his options were. The referee asked Gudjohnsen to retreat, and, without blowing the whistle, gave Titi the all-clear to shoot, which he did and promptly scored. No rule had been broken, despite what many Chelsea fans thought at the time. To set the matter straight afterwards, the ref explained exactly what had happened. He said 'I asked Thierry Henry "Do you want a wall?" Thierry said "Can I take it please?" He was very polite. I said "Yes." I gave the signal for Henry to take it and that's what he did.' José Mourinho was furious afterwards and complained very loudly in the media. But he must have known what the truth of the situation really was. Chelsea were simply guilty of a lack of concentration. Unfortunately, a late miss by Thierry when he sent the ball over the bar from eight yards out with no goalkeeper in front of him, allowed Chelsea to escape with a draw and to maintain a five-point lead in the Premiership. On the other hand, they dropped a point in the return game at Stamford Bridge in April when we drew 0–0. So yes, Chelsea can buy unbelievable players from all over the world but will they want to fight for their club in the same way that the Gunners do? At Arsenal, the players' daily life is quite simply one of pleasure. They are all happy to be Gunners and that's something that is visible for others to see. It is a fantastic club.

On a personal sporting level, I had a mixed season, even though I finished it better than I began. In reality, I underestimated the psychological impact of my on-off departure for Real Madrid. Although I always insisted that I was totally fine about the whole saga, I turned out to be much more unsettled by it than I thought I had been. With hindsight, I can see that I suffered. I could feel a sort of unease, and an increasing responsibility *vis à vis* my club, my team-mates and our fans. Sometimes, I played really well, as in the FA Cup semi-final against Blackburn, but at other times, particularly in the early part of the season, I was frustrated and tense, because I desperately wanted to show everyone that I was still 100 per cent committed to the club and I felt everyone had doubts about that.

I injured the front of my thigh during our pre-season training. In fact, it was a recurrence of my Euro 2004 injury and I am convinced it happened because I was not fully calm mentally. It prevented me from preparing properly for the season ahead, just as Titi and Sol both were by Achilles tendon injuries.

I then injured my ankle in a clash with Jlloyd Samuel against Aston Villa at Highbury in mid-October. It had been a great game, won 3–1 by us, though we might have won 6–1 if it hadn't been for some amazing saves by their Czech keeper Stefan Postma. For a long time after that game, though, I played with a bad ankle. I couldn't even take time out because Gilberto was badly injured and Edu as well. The club needed me and, although my performances were not of the highest level over that period of time, I am proud to say that I did not hide and that I always gave everything I had, even though that may not always have been good enough.

Consequently, I was disappointed on the whole by my 2004/5 season because physically I was never 100 per cent fit. That said, you have to accept that, after a certain age, you can never play without having some little niggle, and that it is impossible to play to 100 per cent of your physical capacity. But it was a handicap not to have been able to do the close season preparation. You pay for those things down the line. The fact that I was not on top form obviously had a negative consequence on my performances. I got criticised a lot and the papers were always saying that the real Vieira was no longer there. That's not a very nice thing to read but I am always very honest when it comes to my performance. When I am not good on the pitch, I don't need to be told or to read it. I know it. And I have to accept that if you have a certain status and are used to operating at a certain level, then when things go less well, people are quick to say that you are not what you were. And when it came to me, there was the perfect excuse with the story of my so-called transfer to Real the previous summer. The British newspapers said that I should have gone, that my mind and my spirit were no longer committed to Arsenal. It didn't bother me because I know myself well enough. At the start of the season, I did not play well but, with time, I began to improve and to find a satisfactory level. I knew that, given what had happened in the summer of 2004, I was going to be a perfect target. For a year and a half, Arsenal won everything there was to win in England. As soon as our level dropped a little, the press had to find a scapegoat. My shoulders were broad enough, though, plus I knew that those sorts of things went with the job.

The up-and-down nature of my season and of Arsenal's was symbolised by the two-week period in the first half of February when we lost 4–2 to Manchester United in a now famously ill-tempered game, despite the fact that I had opened the scoring with a header and that we had led 2–1 at half time. Although that was a very painful defeat, in front of our home crowd, we bounced straight back in the following two matches by beating, first, Aston Villa 3–1 away, in a game where the team as a whole played skilfully and with total determination. It was as if we needed to prove to ourselves and to the fans that we were still capable of playing football of the highest quality and of beating others both stylishly and easily. On top of everything, that game came in the week when Ashley Cole was involved in controversy because it was revealed that he had been illegally approached by Chelsea. His response to that, and to the taunts by the Villa fans along the lines that he looked good in blue (we were wearing our blue away kit), was to score the third goal. It also just happened to be the goal of the season and will probably be the best he ever scores in his career. It was started by Thierry, just beyond the halfway line, when he pushed the ball through the legs of Olof Mellberg, ignored Eric Djemba-Djemba, the Cameroonian mid-fielder who was closing in on him, then sent a 50-yard pass out to the left. Dennis was on the end of it and he quickly sent it on to Ashley who blasted his shot low inside the far post. He couldn't have scored a more meaningful and impressive goal if he had tried, and it sealed his continuing commitment to the club.

The next game was at home to Crystal Palace and that became a 5–1 annihilation. The team line-up was, for the first time ever in the English professional game, made up entirely of foreign players, including those on the bench. The boss countered any raised eyebrows amongst the media by saying, 'I don't look at the passport, only at the quality and attitude'. Either way, his team selection worked pretty well because in the space of seven minutes not long before the end of the first half, we put three goals past Palace keeper Gabor Kiraly. At the start of the second half, Henry sent a through ball to me and I went past the Palace defence, leaving the keeper sprawled on the ground, before walking the ball over the line and scoring the fourth goal. Once Thierry had added a fifth (and his second that evening) half an hour later, we were home and dry, even though I managed to trip England striker Andy Johnson in the box to give Palace a late consolation penalty. Those two games had gone some way to restoring both my confidence and the team's that we were still very much capable of great performances.

Nonetheless, when it came to my level of play, I didn't much like all the press speculation and analysis because I always want to be the best. I still want to be considered one of the best players in the world in my position. In any event, my fitness problems, along with those of the Brazilians Edu and Gilberto, allowed Mathieu Flamini and Cesc Fabregas to play a lot of games, even though that was not part of the plan, especially for Cesc who was incredible, given that he was still just a seventeen-year-old kid at the time. Cesc arrived from Barcelona when he was just sixteen, in the summer of 2003. In October that year, he made his first-team debut against Rotherham United in the Carling Cup and became the youngest-ever person to play for Arsenal. He scored in his second appearance, against Wolves, which made him the club's youngest ever goalscorer. It was an incredible achievement for him to play at that young age in a central midfield position and in such a physically demanding league as the Premiership. He is very talented. Usually, when you start out, the hardest part is getting rid of the fear of playing badly. Cesc, though, has enormous self-belief. He always wants the ball, even in the most heated situations. He is impressively cool-headed and, despite everything that happened to him over the last two seasons, he has not changed the way he is. He is a future great. In fact, he is almost great already.

As for midfielder Mathieu Flamini, he was just twenty when Arsenal signed him in 2004 from Marseilles, the club he had been with for an incredible fourteen years. He too features in the club's long-term plans and he showed his ability by being part of the starting line-up on many occasions last season.

At one stage, a lot of people thought that the Arsenal team was too young but I wouldn't say that was the case. It is simply made up of a mix between young and old and, at one point, there was an imbalance. You mustn't blame the younger ones. Individually, they all have fantastic qualities. It was more on a collective level that we occasionally went wrong during the season.

It doesn't mean that we lowered our expectations. Financially, Arsenal are certainly less well-off than Chelsea or Man U, but there is more to things than money. When it comes to the game and the life at the club, the Gunners are certainly up there with those two clubs. They have other strong points than just their wallet: being a full squad for example.

Obviously, Gilberto's return in April, after he had fractured a vertebra and been out for eight months, was very beneficial for the team and for me. It coincided with the last part of the season when we dropped only four points from our last eight Premiership games. We also played and won the semi-final and final of the FA Cup. Gilberto and I had played together for three seasons and we had developed a really good rapport on the pitch. It's easy to forget that he is a world champion. He is a more defensive player than me and when he was there, I could go forwards more. It reminds me of a phrase that Roger Lemerre, France's coach when we won Euro 2000, used to say about me. He would talk about my role being '60–40', which meant that I had to attack 60 per cent of the time so that I could defend the rest. When I played with Manu Petit, the percentages were reversed because he was more of an attacker than me at the time. But let's be clear: I'm not looking for excuses. That has never been my style. I just know why I had some problems during a few months of the 2004/5 season. And as a result I'm even prouder of the way in which it ended.

Evidently, Arsenal's big priority now is finally to prove what they can do in the Champions League. During the whole time I was there, our lack of success in the competition remained our biggest disappointment. And yet, I know that they have the potential to do really well and even to win the big jug-eared Cup.

Last season, we fell short once again, and failed to get the results we were capable of. In our group, we beat PSV Eindhoven 1–0 at Highbury which we were pleased with because our aim, after a bad Champions League start the year before, was to start the campaign with a win. PSV are a tough, technically strong side and we were in a difficult group anyway, so drawing away to them 1–1 in the return leg was a good result, particularly as we were down to nine men for the last 15 minutes when both Lauren and I got sent off. Since becoming captain of Arsenal, I had only ever been sent off twice (the first time was the previous season at Old Trafford after the notorious incident with van Nistelrooy which still leaves a bitter taste in my mouth), so this was very unusual for me. It had happened after I got a second yellow card. The game had been really tough that evening and Thierry in particular had taken quite a few knocks. PSV's captain Mark van Bommel hadn't stopped fouling all night, yet we ended up being punished much more harshly than our hosts. It required great determination for us not to fall apart at that stage and we showed we were up to the task. Despite those encouraging results against the Dutchmen, though, they were the ones in the end who had a fantastic Champions League, reaching the semi-final, only to be narrowly beaten by AC Milan.

Our defeat by Bayern Munich in the knockout stage of the tournament left us with a lot of regrets because we completely messed up in the first leg in Munich. We were looking good, even though we had conceded a stupid goal by Claudio Pizarro in the opening minutes. After that, we controlled the game until losing Edu through injury after half an hour, after which we became destabilised and lost our shape. Once they scored their second, I found it harder and harder to drag the team forward and we completely went to pieces in the second half. I'm not quite sure why, even though we were missing Sol Campbell in our back line (he was still out with a twisted ankle). But that is not enough to explain why, in attack, we couldn't seem to make any impression. I managed to hit the post in the second half but, with two minutes to go, we were 3–0 down and about to go out of the tournament, when Kolo Touré's late goal gave us that crucial lifeline for the return leg at Highbury. Still, we were really disappointed by the result. 'The only positive thing is that we should be out, but we are still in,' said the boss, and that just about summed up our evening. We needed to win 2–0 at Highbury but unfortunately only managed a 1–0 victory, Henry's goal not being enough to take us through to the next stage.

Between the first leg at the Olympic Stadium and the return leg at Highbury, we nonetheless had other good results. First of all, we qualified for the FA Cup quarter-final in Sheffield thanks to a 4–2 win in the penalty shoot-out. Almunia, a £500,000 signing from Celta Vigo just before the start of the season, was the hero in that game, tipping a stoppage-time Jon Harley header over the bar before saving two penalties from Alan Quinn and Harley again to take us through. We had had to play without an attacking force because Thierry, Robert and Freddie were all injured, and we were also missing Dennis, Robin and José through suspension. That day, though, with the youngsters in the team, we fought like lions. In this kind of hard battle, you become tired, and afterwards some people were surprised that I had played the full 120 minutes. But that's what I'm like. Plus, I was captain and I felt it was my duty to lead this team full of youngsters for the entire match. In any case, I hate losing and in my opinion all cups are worth lifting, so I never gave up. Too bad for those who counted the minutes.

Then, just a few days before the Bayern Munich 2nd leg, we beat Portsmouth 3–0 at home, thanks to a hat-trick by Thierry Henry, who notched up his 20th, 21st and 22nd Premiership goals of the season. I was pleased to set up the second goal for him when I took the ball from Flamini, played it through to Thierry who was left one-on-one with goalkeeper Chalkias and who then nonchalantly clipped the ball over him and into the net. I like to get into those situations whenever I can and I think, now that I am a bit older, that I can read the game better and time passes more accurately. We were pleased to see Titi back in the starting line-up because he had been out with an Achilles injury which had ruled him out of the FA Cup tie earlier that week and we badly wanted him back in time for the Champions League game. Our victory that evening, and Thierry's hat-trick, gave us a lot of confidence for that next game, even if in the end, it wasn't enough to see us through to the Champions League quarter-finals that we so desperately wanted to reach.

The season ended on a high both for Arsenal and for me, personally. I am not counting the final Premiership game away to Birmingham City which we lost because it was a meaningless result by then for both teams and we were missing four key players – Henry, Pires, Reyes and Lauren – in advance of the FA Cup Final the following weekend. Aside from that game, though, we had a good home win against Spurs in April – the return derby after that incredible 5–4 win back in November – where the 1–0 result didn't reflect the fact that we dominated much of the game. By winning, we had also prevented Chelsea winning the title that night and had stayed four points ahead of Manchester United in the race for 2nd place. So that had been a double satisfaction for us and a good result.

An even better one was our 7–0 demolition of Everton at Highbury. It was a game that was full of historic meaning for all sorts of reasons. Firstly, it was the biggest score in Premiership history. On the night, we delivered a performance that made me wonder why we weren't the ones who had won the League, and why we had not been able to progress further in the Champions League. We played with confidence and style; this was Arsenal at their best. Everton, it's true, hadn't won at Highbury in their last ten visits, so they could hardly have been surprised to have lost, but the way in which we scored, three before the break, four after, must still have been depressing for them, given that they did, after all, finish fourth in the Premiership. Sol Campbell was back in central defence, alongside Senderos, for his first game since 1 February and we even had Thierry come on at half time, for the first time in five weeks after being out with a groin injury. Van Persie and Pires opened up the scoring and, eight minutes before the break, Dennis fed me a ball that I chipped over the oncoming Everton keeper, Richard Wright. That goal, though I did not know it at the time, was my last ever Premiership goal for the Gunners and it was fantastic that it turned out to be not only at Highbury but also on such an incredible night. Edu scored the fifth goal from the penalty spot and that, too, was his last Highbury appearance, though in his case, he knew it, which is why he took the penalty.

The match programme had urged the fans to turn Highbury red and white for the very last time because the following season – the last in their current home – the Gunners would be playing in the new home maroon-coloured shirt, the same colour they used to play in when they first moved there all those years ago. So fans had been asked to bring along their flags, scarves, hats, shirts, anything, in fact, that was red and white to give the famous old stadium one final red and white evening. The flashbulbs that illuminated the stadium at the end of the game, almost as if we had won the League, the feeling of elation there was amongst the players and fans, even the fact that the Everton players threw their own shirts into the crowd, all gave me a sense of the enormous significance the game had turned out to have, both for the club and for me, personally.

When I look back at my arrival at Arsenal in 1996, before the manager had arrived from Japan, and I remember how, for the first few weeks, I had trained with the reserves because nobody cared about the fact that I had come from AC Milan, I am so proud of how far I have come. I think that what I represented for the Gunners by the time I left was a real form of accomplishment for me. If you had written in a novel about my last few weeks with Arsenal, or if you had seen them in a film, they would have seemed a bit unlikely and unrealistic. I couldn't have hoped for a better ending to my years with the Gunners. And I hope the fans will feel that way as well.

16

'Patrick Hates Losing'

By Arsène Wenger

During the years that Patrick was at Arsenal, he matured a little bit more each year. I went to Milan when I was still coaching in Japan. I had already come across him when he was playing for Cannes, because he was there when I was at Monaco, although we never actually spoke during that period. The first time I was struck by Patrick was during an end-of-season game. At the time in France, there was a sort of League Cup before it really became an annual competition and the official means of qualifying for a place in Europe. Monaco had played against Cannes, who were in the first division at the time. I had Claude Puel in the middle, a really strong guy who won all his one-on-one match-ups. During the game, Patrick came on at half time and suddenly Puel looked like a kid compared to him. I immediately told myself that this Vieira guy would one day be a great player. It had taken 45 minutes of a League Cup fixture to convince me. Afterwards, I would go and see him at Cannes. I then left for Japan and in January, George Weah was named FIFA's World Player of the Year. He invited me over. At that time, he played for Milan and that's when I met Patrick, during half time of one of the games.

He wasn't playing and he seemed completely demoralised and down, as if he had lost his way. Given how much he loves to play, it must have been torture for him to be at Milan either on the bench or, even worse, in the stands. I tried to cheer him up, saying to him, 'Hang on in there, my friend! You'll get there in the end, and this is AC Milan, after all.' It was terrible to see this young man, who I knew could conquer and dominate the midfield, totally disheartened. At the time, though, there was a lot of talent in AC's midfield.

All that must have taken place in January 1996. In July, I was contacted by Arsenal and Patrick Vieira was in negotiations with Ajax of Amsterdam. I called him in Holland from Japan and I told him to go and sign for Arsenal. And that's how the transfer was done. It was a fairly straightforward one because the fee had been fixed by AC Milan at around $5m, £3.5m at the time, irrespective of who the buyer was going to be. I told David Dein he should not hesitate about the signing because if he wanted Vieira to come to the club, he had to act quickly, otherwise he would lose him. I also convinced his agents at the time, although they were happy for him to go to Arsenal rather than Ajax anyway. They had had a financial problem in Holland because the Dutch had flinched a bit when it had come to Patrick's salary. At Arsenal, on the other hand, they had immediately got everything they asked for.

I arrived with the Gunners on 1 October 1996. Patrick had arrived a few months before, in July. He had suffered a lot at the beginning. Everyone at the club was telling me that Rémi Garde was better. But there had been the Olympics and I thought that Patrick had already left for Atlanta. In fact, he had sprained his knee just a few days before the start of the Games, so he hadn't actually taken part. Instead, he had had a small surgical procedure on the injured knee and needed some further rehabilitation, so perhaps he wasn't in good shape physically when he had finally arrived in London in July and set foot at Highbury for the first time. In any event, they didn't find him all that good at the start. They had quite a mixed structure and there wasn't much difference between the first team and the reserves; everyone more or less trained together. Sometimes there were 15 in the reserves, other times ten and although Patrick sometimes trained with the first team, he trained a lot with the reserves. Much too much in fact. There he was, with no support, when suddenly this unknown new French coach arrives from Japan, of all places. You can imagine how difficult the situation was for him. It wasn't ideal for Arsenal either.

Despite that, when I arrived, I immediately picked him. I never had the slightest doubt. At the time, we were playing 3–5–2. In the middle, I had Vieira, David Platt and Paul Merson. In order to win the ball from Patrick Vieira in 1996, it didn't take one man, it didn't take two, it took at least three men around him! And even those three couldn't be sure of winning the ball! He was huge for me, immediately.

He found a way into people's hearts at once. At the time, the football that was played in England was a lot more physical than it is today. When the English saw that this guy, who had just arrived, and who didn't look like anything special with his long gangly legs, was going to Wimbledon and stopping everyone in their tracks, they loved that! The French had a bit of a reputation for avoiding physical contact, of being the romantics of football, but when all the English teams saw this giant who was crunching into everyone the whole time, they couldn't believe their eyes. When players had a go at him, he gave as good as he got, and when they had a go a second time, he would make sure he returned the favour three times. And the English loved that immediately!

Having said that, the longer time went by, the less he laid into others, even though they laid into him more and more. I can tell you that over the last ten years, this guy certainly took a few knocks. I'll always take my hat off to him for that. He was often the target of the opposing players at the start of the game; he was a player that everyone tried to bring down. But he never backed down, he never avoided getting stuck in. Even if it was an end-of-season game, even if there was nothing much left to play for, if he had to get stuck in, he would get stuck in.

He quickly won me over, as he did everyone. For one reason, because I had the satisfaction of being able to see a player who had been forgotten at AC Milan but was now blossoming and improving. I remember going back to San Siro and the Milanese said to me 'What on earth have you done to us, taking Vieira? How could we have let that guy go?' We soon got the feeling that we had achieved a real coup by signing Patrick, even though we also had to keep a reality check on this seemingly idyllic state of affairs. Patrick was so strong, so dominating in a game. He could destroy, direct and distribute the ball, often all in one go. Whatever one says, there weren't dozens of players of that calibre playing in Europe – there still aren't, for that matter. As Lauren once said, 'He is the lungs of our team.'

As a result, every year, we told ourselves that we were going to feel the heat during the summer because there would be a lot of pressure on us and we would end up selling him. That's because we're not a club with infinite resources. So on the one hand, it was a fantastic feeling to have a player like him, on the other it was a bit concerning as well. We always used to say, 'How will we be able to replace a player like that if he leaves?' And now, of course, that moment has come.

When Tony Adams' exceptional career finally came to an end in 2002, I decided to make Patrick captain. It was self-evident for me. Tony stopped playing but I wasn't 100 per cent sure that he was definitely retiring. I knew that Dixon was no longer an automatic choice. I told my deputies, and notably Pat Rice who plays a big part in shaping my thought process because of his many years of service for Arsenal, 'We don't have a captain any more, who can we nominate? I can only see one, and that's Patrick Vieira. He has authority over the team, and has been at the club for a while.' For Pat, he was the obvious choice as well, and it was important that he gave me his opinion because he is one of the real personalities of the club: he has spent his whole life here. I thought that making Patrick captain might shock some people because Patrick was a foreigner, but it went down incredibly easily with everyone. It seemed the obvious choice, partly because of the charisma he had as a player at the time, and partly because of his sheer presence in the dressing room. I also thought that this appointment would enable him to progress in terms of the role he played on the pitch and his behaviour on it as well. After he became captain, he gained in authority but he also listened more to others. That's why I said that every year he continued to mature. And during his last season with us, he reached yet another level: he managed to distance himself more from things. After all, he was someone who was rather impulsive and once he had got annoyed, he would react really quickly. Last season, though, he controlled himself much better.

That's something I have noticed about myself: sometimes, the job reveals a new facet of our personality, or, rather, it reveals to us a facet of our personality that we were not yet aware we had, either because we lacked confidence or because nobody had ever allowed us to discover it. When you have inner resources, you grow into what is required to do your job. That's why I think the captaincy was a huge positive influence on him. He had a greater sense of responsibility. He was only sent off twice after becoming captain. At first, he was too impulsive. For him, it was an act of courage to respond to provocation. It was a bit like 'If you're looking to provoke me, you're going to find me.' Mind you, 90 per cent of the time, he was the one who was provoked but, unfortunately, it's often those who respond who are punished.

The trophies he won with France obviously gave him a lot of confidence. He's a guy who always has self-doubts. I think that becoming world champion, followed by European champion two years later, were two turning points for him. I like the type of self-doubt that he has, though, because it produces some very positive questioning. It's not the sort of doubt that paralyses you during a game, instead it leads to a process of reflection that makes you self-critical. Patrick was the sort of guy who always analysed his performance with great lucidity. In fact, I think that was one of his principal qualities. He was always very acute when he analysed his matches and he built on that to enable him to analyse in greater detail any problems that came up in the team. Once he became captain, he got into the habit of adapting his behaviour and way of thinking to the life and the development of the squad as a whole. It was also interesting for me to talk to him because he had a good feel for any problems that arose. He got into the habit of analysing not only his own performance, but also that of the team, whilst qualifying his analysis the whole time. He didn't come out with categorical opinions, but rather hypotheses and suggestions. 'Such and such a player has done this but he has also done that. It's true he hogs the ball too much, but he's still young ...' Four years ago, he would just have said, 'That guy's useless.' He was much more moderate than Thierry when he looked at the overall performance of the team and of the individual players within it.

When it came to technique, Patrick was remarkable, and he had an unbelievable instinct for the game. When he was being marked, he was never afraid of taking the ball. Those are the sorts of guys who drive the game forward. When Patrick had his opponent right behind him, he took the ball and turned left or right. Any other player who is heavily marked like this and gets the central defender's ball, will just return it. With him, he always wanted to go forwards. He had an instinct for the game that you either have or you don't. You can't teach that to anyone. He was never afraid and when he played, it was always to go forwards. His reading of the game was outstanding. In a tightly marked midfield, most players will lay a short ball off. Patrick, on the other hand, would turn and suddenly open play up by hitting a long ball to the other wing. That was one of his great qualities.

Patrick almost left on several occasions before finally leaving for Juventus. The closest he came to leaving before was in the summer of 2004 when his saga with Real Madrid went on for ever. What disappointed me at the time, or rather saddened me, was how this whole business kicked off. Some guys give so much of themselves for so many years that there's a real sense of gratitude on the part of the fans. The player has fought hard, he has put his head where some might not even put their feet. But what irritated me was that his desire to leave came at exactly the wrong time for me. I discovered that contact had been made between Patrick and Real right in the middle of Euro 2004, just when I least expected it. And I wondered how I was going to replace a guy like Patrick, especially because we were right in the middle of a major international competition. The least I could do was to find a way of making up for his departure, because I have a responsibility towards this club, which is not rolling in money, and which, from one day to the next, was losing one of its best players. It was a tricky situation. But then I reasoned 'He's going to leave, I'll try to get by, and to find some solutions.' He pushed us into negotiating with Real and we agreed financial terms with the Madrid club. We even exchanged contracts with Real. Then, on the eve of him leaving for Madrid, he decided he wanted to stay. I never completely understood why ... though I think there was one thing that made him change his mind: he went through the pre-season training with the team. If he had been cut off from the squad, things would have been different, but there he spent time with the others and they would all have been telling him not to leave. Every day, they picked away a bit at his decision. He saw that the youngsters were playing well at the start of the season, he saw the quality of the game they played, and that he would once more be able to play some good football. He must have told himself that he would be losing so much.

So Patrick stayed. But his thigh injury was dragging on and it prevented him doing the pre-season physical training with the squad. And, it has to be said, the supporters were not too happy with him. But people took him back into their hearts because the English have a fantastic quality: they forgive those who give their all, and they did not forget what he had done for them. We can still see that today with Dennis: he only had to make three good passes at the end of the season against Everton at Highbury and the whole stadium was singing 'One more year'! It's a form of gratitude which I really like, given the world we live in today where people are discarded so quickly. Only in England do things like that happen.

Now he has signed for Juventus and I understand the sadness our supporters must have felt when they heard the news, but they must trust and support us. His departure will not affect our attempts to regain our Premiership crown. Despite the fact that he has now left, what symbolised Patrick during his final season with Arsenal, in my eyes, even more perhaps than scoring the winning penalty in the FA Cup Final against Manchester United, was what happened at Sheffield United in the FA Cup quarter-final in February where we also went through on penalties. Our team was decimated by injuries and suspensions (Thierry was injured and Dennis was suspended, notably) and Patrick became like a general on the battlefield who, armed with his sword, fights like a demon against the enemy. The following week we were playing a monumentally important Champions League game at home against Bayern Munich (we had to win by two clear goals to stay in the tournament) but he couldn't have cared less! Once he was on the field, in the heat of battle, it wasn't easy to get him to let go! That's why I respected him so much. Although he was a talented player, because I was his coach, I was perfectly aware when he let his standard slip a bit here and there. But I forgave him everything because I knew that he would give his all every time when it mattered and that, even in the most hopeless situation, he would be there until the very end. That was Patrick for you. When he was on the pitch, sometimes he was a little slow to get going, but once he was fired up, there was no stopping him.

Arsenal is the most 'British' club there is. Patrick is black, French as well, yet he came to symbolise the Gunners. But that doesn't surprise me because above all, here, people love their club and they love someone who puts themselves out for their team and for the sheer glory of the club's colours. That's why I maintain that I don't detect any racism here in England. I can't say if it's very present in society at large because I don't really know much about that but in the world of football, at least, there isn't any. What we saw in recent months in Spain and Italy is extraordinary. I thought we had got rid of this sort of behaviour, but clearly not.

The British are very grateful to those who go into battle. That's because they are a nation of fighters themselves. And more than any other foreigner, Patrick symbolised this sort of warrior, in the sporting sense of the word, obviously. When he was out fighting, he wouldn't let you down. So they forgave him all his escapades off the pitch, if you could call them that, because they knew that once he was on, he would always give it his all. He proved it once again in the 2004/5 season by playing a lot of matches with an ankle that was far from right. Those who criticised him were too harsh because, despite the pain he was in, he was always there. He put his body at risk for the club and never complained, and for that he deserves praise. That's also why I liked the symbolism at the end of the FA Cup Final. To see Patrick lining up to take the penalty against Manchester United and their supporters, then giving us that victory, was a fantastic symbol of the love that existed between him and Arsenal. It also turned out to be his last kick of the ball for Arsenal, so it had a double significance and a historic value.

When I hired him back in 1996, I thought he would be a good player, but you can never be sure. To be more precise, I thought it was possible that he might become a great player, as he has now done, but not to the extent he has. The same with Thierry Henry: I did not think he would reach the level he has. In fact, that was more the case with Thierry than it was with Patrick. When I made Thierry play centre forward, he said to me, 'But coach, I don't score goals . . .'

The two men have very different personalities. They are opposites, in fact. Patrick constantly has to be pushed. He will naturally tend to stay in his comfort zone, African-style. But when he is in a situation where he has to fight, he is stimulated and what spurs him on more than anything is the challenge of having to fight for something. When you put him on the battlefield, he manages to dig down deep and find the inner resources he needs. It's all down to his hatred of defeat and his pride in being the best. That's why he is Patrick Vieira. And that's why, by the time he left, he had become one of the greatest players in the club's history.

17

Gunners Past, Present and Future

In my nine seasons at Arsenal, I have played with some incredible players and some fantastic characters. I have listed below some of the guys who left a big impression on me, but really the list could have gone on and on. Before I talk about the players, though, here are a few thoughts on the man who made it all possible.

Arsène Wenger

This man never loses control of his emotions. Even when we won our Doubles, he wasn't going wild or anything, or dancing around the changing room with silly hats on his head. On the other hand, he is someone who made each player take responsibility for his successes or failures. When he arrived, he changed our diet, changed our way of living, but did it by raising our awareness of their importance; he didn't impose things on us. 'There is a time and a place for going out,' he would say. He never said 'I forbid you to go out and enjoy yourselves.' He knew we were young, that there were occasions when we had to let off steam, but he felt it was important for us to take responsibility for our lives, and to learn when we could and couldn't do certain things. His view was that in order to be a top professional player, it was worth making certain sacrifices and he trusted us to recognise that and to live accordingly. I believe that is a much better way to run a team than to impose rigid rules and to treat men as children. The one thing that he cares about is keeping up the image of the club, the one that says 'You don't give up.' That is the key attitude he was always trying to convey to us. The decisions he takes are also taken with that attitude in mind.

Arsène is someone who was always there for me, as he is for all the players. He is someone I could talk to about anything, not just about football. He gave me the responsibility of being captain and that gave me confidence both as a person and as a player and helped me improve personally and professionally. But he also knew when to criticise me, though he would do it behind closed doors. He was known for never publicly criticising his players through the media, which his team always appreciated and which created a much closer bond between him and us. When I was sent off in the first two games of the 2000/1 season, he told me things that were maybe harsh but which were nonetheless true. Again, he made me realise that I had to take responsibility for my actions if I wanted to learn from those mistakes. It wasn't a heated discussion where he was angry with what I had done – it was a calm discussion where he explained things to me simply and clearly. Those sorts of situations happened regularly over the years. After a discussion in his office, I would realise that he was right about something and that I had been wrong, but he had been very intelligent about the way in which he had told me. It meant that I trusted him and respected him enormously.

GUNNERS OF THE PAST

Ian Wright

Without a doubt, the most charismatic of all the players I have ever met. Not just at Arsenal, but at all clubs. As I have already said, off the pitch, he was always having fun, always enjoying himself, always wanting others to share in his enjoyment of life. The life and soul of the team, really. But not in a starry, big-headed way. Ian Wright was a really friendly guy, someone who was easy to like. On the pitch, he was someone who had great skill in front of goal. He had a rare goal-scoring talent. It's amazing to me that it took him so long to reach the top-flight.

He was already twenty-eight when he signed for Arsenal and he had been rejected by Millwall and Brighton when he was younger. All I can say is that he must have had a great inner-confidence and strength of mind to keep going. Deep down, he must have known that his time would come, because most people in his situation would have given up. Maybe it was precisely because success came so late that he wanted to enjoy life to the full once he was able to. In any event, Ian Wright was the biggest character in all my years at Arsenal.

Lee Dixon, Steve Bould, Nigel Winterburn, Tony Adams, Martin Keown

The famous back five that perfectly reflected the 'never give up' image of the club. I have spoken more about Tony Adams in the chapters that cover my arrival at Arsenal, and my captaincy. Along with the others, though, he formed the most effective defence in the English League in the late nineties. The 97/8 Double-winning season was the year we conceded the least number of goals in my entire time at Highbury. We won that Double thanks to our great defending. They weren't spectacular players, but they had strength and organisation and a lot of experience. They read the game superbly and, when the style of play of the team began to change, once the club began to sign more foreign players, they had the knowledge and the intelligence to know how to adapt their game. Although their legs were getting slower, their experience and vision of the game allowed them to learn to play a different style of football, and that is to their great credit. They were really hard workers, they were always there at training, they always tried their hardest, and as a result, even a player like Nigel Winterburn, who really was a one-footed player (beware if he had to use his right foot to kick the ball!), reached the top level of football and stayed there for years.

Martin Keown is the player who I liked the most at the club. He only left Arsenal at the end of the 2003/4 season, aged nearly 38, after more than 400 appearances for the club. He has incredible strength of character and he never gave up, either during training or during a game. His determination to succeed and to keep going meant that you could always count on him. But Martin is also a fantastic, genuine human being. He made me laugh so much, he loved to tease me all the time, and he really is someone you can get close to very easily. His testimonial match in May 2004 was a sell-out and even featured the likes of David Beckham who had insisted on flying over specially from Madrid to play, which said it all about how popular and respected Martin is amongst players from all clubs.

Ray Parlour

I still don't understand why Ray left Arsenal. He was a talented midfielder whose ball-winning and ball-carrying skills all too often went unsung. He captained the team for a while when I was injured during the 2003/4 season and also scored a fantastic goal in the 2002 FA Cup Final which we won against Chelsea. Ray is a really nice, kind guy. He never saw the negative side of things, everything was always a game, he didn't take life too seriously and he was always incredibly welcoming to all the new players. He had a lot of qualities, both as a player and as a person and I was sorry when he left the club.

Marc Overmars

An exciting player, part of our 97/8 Double-winning team, of course, and someone we could always count on for the big games. If you wanted someone to score that one goal that would see you through a crucial match, or a tight situation, then Marc would be the one who would come out of nowhere and knock one in for you. However, the lesser games, the ones that didn't count too much in his eyes, particularly if they were in far-flung places, were less his bag. He was less motivated by those and that sometimes showed in his commitment and performance on the night. He needed the big occasion for his talent to show through at its best.

Emmanuel Petit

I was really close to Manu when he was at the club. Together, we formed a fantastic midfield partnership which began to show fairly soon after his arrival from Monaco in 1997. He liked attacking a bit more than I did, he liked to play the long-ball game whereas I preferred the short passing game, and he was left-footed whereas I was right-footed, so in many ways we complemented each other perfectly. In my career so far, I have to say that he is the player who I have gelled with the most on the pitch.

As a person, Manu is someone who knows no half measures. He is a very genuine person, he either likes you a lot or he doesn't at all, but he is someone you can get very close to. Contrary to what his image sometimes seemed to be, he wasn't into a nightclubbing, high-profile life. But maybe because of his looks, and the fact that he was inevitably a high-profile foreign player, he attracted attention wherever he went, both on and off the pitch. I was bitterly disappointed when, along with Marc Overmars, he signed for Barcelona in the summer of 2000.

Nicolas Anelka

As a striker, his talent has never been in doubt. When he first arrived at Arsenal from Paris St Germain during my first season at Highbury, he was still only 17. But the following season, 1997/8, he broke into the first team and contributed enormously to us winning the Double. He was, and is, very quick and has great finishing ability. Like many talented players, I remember he didn't need to work as hard as others but, if he had stayed at the club, I'm convinced he would have become one of the great Arsenal strikers of all time. He even won the PFA Young Player of the Year award in 1999, which showed how much potential everyone thought he had. He was playing next to Dennis, the boss obviously knew him well, the team was supporting him in midfield and defence, in fact everything was in place for him to do well at the club. So in my view, he made a big mistake in leaving at the end of the 1998/9 season.

Nicolas is much shyer than people think. He can come across as arrogant but that is often the way with shy people: they avoid eye contact, or talking to people, simply because they are ill at ease in social situations. When you get to know him, he is actually a really nice guy to have around. In addition, he has one big quality: he never runs away from his responsibilities. If he has done something wrong, he will acknowledge the fact.

David Seaman

His track record at Arsenal speaks for itself. And in our Double-winning seasons, if we had not had David in goal, we would not have had the success we did. If you don't have a great goalkeeper, you don't win trophies, simple as that. He symbolised the Arsenal spirit in those years. He had a great physical presence in goal, which is always crucial. Plus, he could anticipate and read the game so well, thanks to his enormous experience. At his peak, he was one of the best keepers in Europe.

As I have already said, but it's worth emphasising, I have never known someone who smiles as much as David. He and Martin Keown are the two players that I have stayed in close touch with since leaving Highbury. He is quite simply what you call a nice human being. There's no edge to him, no malice. He's a great man.

Edu

Edu arrived at Arsenal at sadly the wrong time for him and the club, as he had to compete against Gilberto and myself, both World Cup winners. He perhaps deserved to play more serious games which could have seen him become one of the great Arsenal midfield players. Unfortunately, his bad luck has continued at Valencia with a terrible injury. I hope he makes the speediest of recoveries and fulfils his potential.

GUNNERS OF THE PRESENT

Dennis Bergkamp

The one and only Dennis. Along with me, one of the longest-serving Gunners by the time I left. Dennis is pure talent. He enables the team to live and breathe. It all comes so easily to him, he never has to force things, either in training or in match situations. There's a fluidity about his game that is unique. There are only two players in the game today that I would pay to go and watch. Zizou is one. Dennis is the other. What more can I say?

As a man, Dennis is much more relaxed and gregarious than his 'Ice Man' nickname might imply. He likes to have a laugh, to tease people, to have a good time. When I left Arsenal, he was one of the players that I found hardest to leave behind. It feels really odd knowing that I will not be seeing him on a daily basis. It's like changing schools when you are a kid and leaving all your friends behind. Dennis is one of the guys I miss.

Freddie Ljungberg

Took over Ian Wright's number 8 shirt and, in 2001/2 in particular, formed an incredible partnership with Dennis which contributed enormously to our success that season. He's the sort of player who sometimes doesn't touch the ball for five minutes but who can then turn a match with one touch of the ball, either because he creates the goal or scores it himself. He is a match-winner. He likes playing deep and, because he is highly intelligent and reads the game so well, he is very difficult to mark. He always has time for people and is very easy to get on with. I always enjoyed his company a lot.

Sol Campbell

The rock. He has a huge physical presence on the pitch and I think he strikes awe in opponents. He showed great courage in transferring from Spurs to Arsenal but it's a reflection of the man: not afraid of anything, either on or off the pitch. What also impressed me when he arrived was that, given his size, he was a lot quicker than I might have thought.

In everyday life, Sol is someone who reveals his emotions, who I felt close to, and who I liked enormously. He likes playing the piano, he has interests beyond football and sport and, as a result, you can talk to him about anything, he'll have an opinion on it. That made him an interesting team-mate to have around.

Gilberto

Gilberto Silva, to give the Brazilian his full name, arrived at the club in 2002 and the idea was for him to partner me in midfield. It took a while for us to gel but when we did, we formed a great duo. The more we played together, the better we were. It was a real shame that in my last season at Highbury, he was injured for so long. As soon as he came back, in April, the difference began to show at once and was reflected in our results. Gilberto is someone who is essential in a team, a holding player like Makelele, but whose contribution doesn't necessarily get noticed that much. He's just there. He distributes the ball, he is effective, he is there when he is needed. He plays more defensively than Manu did, so that enabled me to push up front more in my last three seasons at the club. It meant that I was able to create more goal-scoring opportunities as well.

Lauren

Born in the Cameroon, he arrived at Arsenal in the summer of 2000 but didn't really get into his stride until the following season when we did the Double. He is the sort of player that managers love having in their team because he knows what he has to do on the pitch. He knows what his role is, he is a pillar of the team in many ways, and he was always someone we could count on. I knew he would always fight and keep going in a game, and that is the sort of quality that is worth a lot to a team.

He is reserved as a person, and low key. He is not at all one for the limelight and off the pitch he is quiet and unassuming.

Robert Pires

Technically, Robert is way up there. He stands out from the vast majority of players. He is incredibly versatile, can play on the right or on the left. With his slightly flat-flooted stance – we say in French that his feet are in the 'ten past ten' position, he gives the impression that he won't be one of the fastest on the pitch, whereas in reality he is deceptively quick. He can read the game unbelievably well, and so can create space, slot balls through to team-mates and make and finish moves that leave the opposition constantly surprised. He is very canny and shrewd as a player.

Robert is one of those guys who is too nice for his own good. He is a gentle, easy-going soul and trusts people too quickly, which can cause him problems. He is intelligent and interested in all sorts of things beyond football and, if you met him and didn't know who he was, you would probably never guess he was a professional footballer. You'd probably mistake him for a model (he has modelled for a make of jeans in the past) or a rock star.

Thierry Henry

Titi, as all his French team-mates call him, has overtaken Ian Wright's goalscoring record for Arsenal to become the Gunners' most prolific-ever scorer. When Ian achieved his record, no one thought – myself included – that it would be overtaken so soon. And when Thierry first arrived at Arsenal, he was an unlikely candidate for that honour, having spent most of his career up until then playing on the wing. Arsène Wenger's vision was to move him to striker and since then, he has never looked back – and nor has the club. He actually had a bit of difficulty at the beginning: the goals didn't start flowing the minute he arrived. But one of Thierry's great qualities is that he is a really hard worker. He often stays behind after training to put in extra sessions, he is never satisfied and constantly believes he can progress. What he has achieved today has largely been the result of sheer hard work and dedication allied to passion and natural talent. He is also incredibly quick and, above all, he has a passion for football. Once those three qualities came together at Arsenal, he began to notch up goals as if that was what he had done his entire career. The other great thing about Thierry is that he is a very unselfish player. He is a real team-player, largely because he loves the sport so much. He is not in it for the star status, but because he wants the team to win.

He is a reserved kind of guy who can nonetheless be charming and engaging. Like Manu, when he likes you, he really likes you. For him, it's all or nothing in his relationships with people. Thierry was the person I used to room with at Arsenal and who I felt very close to. Although I miss him, I see him whenever we get together to play for France and that, for me, makes our separation easier.

GUNNERS OF THE FUTURE

Kolo Touré

Originally from the Ivory Coast where he was born in 1981 and whose colours he still represents at international level, Kolo Touré arrived in 2002 and really started to make his mark in the 2003/4 season. He is one of the young generation of players at Arsenal who has great potential. Young players need to be surrounded by more experienced players so that they can learn; then, when they have matured, they can truly flourish, as he has. He has exceptional talent, in my opinion, and he is part of the future of the club. Arsenal need to hold on to him.

Ashley Cole

The same can be said, of course, for Ashley, who has been a Gunner all his life. He very nearly left the club, as everyone knows, in 2005 but, thankfully, he now seems to be happy and settled there again. I can't praise his talents enough. I think Ashley has the ability and potential to become the best left back in the world. He should go on to captain the team. He has everything it takes to be to Arsenal what Paolo Maldini has been to AC Milan: a player who is so strongly linked to a club (Maldini has spent his whole career at AC) that he will be forever associated with it and come to symbolise it. That could and should happen to Ashley. Ashley is the future for Arsenal and they should make sure they are aware of it.

Like Sol Campbell, Ashley is also one of those open-minded people, someone who has an intelligence and a curiosity about things that make them interesting. Ashley will talk about anything, and he has a lot to offer others.

Robin van Persie

He has a magnificent left foot and, as a striker, he has already shown what he can do on a number of occasions. His two fantastic goals against Blackburn in the 2004/5 FA Cup semi-final will be remembered for a long time, because he had only just come on as a substitute. Robin has exceptional talent and, now that he is at Arsenal, surrounded by more experienced team-mates, he will hopefully mature that talent and learn how best to use it. He just needs to learn to play as part of a team a bit more, then he really will be able to fulfil his potential and do his best for the club.

José Antonio Reyes

One of two brilliant young Spanish signings. He has incredible talent, he dribbles with amazing ease, he is great one on one. He hasn't yet shown the fans what he can do but I'm sure that, once he has learned to adapt a bit more to the physical English game, he will fulfil the huge potential that he has. Having recently signed a five-year contract with the club, it seems he is determined to stay at Highbury which will be good news for the team.

Cesc Fabregas

The goal he scored for Arsenal (against Wolves in 2004 in the Carling Cup) when he was still sixteen years old showed just how much potential he has. He reads the game incredibly quickly. On top of that, he is not frightened of sticking his foot in and of getting stuck in when necessary. When he first arrived in England in 2003 (he was signed from Barcelona) he played with the Arsenal youth team, and that's probably where he learned to cope with the physicality of English football. That's why, when he progressed to the first team, he knew exactly what to expect. He has enormous self-confidence, and therefore maturity, and now that he is surrounded by players and a manager who share that confidence in him, he can only continue to flourish and to impress everyone who sees him play. He needs to stay at Highbury and he too is part of the future of Arsenal.

The Arsenal that I have left behind still has that unique spirit. The club has a lot of talented youngsters who, when they arrived, settled in easily to the way of thinking and playing of the rest of the squad. The older foreign players who were already there helped the younger foreign ones to adapt to life at Highbury and in London. The club also helped them a lot, much more so than when I first arrived. Things are much more professionally organised now for young players when they are first signed. This means they can immediately focus on their football and on doing their best for Arsenal. I am really surprised, though, that the club did not sign any big names over the summer of 2005. I have to confess that I also find it hard to comprehend how they could have agreed to let me go without having someone in mind who they could replace me with. I believe it shows at the moment that the squad as a whole lacks experience. I can understand why the boss says the fans must trust him and be patient. I am sure he knows what he is doing and has a very clear idea about what sort of team he is building. The problem is that, when I look at the enormous success that the team has had since 1998 and the success that a team like Chelsea looks like having in the immediate future, I wonder how much patience the fans are going to have. I think it's going to be difficult. But I hope they can keep the faith because I believe it will pay off for them. Arsenal is, and will always remain, a great club.

POSTSCRIPT

Mama Rose

What can I say about my second son, Patrick? What insights can I give about what he was like as a boy? Was it obvious that a great career awaited him? All I can say is that the one abiding image I have of Patrick when he was a boy was that he was forever kicking a football about. To be honest, I don't remember him doing anything else. He was completely obsessed, to such an extent that if he didn't have a ball to kick, he would find some other rolling object and improvise with that instead. Sometimes I even remember him kicking small marbles around, because they were better than nothing. No other sport seemed to interest him, no other game; it was always football, football, football. He hated it though when others were better than him: that would put him in a bad mood. Similarly, he hated losing which was why he always gave his all in every game. He would do anything to avoid defeat.

As a person, he has always been calm and reserved around his family. When he came home from games and he had won, he wouldn't go on about it, or show off. That's not his style at all. He would never talk much about what had happened, but when things had gone well, it was always obvious from his eyes and from the expression on his face that he was happy. As a family, we are very close, and Patrick has always respected our privacy. He has never been one to talk about his private life in the media, and he has also avoided talking about me or his brother. But he is always calling us, always asking for our opinion. He is very close to his brother, Nicko, talks to him on the phone a lot, and there has never been the slightest problem between them. Nicko has always been incredibly proud of his little brother, and has never felt any rivalry. Obviously, I too am proud of everything Patrick has achieved in his career, but what I am most proud of is the fact that both my sons have stayed close to me and to each other, and that Patrick, given the life he leads, has stayed as honest, caring and true to himself as he was when he was a child.

Lilian Thuram

I first saw Patrick play when he was a tall, gangly seventeen-year-old at AS Cannes when I was at AS Monaco. He immediately made an impression on me. He had a confidence about him that I had never seen before in someone so young and he was quite clearly a cut above the rest of the team. I was doubly struck by him because, at that stage, I was harbouring thoughts of playing in midfield myself, so here was someone who was showing me, even at seventeen, how to play in that position. Obviously, since then, he's got even better and his personality has developed so that the package he brings to a game is truly impressive. He exudes an air of superiority and calm and naturally commands the respect of others, which is why he has captained so many of the teams he has played for, including France. When the going gets tough, his team-mates know they can count on him. It's a bit like when a plane hits turbulence: the passengers will look at the air hostesses to read their body language. If they look calm and authoritative, the passengers will take their cue from that and be reassured. That's what it's like playing in Patrick's teams. He'll always be there, fearless, never giving up.

I know he can get into trouble with referees but when he does it's not because he has gone in for a tackle maliciously or cynically. Of course he's human, he can get carried away, but in essence Patrick is not an aggressive guy. He might be driven to distraction and frustration by what is going on in a game, but he won't go looking for trouble, unlike some players. It's just that he is totally committed in a game, he will go for every ball and keep trying until the final whistle and it is that attitude which is an example for all the team. That's why he leads by example rather than by words.

His transfer to Juventus is a great move, not just selfish (because he's a great mate of mine) but also because it does a player's career good to change clubs. You push yourself more when you join a new club, you force yourself to reach for even greater heights, you can't stand still in the way that you sometimes can when you stay somewhere for a long time (it's the same as any job, let's face it!). There is a lot of respect for Patrick amongst his new team-mates because of his intelligence and his personal qualities, as well as his footballing skills, so I'm sure that his move to Juventus will prove to be a success for him.

Dennis Bergkamp

Patrick and I go back a long way. I had been a Gunner for a year when Patrick arrived in 1996. Immediately, his courage on the pitch stood out and it took only a little while – and in particular Arsène Wenger's arrival – for others to notice how good he was. After that, he never looked back. His footballing skills and commitment have never been called into question but sometimes he has got into trouble on the pitch. Off it, though, it's a different story. He is a genuinely nice guy. I know that word 'nice' can sometimes seem a bit vague but that's a very accurate way of describing him. He is laid back, caring towards others and doesn't lose his temper. When he captained Arsenal, if a player ever had a problem and told Patrick about it, he would be there to help him and would go and talk to the boss if necessary on behalf of that player. He also treated everyone just the same, whether they were the backroom staff, the secretaries at the club, or the directors. I never came across anyone who had a bad word to say about him.

I got to know him more over the last four or five years because our wives got on very well, so the four of us would really enjoy going out to dinner, for example in Hampstead, where he lived, and we would have incredibly relaxed, low-key evenings. The paparazzi were never tipped off, flashbulbs never went off, we would simply have a normal, fun evening amongst friends. My wife and I definitely miss those times with Patrick and Cheryl. And both on and off the pitch, I miss Patrick as a close friend and as a hard-to-replace team-mate.

INDEX